America's History Revealed
Keeping America Free

To Larry
I hope you enjoy this look at
our history.
Philip W. Winkler
12/18/2010

America's History Revealed

Keeping America Free

Since 450 A.D. – What Other Histories Won't Tell You

Philip W. Winkler

LIBERTY & INDEPENDENCE PRESS

(www.PhilWinklerSpeaker.com)

Liberty & Independence Press
107 East 107th Avenue
Northglenn, Colorado 80233
www.LibertyIndependence.com
e-mail: LibertyIndependence@gmail.com

Liberty & Independence Press is a tradename of
We Solve Problems, Inc.

Book design by Rebecca Finkel

Library of Congress Control Number: 2009909638

ISBN: 978-0-9825297-4-4 (Softcover)
978-0-9825297-0-6 (e-book)

To all those who love liberty.

Acknowledgments

The writer owes a debt of gratitude to many: to those such as Washington, Franklin, Jefferson, Madison, Lincoln, Smith, Say and Bastiat, and many others, who gave us our Declaration of Independence, our Constitution, and in other ways blazed the trail of freedom; to those who have fought to preserve freedom; to historians such as Mark H. Brown, Walter Lord, Thomas Fleming, Francis Parkman and William Shirer, from whom I have learned much and from whose writings I have drawn information; to my friend, attorney and State Senator Shawn Mitchell, who read an early draft and gave suggestions for improvement; to my editor, John Maling, and my designer, Rebecca Finkel. There have also been friends and family who encouraged me, parents and others who helped teach me a love of truth, and my wife who has endured the trials that have come with this effort.

Table of Contents

List of Illustrations
Tables, Maps and Figures

Introduction

"As a nation of freemen we must live through all time, or die by suicide."
—ABRAHAM LINCOLN[1]

L incoln, in the speech just quoted, asserted that the armies of the world could not conquer America. He continued, "At what point, then, is the approach of danger to be expected? I answer, If it ever reach us it must spring up amongst us; it cannot reach us from abroad. If destruction be our lot we must ourselves be its author and finisher." If Americans lose our freedom, it will not be by conquest, but by our failure to preserve our heritage and to abide by our Constitution.

As a nation of freemen, to prevent such suicide, we must remember and understand America's history and heritage, and what makes us free.

History is more than names, dates and events. It's like a national memory, one that helps us understand present issues by the light of past events. It's about ideas as well as events. Ideas affect attitudes, attitudes affect actions, and actions have consequences. History matters.

In Colorado, recently a court sought to determine whether a university properly fired a professor accused by his peers of not only plagiarism, but of falsifying history. The questions there at issue form only the tip of a larger iceberg.

Many textbooks for survey courses on U.S. history contain numerous factual errors and are strongly biased. Much of that bias has an anti-American, anti-freedom flavor. I have repeatedly found instances of critical facts misstated, misrepresented or omitted. Sometimes texts relate facts correctly, but by presenting them in an odd order and omitting other relevant facts, they still give false impressions.

I know this because in 1994, my wife and I helped found a charter school. The school now serves about 1,150 students, kindergarten through twelfth grade. For the first fourteen years of the school's life, I served on the governing board, eight years as chairman. During that time, I reviewed many textbooks on economics, government, and history. I have also read or examined some college history books. Good ones are hard to find.

"Historians" have misused history this way before. Sometimes, they do it with a purpose.

Warped history produces warped political views. In the 1750s, Scotsman David Hume wrote a history of England. Hume's books served for many as texts for the study of English history. Thomas Jefferson, who read Hume while young, said of him later:

> . . . he suppressed truths, advanced falsehoods, forged authorities, and falsified records. All this is proved on him unanswerably by Brodie. . . . It was all-important [to Hume] to maintain the thesis . . . that "it was the people who encroached on the sovereign, not the sovereign who usurped on the rights of the people."[2]
>
> . . . Everyone knows that judicious matter and charms of style have rendered Hume's history the manual of every student. I remember well the enthusiasm with which I devoured it when young, and the length of time, the research and reflection which were necessary to eradicate the poison it had instilled into my mind. . . . he still continues to be put into the hands of all our young people, and to infect them with the poison of his own principles of government. It is this book which has undermined the free principles of the English government.[3]

I have seen all too much of such tactics in modern books on American history. Some of the errors appear deliberate. Some of the authors may have followed the errors taught them by others. Yet, Ph.D.s in history should know better. Jefferson's comments on Hume show that truth should matter more than style.

From childhood, my passions have embraced American history and government, especially the Declaration of Independence and the U.S. Constitution. This passion grew from my love of freedom and respect and admiration for America's unique role in the world.

Because of what I have seen in many survey texts, I decided to write this book to counter the harm they do; to point out some of the common myths, bring to light some of the commonly omitted facts, and present another point of view–to present our nation's history more truthfully.

In addition, I have included material to help the reader delve more deeply into some topics either not usually mentioned, or of great importance such as the Declaration of Independence and the Constitution. Part of this material comes from my own research and analysis.

I have included an economics primer. Some readers will question how I can call it that. It does not cover the theory of value, marginal utility or other common topics. It covers basic principles for understanding the free market and identifies myths and errors—things that relate to the use or abuse of government force. Hence, it relates to choices we must make as citizens.

Themes of this book

As this book's major theme, I intend to convey information and principles needed for America to remain free. That major theme includes the following subsidiary themes:

1. the principles of the Declaration of Independence and the Constitution;
2. the principles of the free market and economics;
3. an understanding of why the Founders had to declare Independence;
4. that freedom requires personal responsibility;
5. that freedom requires obedience to law, not anarchy nor mob rule;
6. that illegal or immoral orders must not be followed;
7. that peace and freedom require strength and opposing tyranny, and that in war there is no substitute for victory;
8. that true history is not the captive nor the enemy of any one race or ethnic group; and finally,
9. that we must pursue truth wherever it leads.

The subjects that I have chosen to include, appear in this book because they relate to one or more of the above themes. Special emphasis is placed on the Declaration of Independence and the circumstances that caused it, and upon the Constitution. These documents form the foundation of our freedom. Americans need to understand the Founding Fathers and why they did what they did, because if they do not respect the Founders, they will not respect the foundation they gave us, and will not seek to keep it. Without that foundation, freedom would disappear. Indeed, only the truth can help us keep our freedom.

How should history be written, taught, or studied?

Please see the Model Vision for a History Department just after this introduction.

Bibliographic References

Sometimes I refer to parts of the Declaration of Independence by what I call a clause or paragraph number, such as DI-2, DI-30, etc. Similarly, I refer to paragraphs of the Olive Branch Petition as OBP-1, OBP-2, etc. I refer to parts of the Constitution by the usual Article, Section, and Clause designations.

Quotations

A number of quotations or other references are derived from the following:

Regarding Jefferson: *The Life and Selected Writings of Thomas Jefferson*, edited by Adrienne Koch and William Peden, Random House, New York, 1944, 1972, 1993. These could be taken instead from *The Works of Thomas Jefferson*, 12 vols., edited by Paul L. Ford, G. P. Putnam's Sons, New York, 1904-05, or *The Writings of Thomas Jefferson*, 9 vols., edited by Henry A. Washington, 1853-54, or *The Writings of Thomas Jefferson*, 20 vols., edited by Albert Ellery Bergh, Thomas Jefferson Memorial Association, Washington, 1907. Koch and Peden's book may be more readily accessible. However, it doesn't include all the Jefferson quotes I use.

Regarding Franklin: *The Man Who Dared the Lightning*, by Thomas Fleming, William Morrow and Company, New York, 1971.

Regarding Lincoln: *The Life and Writings of Abraham Lincoln*, Edited by Philip Van Doren Stern, The Modern Library, Random House, New York, 1940.

Sources Online

There are a number of sources that are now available online, for example:

Jefferson's *Notes on Virginia*: *www.yale.edu/lawweb/avalon/jevifram.htm*;

    or: *etext.lib.virginia.edu/toc/modeng/public/JefBv021.html*;

    or: *oll.libertyfund.org/ToC/0287.php*.

Jefferson's *Autobiography*: *www.yale.edu/lawweb/avalon/jeffauto.htm*;

    or: *libertyonline.hypermall.com/Jefferson/Autobiography.html*.

Jefferson's *A Summary View of the Rights of British America*:

    libertyonline.hypermall.com/Jefferson/Summaryview.html.

The *Olive Branch Petition*, from the Second Continental Congress, July 8,
   1775, can be found online at: *ahp.gatech.edu/olive_branch_1775.html*; or:
   www.learner.org/channel/workshops/primarysources/revolution/docs/olive.html;
   or: *www.lexrex.com/enlightened/laws/olive_pet.htm.*
   (As of this writing, the document found at */personal.pitnet.net/primary
sources/olive.html* is not the Olive Branch Petition as above named, but is
an earlier document.)

From time to time in this work, I give my opinion. The reader will also see
the facts that form the basis for that opinion, and can make his or her own
judgement. Should I find that any relevant perceived "facts" prove erroneous,
I shall seek to correct them in a future edition. This book is the result of extensive reading, study, and research. I have sought truthfulness and accuracy.
What does the book bring to light, not found in the usual survey texts? How
many lies, errors, myths, omissions and misrepresentations in other books,
written by Ph.D.s in history, do I correct? It gets difficult to count, but I estimate at least forty to fifty of each.

Thomas Jefferson said, "I have sworn upon the altar of God, eternal hostility against every form of tyranny over the mind of man."[4]

I find those who perpetuate myths and spread historical falsehoods guilty
of a form of tyranny over the minds of mankind. That is the reason for this
book. For, as written elsewhere, "And ye shall know the truth, and the truth
shall make you free."[5]

A Model Vision Statement
for a School or College History Department

We teach history and government from a pro-freedom, generally pro-American perspective, and economics from a pro free-market perspective.

We have observed that many of the texts in use in high schools and colleges are written from an opposing point of view. We find the tactics that many of them use reprehensible. Our Mission calls for providing students with foundational knowledge, and preparing them to be exemplary citizens. Our Vision calls for intellectual honesty, fairness, and objectivity. Therefore, in accordance with our overall Mission and Vision, our vision for the department proclaims that we present the facts as truly and fully as we know them and as time allows. Furthermore,

- we do not suppress or omit critical facts
- we do not present theory as fact
- we do not present falsehood as fact
- we do not present some facts and omit others in order to give a false impression
- we do not present facts in an unnatural order, to alter perception of cause and effect or to give a false impression.

We model a willingness to learn and to progress in our knowledge and understanding of historical events, economics, and the principles of the Declaration of Independence and the United States Constitution.

We strive to use human interest, stories, reason and passion, to make the subject alive and interesting for our students; the subject is vital—the future of our freedom depends on our students' understanding.

Americans have made many mistakes; in the discourse we acknowledge those mistakes. We do not avoid discussing them; yet neither do we keep from our students the great good that America and Americans have done.

America
Land of Freedom and Opportunity

A merica has a unique role in the world. From the period of her Declaration of Independence and her Constitution, she has set an example for the world—in freedom, in the resultant inventiveness, productivity and prosperity; in order, justice, and opposition to oppression. She has not been perfect, just far better than other places—so much better that people have flocked to her from all over the globe. They have come to escape oppression. They have come primarily for two things: freedom and opportunity.

America's "Founding Fathers" believed they were setting a standard for the world that would eventually bless all of humanity.

James Madison wrote, "Happily for Americans, happily we trust for the whole human race, they [the founders] pursued a new and more noble course."[1]

John Adams considered the settlement of America "as the opening of a grand scene and design in Providence for the illumination of the ignorant and the emancipation of the slavish part of mankind all over the earth."[2]

Before his death, Thomas Jefferson saw America's influence spreading over the earth. America chose to declare Independence rather than submit to tyranny. Speaking of this, he said, "May it be to the world, what I believe it will be (to some parts sooner, to others later, but finally to all), the signal of arousing men to burst [their] chains . . . All eyes are opened, or opening, to the rights of man. The general spread of the light of science has already laid open to every view the palpable truth, that the mass of mankind has not been born with saddles on their backs, nor a favored few booted and spurred, ready to ride them legitimately, by the grace of God."[3]

Albert P. Blaustein, professor of law at Rutgers, in 1984, wrote, "The United States Constitution is the nation's most important export. . . . Every nation that has a one-document constitution (or is committed in principle to having one) is inevitably following the United States precedent-model. And that applies to all but six countries."[4]

The American example gradually spread to other countries. Tens of millions of people from around the world have also chosen to come here. Beginning with the British Isles and western Europe, then southern and eastern Europe and parts of Asia and Central and South America, immigration has played a major role in populating the United States. Many were brought from Africa, kidnaped and sold as slaves. During the colonial period some colonies tried to stop the slave trade. America finally outlawed it in 1808. Most of America's immigrants came in hopes of a better life, a freer life, a life of more opportunity. Usually, they found it.

In America, not only immigrants, but others starting out in the working world begin as described by Lincoln. "The prudent, penniless beginner in the world labors for wages awhile, saves a surplus with which to buy tools or land for himself, then labors on his own account another while, and at length hires another new beginner to help him. This, say its advocates, is free labor–the just, and generous, and prosperous system, which opens the way for all, gives hope to all, and energy, and progress, and improvement of condition to all."[5]

Often people advance through education or apprenticeship. They gain knowledge and learn new skills. Lincoln studied to become a lawyer. While not all move beyond working for someone else, generally they don't continue in the same position indefinitely. While some politicians like to quote statistics regarding the plight of the poor, using numbers of those working for "minimum wage" at different dates years apart, most of those so employed at different dates are different people. They work for a time at minimum wage, but they do not stay there.

The story of a young blacksmith well illustrates the process Lincoln described. When farmers in Illinois had problems plowing the prairie sod in the 1830s, he fashioned a steel plow share that solved the problem. His sale of plows grew slowly for a time. Yet after just a few years, the blacksmith, John Deere, built a factory.

We could cite many such stories. Many large business enterprises rose from humble beginnings. Many people, like Benjamin Franklin, began their careers working for others and became business owners and employers. In some cases, as with John Deere, they rose through an invention. Others rose by other means.

Its great freedom and opportunity led to America serving as home for many inventions. Eli Whitney: the cotton gin; Cyrus McCormick: the reaper; Samuel F. B. Morse: the telegraph; Alexander Graham Bell: the telephone; Marconi: the wireless (forerunner of radio); Charles Goodyear: vulcanized rubber; Nicola Tesla: radio tubes, and practical alternating current; Thomas Edison: the electric light, motion pictures, the phonograph to record sound, and a host of other inventions; Orville and Wilbur Wright: the airplane (or at least, manned flight); Philo Farnsworth: the television. While these are among the more famous, such a list of American inventors and their practical inventions could be expanded into the thousands. The twentieth century saw a flood of scientific and technological advances, many of them originating in the United States. Indeed, the advances in the U.S. helped spark advances elsewhere.

In the words of Donzella Cross Boyle, "The achievements of man are boundless when his spirit is set at liberty."[6]

• • •

Among the major powers of the earth, America stands out for her motivations in war. In general, she has not sought to gain territory and power by conquest. Her first war was defensive, fought for freedom and independence. By the treaty that settled that war, America held title to land from the Atlantic to the Mississippi River. The largest part of additional territory came with the Louisiana Purchase from France. In the War of 1812, there were some who wanted to conquer Canada, but war came primarily because of British impressment of American sailors, and British failure to respect America's rights as a neutral country in Britain's war with France. In 1845 the U.S. annexed Texas. Soon after, came war with Mexico. Most people do not know all the causes that we will discuss later. The United States acquired a large part of what is now the American Southwest in the treaty that settled this war. The territory so acquired is often referred to as the Mexican Cession, for which the United States paid Mexico $15 million, plus assuming some $3 million in claims against Mexico. Shortly thereafter (1853), the U.S. paid Mexico another $10 million for a much smaller area ceded to us in the Gadsden Purchase. The boundary with Canada in the Northwest was settled by negotiated treaty without conflict, which confirmed title to Oregon and Washington. America bought Alaska from Russia.

The Spanish-American War in 1898, begun for largely humanitarian reasons, brought possession of Cuba and the Philippines. Later, we allowed both to become independent countries. From World War I, we took no territory. America fought in World War II to defend freedom and to defeat three of the worst totalitarian aggressors in history. We kept the island of Okinawa for many years, but have since given it back to Japan. In Korea and Vietnam, the U.S. sought to protect the freedom of an allied country from a Communist aggressor. We took no territory. Since then we have fought Iraq in the first Gulf War to eject them from Kuwait, and Afghanistan and Iraq in the "War on Terror." We took no territory. Indeed, after World War II the U.S. made significant and expensive efforts toward the rebuilding or rejuvenation of Germany and Japan, and has made similar efforts during the recent, ongoing conflicts in Afghanistan and Iraq.

This unique nation does not and cannot remain free solely by military power or by economic might. The hearts and minds of Americans determine the country's destiny. Abraham Lincoln said, "What constitutes the bulwark of our own liberty and independence? It is not our frowning battlements, our bristling sea coasts, our army and our navy. These are not our reliance against tyranny . . . Our reliance is in the love of liberty which God has planted in us. Our defense is in the spirit which prized liberty as the heritage of all men, in all lands everywhere."[7]

The love of liberty, and even the understanding of liberty, cannot survive without care and effort. Ignorance is one of many enemies of freedom. Thomas Jefferson said, "If a nation expects to be ignorant and free, in a state of civilization, it expects what never was and never will be."[8]

That's the reason for this book. That is why the next section will discuss the traditions of the common law.

CHAPTER ONE

For a Foundation of Freedom

Colonial and Pre-Colonial Issues

The Common Law
Foundation of Freedom

THEME: Principles of Freedom and of America's Founding

The roots of America's system of law come from England's common law. It formed the basis for the tradition of freedom that came with the colonists from England. It is important to understand the common law and how it differs from civil law, or as it may also be called, "ruler's law."

The differences between these two systems are described, in part, as follows, by J. Reuben Clark, Jr., former Ambassador to Mexico, and constitutional lawyer.

> As of the time of the writing of the Constitution, there were two great systems of law in the world—the Civil Law (the law of continental Europe) and the Common Law (the law of England and her colonies, including the 13 American Colonies).
>
> Briefly, and stated in general terms, the basic concept of these two systems was as opposite as the poles—in the Civil Law the source of all law is the personal ruler; whether prince, king, or emperor—he is sovereign. In the Common Law, certainly as finally developed in America, the source of all law is the people . . .
>
> The people under this system [of Roman or civil law] have those rights, powers, and privileges, and those only which the sovereign considers are for their good or for his advantage. . . . *Under this system, the people look into the law to see what they may do. . . . under our common law system, we look into the law to see what we may not do, for we may do everything we are not forbidden to do.*[1]

Where did the common law come from? This ancient system differs greatly from what some scholars in our day have said of it. For example, one author (Arthur Hogue) believes the common law comes from the royal courts of

England. He considers it to have developed in its early phase between about 1154 and 1307.[2] Another (Walter Ullmann) asserts that it grew out of feudalism.[3] Thomas Jefferson, a couple of hundred years closer than these authors to the common law, defined it differently.

Jefferson describes it thus: "The common law of England, by which is meant, that part of the English law which was anterior to the date of the oldest statutes extant."[4] [anterior: prior; extant: can still be found.] Jefferson could read and write Anglo-Saxon. He was able to study ancient sources, and found that the common law came from the law the Anglo-Saxons brought to England about 450 A.D.[5] Hence, according to Jefferson, the common law, or its origin, is far older than 1154; in fact, far older than 1066 (the year of the Norman invasion of England). Jefferson asserted forcefully, that feudalism and the common law clashed with one another.

How could we know of law without a written record? To illustrate, regarding land law among the English prior to the Norman Conquest, J. E. A. Jolliffe, Emeritus Fellow of Keble College, Oxford, says: "In common with many of the Germanic codes the laws of the English contain no complete statement of the custom of landright. It was known to all, needed no written record, and was spoken by verbal memory in the courts."[6]

In addition, Jefferson speaks of various fragments of the ancient laws of the Anglo-Saxons as still available. ". . . their substance has been committed to many ancient books and writings, so faithfully as to have been deemed genuine from generation to generation."[7] He also said the common law could be "collected from the usual monuments of it,"[8]—that is, old writings containing some of the principles of the common law.

W. Cleon Skousen discusses the origins of the common law in his *The Making of America,* describing the organization and principles of Anglo-Saxon society and law. (See his Chapter 2, Discovery of the Ancient Principles.) Thomas Jefferson wanted many of our laws restored to those of the Anglo-Saxons as they were before the eighth century.[9] The Norman invasion in 1066 brought much of the Roman or "civil" law to England, and episodes such as that of the Magna Charta, represent the efforts of the English to regain the rights they formerly held under the common law.

Feudalism grew out of the civil law. A significant part of the difference between feudalism and the common law deals with ownership of land. Jefferson
said, "Our Saxon ancestors held their lands, as they did their personal property
in absolute dominion."[10] Such ownership is sometimes called, "allodial." This
was the common law in England before 1066. Thus Jolliffe says, ". . . the dis-
tinctive fact of Saxon custom is that it is governed by the notion . . . of property, and almost entirely by the right of individuals.[11] . . . We are brought,
therefore, to conclude that in the tenth and eleventh centuries the Saxon land-
holder was free both from customary rules such as may have prevailed in a re-
mote past, and from the manifold restrictions upon tenant right and lord's
right which were the essence of feudal *dominium*. The Saxon's right was, in
short, not tenure but property."[12]

Under feudalism, any land holder had a "lord" to whom he and his land
were subject, and from whom he held the land ("tenure," or being merely a
tenant of someone else). Feudalism came to England with the Norman conquest.[13] After 1066 then, as Jefferson describes, "A general principle was introduced, that 'all lands in England were held either mediately or immediately of
the Crown;'" or in other words, "The fictitious principle, that all lands belong
originally to the King."[14] "The Norman lawyers soon found means to saddle"
the English people with the burdens and taxes of feudalism.[15] Hogue asserts
that there were no allodial lands under the English common law.[16] However,
Jefferson answers, "Feudal holdings were, therefore, but exceptions out of the
Saxon laws of possession, under which all lands were held in absolute right.
These, therefore, still form the basis or groundwork of the Common law."[17]

Hogue and Ullman have mistaken feudalism, a form of the civil law, for the
common law. They say of the allodial concept of the right to property, that it
did not exist in the common law, while Jefferson says it was a foundation of the
common law. In this difference of definition, I choose to trust the wisdom,
knowledge and depth of understanding of Jefferson. Applying this here, "America was not conquered by William the Norman, nor its lands surrendered to
him or any of his successors. Possessions there are, undoubtedly, of the Allodial
nature."[18]

Under civil law, rights are bestowed upon the people by their government.
Hence they only have those rights that government allows them; they may only

do what they are allowed to do. Under common law, the people "are endowed by their Creator with inherent and inalienable rights."[19] In this tradition, government makes laws to keep people from hurting each other, but otherwise leaves them free. Government in the United States developed the way it did, at least in part, because its first settlers came from England, bringing the tradition of the common law.

Questions

Question 1: What do the words *inherent* and *inalienable* mean?

Question 2: Which would give a person more personal choice and freedom, civil or common law, and why?

Question 3: About 1990, a family moved from a city in Colorado to a rural area in Kentucky. They purchased land, and planned to put up additional buildings on it. Having become accustomed to the restrictions and the need for permits in the city they came from, they went to the county about their plans. No permits were required. They needed to comply with law about the disposal of sewage. Aside from that, each time they asked, "Can we do this . . .?", they were told, "It's your land. Do whatever you want."

Which approach shows characteristics of the common law, and which shows characteristics of the civil law? Which approach implies greater freedom?

Origin of the "Native American" or "American Indian"

THEMES: Seeking Truth, Including Truth About Race Relations; Peace Requires Justice

When the first English settlers came to America, bringing those traditions of the common law, they met a race that was already here. Who were they? Where did they come from?

History books commonly present the theory that the ancestors of these people came from eastern Asia over a land bridge between Siberia and Alaska. Usually this is said to have occurred during an ice age, with the northern part of North America covered by thick sheets of ice. Often a map purports to show the route of migration. In some books, the map shows a convenient, comparatively narrow path through open land between large glaciated areas–a different path depending on which book. In others, the migration route crosses over a thousand miles of glacier. One book refers to the ice as two miles thick. One book expresses the ultimate in silliness with a passage describing the first Americans hunting deer and elephants over these ice sheets.

If that were true, they would have all died together, for the deer and elephants would have nothing to eat. Even with the theoretical path between large glaciated areas, a climate that would keep such huge areas under ice would certainly not allow much vegetation to grow in a narrow strip between them. It takes a lot of green stuff to feed an elephant, or a mammoth. A discerning student should recognize this as ridiculous; yet we have adult college professors writing and teaching this nonsense.

Humans are very mobile creatures. They build boats. Whether the first Americans came from eastern Asia or from somewhere else, they would not need a land bridge to get here. There could have been multiple places of origin. Whichever way they came, they didn't follow herds across a thousand miles of ice.

We do not have a good term in common usage for these people. The term Indian derives from Columbus' mistake in thinking he had reached the East

Indies. The term Native American does not distinguish them from a couple of hundred million of us not of their race, but who are native Americans because we were born here. Amerindian is somewhat clumsy, and still uses, in part, Columbus' mistake, but at least it's a designation that distinguishes them from other Americans, and from Indians from India. It is therefore the nearest to a neutral term.

Amerindians, especially Eskimos, have some characteristics in common with east Asians. However, some of what has been known for decades does not fit the theory. Blood type is inherited. About 30 percent or more of east Asians and south Asians have type B blood. It is more common among them than in any other group. By contrast, among Amerindians that blood type is virtually absent.

In addition to the OAB system of blood classification, there are (or have been) other systems. One of these is the MNS system. Among Amerindians, "the frequency of blood type M is extremely high (nearly 90 per cent). This sets off the Amerindian geographical race from all other geographical races."[20]

Some evidence from archeology (pyramid building and dimensions, for example, in Egypt and Central America) and other sources indicates the possibility of a middle eastern origin for the Amerindian. Thor Heyerdahl pointed out the similarity between the making of reed boats in Egypt and Peru. He and others constructed reed boats that he called Ra, and Ra II, which they sailed from the middle east to the West Indies. Thus he showed that people could have come that way to America, even with comparatively primitive technology. This does not prove that they came that way, just that they could have.

Many current history books give a one-sided picture of relations between Amerindians and English settlers, or Americans of European descent. In this picture, English or Americans are always in the wrong. Land purchases from the Amerindians, such as that of Roger Williams in Rhode Island, are often ignored. There were many purchases, some very large. Some of those may have been made by duress, but others were not. Roger Williams recognized the Amerindians as the rightful owners of the land, and therefore bought land from them. While his purchase was one of the more famous ones, his was not the only one.

Francis Parkman,[21] in *The Conspiracy of Pontiac*, quotes Bancroft as follows: "The inhabitants of New England had never, except in the territory of the

Pequods, taken possession of a foot of land without first obtaining a title from the Indians." Parkman also quotes instructions to purchase such title, from 1629. "Several of the other colonies had more recently pursued the same just and prudent course."[22] William Penn actually paid two tribes for the same lands–the Delawares, who occupied them, and the powerful Iroquois, "who claimed them by right of conquest."[23]

Parkman also mentions instances where land was taken without title, and the infamous "walking purchase," about 1737, by which the Pennsylvania proprietors cheated the Delawares.[24]

The landing of the Pilgrims at Plymouth in 1620, presents a different scenario. They took over land with no occupants. The tribe that previously lived in that area had all died from disease, except for Squanto. He had spent time in England, spoke English, and came to the Pilgrims and helped them adapt to the land.

Some histories imply that it was always the white man who broke the treaties. Perhaps in the past some histories presented this the other way around. Both sides broke treaties. It is certainly a mistake to think that the fault always belonged to one and the same side. There were some English (before 1776) or Americans who did not respect the rights of Amerindians. There were also some who strove to deal with the Amerindians honestly, justly, uprightly, and honorably. The latter included Roger Williams, Benjamin Franklin, Thomas Jefferson and Abraham Lincoln. Some Amerindians dealt in treachery and bloodshed, and were truly savages; some strove to keep their word and to live in peace. The true picture of relations between these races is mixed and complex. The sections on Franklin and the Confrontation at Germantown, and Roots of the Sioux War of 1876, illustrate this.

Franklin and the Confrontation at Germantown

THEMES: Complexity of Race Relations; Whites Defending Amerindians from Other Whites; true history is not the captive nor the enemy of any one race or ethnic group; pursue truth wherever it leads.

In 1763 the English had just won the French and Indian War and took over Canada from the French. The Amerindians along the frontier commenced another war upon the "English," largely at the instigation of the chief Pontiac. The war took place from New York to Virginia, and west to what is now Michigan. An extensive account may be found in *The Conspiracy of Pontiac* by Francis Parkman (1851, 1870).[25] This war had several causes. Blame may probably be shared by the English, the French Canadians, and the Amerindians. The English made some mistakes in their treatment of the Amerindians.[26] In some areas the English had settled on land without permission.[27] The tribes had allowed themselves to become dependent on the gifts from the French,[28] which they did not receive from the English, and began the war through treachery. By treachery they massacred the garrison at Michillimackinac. The Ojibwas and Sacs professed friendship to the English, and pretended to engage in a ball game. The game was a mere device used to bring about the massacre. This is an account of true savagery, marked by the drinking of the blood of the slain, the murder of prisoners and cannibalism.[29] By treachery, Pontiac sought to kill the English at Detroit, professing friendship at the moment he had planned to start the killing.[30] Some of the French who remained in Canada and what Americans later called the Northwest Territory, were only too happy to incite a war between the other two parties. These French told various lies to the Amerindians and encouraged them to make war on the English.[31]

By the fall of 1763 more than two thousand English colonists had been killed. In Pennsylvania, those on the frontier had suffered many atrocities—such as the massacres at Greenbrier and Wyoming, and the murder of a school teacher and eight of his students.[32] They were also angry over the government's failure to help with their defense. Near the town of Lancaster, lived a group of twenty Amerindians, called the Conestogas. They were apparently a peaceful tribe; they had made a treaty with William Penn as early as 1701, and many of them had English names: John, Harry, Peggy, etc. There is some "evidence" that *may* implicate from one to four of the Conestogas in some hostile acts. Some of this evidence is merely speculative. In mid-December, a group of frontiersmen from Paxton and Donegal attacked the village of the Conestogas at night, killing all six that were at home. Local authorities gathered the other fourteen from the surrounding neighborhood, and put them in the stone jail at Lancaster for their safety. On December 27th, about fifty to one hundred armed men stormed the jail and killed the other fourteen Conestogas, mostly women and children.

Not satisfied with this deed, they announced their intention to go to Philadelphia to kill the 140 Amerindians housed there. These people had been brought there months before to keep them out of harm's way, as well as to be sure they did no harm. Most of them were Moravian converts to Christianity. The Paxton men raised an army variously reported as from 500 to 1,500 and marched toward Philadelphia in February, 1764. The governor appealed to Benjamin Franklin for help. Franklin took the lead in raising an army to defend the city, and the Amerindians.

On hearing of preparations in Philadelphia, the Paxton men stopped in Germantown. A delegation of four went to meet them, including Franklin. He had publicly called them murderers, so this involved considerable personal risk. When he told them that if they came, they would be met by 1,000 men, dug in, with cannon, the Paxton men backed down. The delegation assured them that their concerns about the safety of the frontier would be considered by the governor and the Assembly. The Paxton men dispersed, most returning home. A few were allowed to come into Philadelphia to examine the Amerindians, to look for any that had committed hostile acts. They could not identify any who had.

None of the Paxton men were punished for what they had done, a fact that Franklin found bitterly disappointing.[33]

Common Storehouse and Starvation; Freedom and Plenty

THEME: Principles of Economics, Private Property, and the Free Market

When the first permanent English settlement in America was founded in 1607 at Jamestown, Virginia, at first the settlers used a common storehouse. When the Pilgrims and those with them landed at Plymouth, in Massachusetts in 1620, they also used a common storehouse. Those who worked and those who didn't were fed the same. This did not work well at either place. Both colonies went through a "starving time." In Jamestown, Captain John Smith had to tell the men, "If you don't work, you don't eat." During one period they survived mainly because of the generosity of the local Amerindians. A later governor tried to make the system work by means of martial law. In Massachusetts they endured the common storehouse system for seven years; in Virginia, it lasted a little longer.

In each colony, they did not achieve abundance until they stopped using a common storehouse, and adopted freedom and private property. Once each person, or each family, could have their own land and could benefit from what they produced, then the colony was on a firm economic footing. Then they prospered.

The Development of Religious Freedom

THEME: Principles of Freedom and of America's Founding—A Long Time Coming

One of the most basic of all freedoms, is freedom of conscience. This means the right to believe and worship (or not) as we choose. This freedom developed slowly over centuries, and did not come to full fruition until America became a nation.

The Romans persecuted Christianity off and on for the first three hundred years from the time of Christ. After the emperor Constantine gave Christianity official recognition and favoritism in the Roman Empire, about 325 A.D., that changed. By 390, ironically, Christians were persecuting pagans.

In the mid-seventh century, the Muslim religion arose, and was spread by the sword. Some dispute over whether Muhammad, its founder, so intended, or his followers erred in interpreting his teachings. For centuries, uniformity of Christian viewpoint was enforced by the sword. This was clearly not the intent of Christ.

One means of enforcing Christian uniformity was called the Inquisition. The Inquisition was used in the 1200s, revived in the 1400s, and thereafter brought terror for nearly 300 years. Suspects were sometimes tortured to admit their guilt while a recorder sat by to take down every word, to be used against them. Those judged heretics could be publicly tied to a stake and burned. The Inquisition was strongest in Spain, but was also strong in Italy, and was used in the 1200s in France.[34] It was not the only form of religious intolerance of that age, just the most infamous.

In England, William Sawtre in 1400, and John Badby in 1409, were executed for "heresy," which means that those in power found their religious opinions unacceptable. Officials offered Badby a yearly stipend of three pence a day out of the king's treasury for as long as he lived, to deny his beliefs. He refused, and they burned him to death.[35]

About the year 1447, Johann Gutenberg was the first in Europe to use movable metal type in his printing press. One of the first things he printed was the Bible. Before that time, most people had no access to the Bible.

William Tyndale translated the New Testament and the Pentateuch (the first five books of the Bible) into English. The translation was published outside of England and smuggled into the country, where the Archbishop ordered any copies of the book confiscated and burned. Tyndale was tried for heresy and killed for his beliefs in 1536.

Also in the early 1500s, many other people and events contributed to the breaking of what was previously a religious monopoly over most of Europe. In 1517 Martin Luther protested the sale of "indulgences," by nailing to the door of his local church, a list of 95 "theses" against the practice. In 1521 the Catholic Church excommunicated him, but protected by his prince, Frederic "the Wise," he formed a new church, the Lutheran sect. Meanwhile Zwingli and Calvin began a new church in Switzerland.

The king of England at that time was Henry VIII. Henry wanted a son, and sought to divorce his wife Catherine of Aragon, or to have their marriage annulled. In eighteen years, they had only one child, Mary. When he couldn't get his way with the Catholic Church, Henry broke away and formed the Church of England. After a few more wives, he had another daughter and a son.

At the death of Henry VIII, his son Edward VI became king of England. Edward died after ruling for only six years, and Mary Tudor became queen. Her persecution of those with differing religious beliefs earned her the title, "Bloody Mary." She reigned from 1553 to 1558, and was succeeded by her half sister, Elizabeth. Mary Tudor married Prince Philip of Spain, who in 1556 became Philip II, king of Spain, which he ruled until 1598. With his encouragement, during his reign the Inquisition gained the greatest strength and power in its history, and the burning of heretics was a common sight.

During her brief reign, Mary had tried to turn England back to Catholicism, but Elizabeth was Protestant, and she ruled from 1558 to 1603. While she was queen, the first efforts were made to plant an English colony in America. During this period, and during much of the next century, from time to time and by turns, England persecuted Catholics, Puritans, and Quakers.[36]

In 1689 Parliament passed the Toleration Act, which gave most sects some freedom of religion. That freedom still did not apply to Catholics and Unitarians.[37]

On the eve of the Reformation, but after Gutenberg, Columbus had discovered America. Other explorers had apparently discovered the existence of the American continents hundreds of years earlier, but the knowledge had not spread, nor was it retained. Most of Europe remained ignorant of this land's existence. This time the knowledge of it spread. At first some in Europe thought mainly of America as a place to seek gold and conquest. Eventually groups in England began to think of America as a place to escape the oppression of the Old World, especially religious oppression.

Hence, in 1620 the Plymouth colony was founded by the Pilgrims in search of religious freedom. They were Puritans, and had gone from England to Holland, but did not want their children growing up learning the ways of the Dutch. Hence they sought freedom by leaving Europe and going to America. Not all of those aboard the Mayflower were from this religious group. Other Puritans, perhaps of a different religious persuasion, for there were several types of "Puritans," left England for Massachusetts a few years later. When they also persecuted those of different religious views, Roger Williams went to what is now Providence, Rhode Island. There he purchased land from the Amerindians, and founded a colony based on religious freedom. In Rhode Island, all were free to worship as they chose, without persecution.

Lord Baltimore founded the colony of Maryland in 1632 as a place where Catholics could go to freely follow their religion. Likewise, William Penn founded Pennsylvania in 1681 seeking freedom for Quakers.

The success of these colonies as places of religious tolerance was mixed. Still, more religious freedom grew in America than anywhere else, and after Independence it soon burst into full bloom.

Thomas Jefferson introduced into the Virginia legislature a bill for religious freedom which eventually passed. This bill provided that "no man shall be compelled to frequent or support any religious worship, place, or ministry," nor "suffer on account of his religious opinions or belief; but that all men shall be free to profess . . . their opinions in matters of religion, and" this shall not "affect their civil capacities."[38] By saying that a person's religion would not "affect their civil capacities," Jefferson meant that it would not affect their ability to hold public office, to give testimony in court or serve on a jury, to sue or be sued, or their legal guardianship over their children.

Not long after, the U. S. Constitution, in Article VI Clause 3, said that "no religious test shall ever be required as a qualification to any office or public trust under the United States." A few states still had such religious tests as a qualification to state office (for instance, that one had to be a Christian, or a Protestant Christian), but those disappeared over the next few decades. The first Congress under the Constitution passed the Bill of Rights, and once ratified, the First Amendment forbid Congress from making a state religion for America, or interfering with the right of the people to worship according to their own conscience–thus, "Congress shall make no law respecting an establishment of religion, or prohibiting the free exercise thereof."

CHAPTER TWO

Roots of America's Declaration of Independence

American Colonial Foundations

THEME: Rights of Colonial Americans by Charters, Treaty, and Natural Law—Beginning of American Freedom—Legal and Moral Foundation for Independence

To understand the roots of America's independence, we need to consider the way the colonies were founded, and the rights promised them.

Every colony except Georgia, was privately financed. From Virginia's first permanent settlement in Jamestown in 1607, to Pennsylvania in 1681, the first twelve colonies were each the product of the vision, money, and enterprise of private parties. For commercial venture or to create a haven for certain religious groups, individuals or joint stock companies provided the financing.[1] For instance, the London Company financed the founding of Virginia; Thomas Weston provided backing for the Pilgrims' migration to Plymouth on the Mayflower.[2] When Charles I granted the Charter of Maryland to George Calvert, Lord Baltimore, in 1632, it provided "that he may transport [people to the new colony], by his own Industry, and Expense."[3]

Georgia was the brainchild of James Oglethorpe, a place to send people freed from debtors' prison. George II granted a Charter for Georgia in 1732. Parliament gave repeated monetary grants to this undertaking, making it the only colony to ever receive government money for its founding. Even so, most of the cost was met through numerous private gifts of both money and supplies of all kinds.[4]

Significantly, the colonies in America were never an effort of the English government.

However, the English government made commitments to many of the colonies from very early in their existance. By treaty or charter, with documents varying in their language, England committed to honor the following rights of the colonists:

1. Americans had all rights that Englishmen had.

2. Americans had the same rights as Englishmen to trade freely with any nation or place in the world. This is plainly implied by point one; it's also specifically mentioned for Virginia.

3. Americans could not be taxed without the consent of their legislatures. This is also implied by point one, and is specifically mentioned in the case of Virginia.

4. England could not send troops to an American colony without the colony's consent.

5. Americans had the right to resist any invasion by force.

The legal rights in points one to three were repeatedly violated. When point four was also violated, Americans eventually resorted to the use of point five. It was the only choice left to them to retain, or regain, their freedom.

For instance, when Charles I was deposed, for a time, the colony of Virginia opposed the rule of Cromwell and the Parliament. Eventually they were persuaded to accept it. Virginia then entered into a treaty or agreement with England on March 12, 1651. This "solemn convention," as Jefferson called it, contained among its terms the following:

> . . . inhabitants [of Virginia] . . . shall have and enjoy such freedoms and privileges as belong to the free born people of England. . . . 7ly. ["Seventhly"] That the people of Virginia have free trade as the people of England do enjoy to all places and with all nations . . . 8ly. That Virginia shall be free from all taxes, customs, and impositions whatsoever, and none to be imposed on them without consent of the [Virginia] assembly; . . . that neither forts nor castle be erected or garrisons maintained without their consent.

The "commissioners for the parliament" that signed this on behalf of England, committed to "engage themselves and the honor of parliament for the full performance thereof."[5]

This Virginia agreement is very clear about points two, three, and four. For other colonies we do not have the same degree of clarity, yet for most of them the charters imply the same points.

POINT 1.–THE SAME RIGHTS AS ENGLISHMEN

Virginia's charters of both 1606 and 1609 contain a clause about its citizens having all rights of those born and abiding in England. Those of Massachusetts and Rhode Island contain similar clauses except they leave out "abiding,"[6] as does North Carolina's. The charter of Connecticut (1662) promised that all in that colony "shall have and enjoy all Liberties and Immunities of free and natural subjects within any of the Dominions" of the British crown, "as if they . . . were born within the realm of England."[7] The charter of Georgia (1732) promised that "all . . . persons . . . born within the said province, . . . shall have and enjoy all liberties, franchises and immunities of free denizens and natural born subjects, within any of our dominions, to all intents and purposes, as if abiding and born within this our kingdom of Great-Britain."[8] (England united with Scotland in 1707 to become Great Britain, hence that difference in the wording of Georgia's charter.)

BINDING ON THE KING'S HEIRS–MOST FAVORABLE INTERPRETATION–CONTRARY THINGS NOTWITHSTANDING

Maryland's charter (1632) promises that all citizens and their descendants, will have all liberties as if they were born in England. In contractual language, it binds not only King Charles I and the English government of the time, but also their "Heirs or Successors." Charters for at least nine colonies contain language making each charter's promise binding on the king's heirs or successors. Maryland's charter firmly states its constitutional supremacy to acts of Parliament or other English governmental bodies: "any Statute, Act, Ordinance, or Provision to the contrary thereof, notwithstanding."[9] Hence many of the acts of Parliament that aggrieved America, as applied to Maryland, were legally null and void. The same principle applies to several other colonies.

Some of the charters, for instance those for Connecticut and Georgia, contain wording similar to that of Maryland's described above, about "anything to the contrary notwithstanding." In Connecticut's case the language is not quite as clear, but Georgia's declares that the charter must be "construed and adjudged, in all courts and elsewhere in the most favorable and beneficial sense, and for the best advantage" of the colony "any omission, imperfection, defect, matter or cause, or thing whatsoever to the contrary, in any wise notwithstanding."[10]

This mandate that the charter be interpreted in the way most favorable to the colony is also found in other charters. Virginia's says "that in all Questions and Doubts that shall arise upon any difficulty of Construction or Interpretation of any Thing . . . in this . . . the same shall be taken and interpreted in most ample and beneficial Manner for the . . . Company and their Successors, and every Member thereof."[11] The Massachusetts (1620), North Carolina and Rhode Island charters express a similar idea.[12] Thus any doubt about the meaning is to be resolved in favor of the colonists or the associated corporation, *not in favor of the British government.*

POINTS 3. AND 4. AND THE ENGLISH BILL OF RIGHTS

The English Bill of Rights passed in 1689, forbid the king from taxing the English or keeping a standing army among them, without the consent of Parliament. Points three and four above are nothing more than logically applying the same rights to the colonies. By point one, the same rights must apply. Hence the American colonists could not legally be taxed, nor standing armies kept among them, without the consent of their own legislatures.

POINTS 4. AND 5.—THE RIGHT TO RESIST ANY INVASION BY FORCE

Connecticut's charter recognized the colony's right to resist any invasion by force.[13] This, of course, is a natural right. The charter makes it also a legal right. *As both a natural and legal right, it could be exercised even against England.* Charters for Massachusetts, Rhode Island, Virginia and Georgia, also contain similar clauses for their right to defend themselves against invasion. For instance, the Massachusetts charter of 1691 states the colony's right to resist by force of arms "all and every such Person or Persons as shall at any time hereafter Attempt or Enterprise the destruction, Invasion, Detriment or Annoyance" of the colony.[14] (Spelling and punctuation slightly modernized.)

Most of the charters contain this same right of defense. A number of them even say that the colonists may prevent anyone else from attempting to inhabit the colony without their consent. That certainly applies to British troops, as in point four above.

POINT 2.–THE RIGHT TO TRADE

Regarding the right to trade, while the 1651 agreement with Virginia was very clear, the charters were a hodgepodge. Some of the grants, patents, commissions, or charters did not mention trade at all. Hence, one could presume those colonies free of restrictions. Others contained minimal restrictions. Pennsylvania's was very restrictive. Some fell in between. For colonies with multiple charters of different dates, the later charters tended to impose more trade restrictions. Usually, when taxes on trade were mentioned, the charter called for the same duties on colonial trade as on British trade. Sometimes taxes on imports into the colony were authorized but not mandated. In a number of cases, the terms contained inherent ambiguity.

For instance, consider the question of whether a colony could ship goods directly to a foreign country. Some of these documents outlined the following procedure: they authorized the colony to ship products to England or any British dominion, there to be unloaded and taxed. Then if desired, they could load the same products again, and ship them "duty free" to foreign countries. Clearly, the British government did not impose this burden on those shipping initially from England. In most cases however, these charters did not mention whether the colony might ship directly to a foreign country.

In the case of Pennsylvania, the charter also forbid the colony from shipping directly to any other country. A number of other charters authorized the described procedure, but did not forbid direct shipment. To interpret this to forbid the colonists from doing so, would conflict with the requirements that they have the same rights as those in England, and that the charter be interpreted most favorably for the colony or its associated company.

This presents us with an interesting comparison between the view of the civil law and that of the common law. Under the civil law, we look to the law to see what we are allowed to do. With that view, the colonies could only do as authorized; hence even though direct shipping was not mentioned, it would not be allowed. Under the common law, we look to the law to see what is forbidden, and we are allowed to do anything else. With that view, if direct shipping was not mentioned, then it was permissible. Certainly, with the same rights as Englishmen in England, and the most favorable interpretation, we must so conclude.

That view, I believe, should have prevailed for most of the colonies.

Many texts refer to seafaring Americans as smugglers who during this period traded with other countries and evaded enforcement of Parliament's trade regulations. Certainly the British considered them smugglers. Yet if we take the common law view, they were exercising legal rights under colonial charters.

We could look at Parliamentary legislation, such as the Navigation Acts, to judge the meaning of the charters. In that case, we would have to conclude that the charters intended to forbid some colonies from trading directly with foreign countries. However, to me that is logically backward. It's contrary to my premise, that *considering the charters more fundamental and superior to the legislation, the legislation should be judged by the charters.*

Either way, there still remains the presumed guarantee of the same rights as those in England, the right of control over immigration or the influx of British troops, the most favorable interpretation, and the right to resist invasion by force.

British Denial of the Same Rights as Those Born and Abiding in England

When Parliament tried to outlaw the building of iron mills in America (the Iron Act of 1750), or restrict the making of hats in America (the Hat Act of 1732), or to regulate trade coming to or from America differently (more restrictively and with more taxes, sometimes only in ships built in Great Britain) than trade coming to or from England, it was seeking to deny to Americans rights of Englishmen. Parliament sought to take away trial by jury regarding alleged violations of the Sugar Act of 1764, and the trade act of 1768. This violated the English Bill of Rights of 1689.

Thus many of the British actions were violations of the treaty with Virginia and of these charters. When Americans resisted these actions, Britain sent troops to America. That was also a violation of the Virginia treaty, and of both natural and legal rights. Jefferson spoke of it thus:

> . . . to enforce the arbitrary measures before complained of, his
> Majesty has . . . sent among us large bodies of armed forces . . . Did

his Majesty possess such a right as this, it might swallow up all our other rights, whenever he should think proper. But his Majesty has no right to land a single armed man on our shores; and those whom he sends here are liable to our laws . . . or are hostile bodies invading us in defiance of law.[15]

I have above, in honesty, admitted those items of evidence that could weigh against my conclusion. However, I still arrive at this conclusion:

America's resistance, and her Declaration of Independence, stood on a rock solid moral and legal foundation.

TABLE 1: **Features of Colonial Charters by Colony**

Charter	Year	All Liberties of English or British	Most Favorable Construction	Defense Against Invasion
Walter Raleigh	1585		Yes	Yes
Connecticut	1662	shall have and enjoy all Liberties ... as if they ... were born within the realm of England	shall be construed ... most favorable ... of the said ... Company and their Successors	to ... resist by Force of Arms ... and to kill ... every such Person ... as shall attempt ... Invasion ...
Delaware	1701	[refers to right to] an Assembly, according to the Rights of the Free-born Subjects of England, and as is usual in any of the King's Plantations in America.		
Georgia	1732	that all and every the persons which shall ... be born within the said province, ... shall have and enjoy all liberties ... as if abiding and born within this our kingdom of Great-Britain	shall be... con-strued and ad-judged, in all courts and else-where in the most favorable ... sense, and for the best ad-vantage of the said corporation and their successors any ... defect ...or thing whatsoever to the contrary, ... notwithstanding.	repel, resist and pursue by force of arms ... every such person ... as shall at any time ... in any hostile manner attempt ... invasion ..invade or attempt the invading, con-quering or annoy-ing of said colony.

TABLE 1: Features of Colonial Charters by Colony (continued)

Charter	Year	All Liberties of English or British	Most Favorable Construction	Defense Against Invasion
Maryland	1632 1681	all ... Liberties of this our Kingdom of England, ... in the same manner as our Liege-Men born ... within our said Kingdom of England, without Impediment, ... Vexation, ... or Grievance of Us		
Massachusetts	1620 1629 1691	shall have and enjoy all Liberties ... as if they ... were borne within this our Realm of England	[Yes, in the 1620 charter]	[very similar to Georgia's wording]
New Jersey	1664 1712			[1664] to make war ... as they shall see cause [1712] resist, by force of arms ... every such ... persons ... as shall ... attempt ... invasion
North Carolina	1663 1665	all liberties ... of this our kingdom of England, ... as our liege people born within the same, without the least molestation ... of us	most . . . favorable to [proprietors] their heirs and assigns	[1663] to muster . . . to make war [1665] to make war . . . as they shall see cause
Rhode Island	1663	shall have and enjoy all Liberties ... as if they ... were borne within the Realm of England	shall be construed, ... and adjudged in all cases most favorably ... for the benefit ...	resist by force of arms ... every such person ... as shall at any time ... attempt ... invasion
Virginia	1606 1609	all ... Persons ... which shall ... inhabit within the said Colony and ... their children ... shall have ... all Liberties ... as if ... abiding and born, within this our Realm of England	in all Questions ... of ... Interpretation ... the same shall be ... interpreted in most ... beneficial Manner for the ... Company, and their Successors, and every Member thereof.	resist by Force and Arms, ... all ... Persons whatsoever as ... shall ... attempt at any Time hereafter, Destruction, Invasion, Hurt ... to the said Colony

TABLE 1: **Features of Colonial Charters by Colony** (continued)

Charter	Year	Liberties promised binding on the king's heirs or successors	Binding regardless of other ordinances or statutes
Walter Raleigh	1585	Yes	Yes
Connecticut	1662	We do for Us, Our Heirs and Successors, ordain, declare, and grant unto the said Governor and Company, and their Successors ...	That these Our Letters Patents, shall be firm, good and effectual in the Law, [passage on most favorable for company] ... any Statute, Act, Ordinance, Provision, ... heretofore ... made, ... or any other Matter, Cause, or Thing whatsoever, to the contrary thereof, in any wise notwithstanding.
Delaware	1701	Yes	sort of
Georgia	1732	we do, for ourselves and successors, declare, by these presents, ...	these our letters patent, ... shall be ... valid ... in the law, ... in the most favorable ... sense, and for the best advantage of the said corporation and their successors any omission, imperfection, defect, matter or cause, or thing whatsoever to the contrary, in any wise notwithstanding.
Maryland	1632 1681	We ... for Us, our Heirs and Successors, do firmly charge, constitute, ordain ... [liberty passage] without Impediment, Molestation, Vexation, Impeachment, or Grievance of Us, or any of our Heirs or Successors;	[the passage to the left] any Statute, Act, Ordinance, or Provision to the contrary thereof, notwithstanding.
Massachusetts	1620 1629 1691	We do hereby for Us Our Heirs and Successors Grant Establish and Ordain ...	
New Jersey	1664		
NorthCarolina	1663	Yes	Yes
Rhode Island	1663	we do, for us our heirs and successors, ordain, declare and grant ...	Yes
Virginia	1606 1609	Also we do for Us, our Heirs and Successors, Declare by these Presents, ...	

Regarding Omissions from Table 1

Pennsylvania's charter was one of the worst, containing trade restrictions and allowing for taxation by Parliament.

In Thorpe's *American Charters, Constitutions and Organic Laws 1492-1908*, there is no reference to a specific charter for New York or South Carolina. Under New York, Thorpe refers to the charters for Virginia, New England, Massachusetts, Connecticut and a few other things. Under South Carolina, he refers to the charters given Walter Raleigh and the colony of Virginia.

For New Hampshire, Thorpe refers to charters given to Virginia, New England, and Massachusetts, plus such things as the Grant to John Mason and the Commission of John Cutt. In those latter documents, there's not much relating to our subject, except for the right to defend against invasion, found on page 2448 in Volume 4.

Whenever Any Government Becomes Destructive of These Ends

THEME: England's Violation of American Rights

In DI-2, Jefferson wrote that people had inherent and inalienable rights, and that "whenever any form of government becomes destructive of these ends, it is the right of the people to alter or to abolish it, and to institute new government."

Jefferson summed up the actions of England toward America succinctly, thus:

> Their trade with foreigners was totally suppressed, and when carried to Great Britain, was there loaded with imposts [i.e. taxes]. It is unnecessary, however, to glean up the several instances of injury, as scattered through American and British history, and the more especially as, by passing on to the accession of the present king [George III], we shall find specimens of them all, aggravated, multiplied and crowded within a small compass of time, so as to evince [show] a fixed design of considering our rights natural, conventional and chartered as mere nullities. [nullity: null and void, invalid, having no effect] The following is an epitome of the first sixteen years of his reign: The colonies were taxed internally and externally; their essential interests sacrificed to individuals in Great Britain; their legislatures suspended; charters annulled; trials by juries taken away; their persons subjected to transportation across the Atlantic, and to trial before foreign judicatories [i.e. courts]; their supplications for redress thought beneath answer; . . . armed troops sent among them to enforce submission to these violences; and actual hostilities commenced against them. No alternative was presented but resistance, or unconditional submission.[16]

Corruption in the British Government

THEME: Should America's Rights Remain Subject to a Corrupt British Government?

Jefferson described the British government in his day as having "an heredi-tary King, with a House of Lords and Commons corrupted to his will, and standing between him and the people."[17]

Some towns or areas of small population, sometimes called "rotten boroughs," elected representatives to Parliament, while some large cities had no representation. Although England's population at the time of the Revolution was about seven or eight million, Jefferson estimated that those who were entitled to vote came to only "one hundred and sixty thousand electors in the island of Great Britain."[18]

While Franklin was in England acting as agent for some of the colonies, he observed the Parliamentary elections of 1768 and 1774. Some men were spend-ing 4,000 pounds to bribe their way into Parliament. Because there were no res-idency requirements for election to the House of Commons, sufficient money put into the right hands would get a man elected from a district that could be anywhere in Britain. Members of Parliament could serve in other government positions at the same time. Those in Parliament who supported the Prime Min-ister could expect appointment to profitable offices, even during their term in Parliament.

Thus Franklin said that "most of the members are bribing or purchasing to get in. . . . there was little doubt of selling their votes to the Minister for the time being, to reimburse themselves."[19]

While those in the House of Lords were not elected, the same system of re-warding friends of the ministry (that is, the ruling group) prevailed there also. Thus when Franklin saw William Pitt's motion calling for the King to withdraw British troops from Boston rejected by the House of Lords, he said: "Sixteen Scotch peers and twenty four bishops, with all the Lords in possession or ex-pectation of places, when they vote together unanimously, as they generally do for ministerial measures, make a dead majority."[20]

Alexander Wedderburn, the man who so abused Franklin before the Privy Council, [see below, under Repeated Petitions, Repeated Injuries.] had been changed from the ministry's opponent to its supporter, by appointment to high office. In 1774, Lord Howe had conversed privately with Franklin in an effort to find a way to reconcile England and America. Apparently speaking for the ministry, Lord Howe had offered to Franklin "any reward in the power of the government to bestow."[21] The offer deeply offended Franklin.

Jefferson, knowing how things worked in England, in 1775 wrote: "the dignity of Parliament, it seems, can brook no opposition to its power. Strange, that a set of men, who have made sale of their virtue to the Minister, should yet talk of retaining dignity!"[22]

At the bottom of this corrupt system were the power, money, and influence of the king. So concluded both Franklin and Jefferson.

Speaking of ways to structure a legislature, Jefferson wrote, "in Great Britain it is said their constitution relies on the house of commons for honesty, and the lords for wisdom; which would be a rational reliance, if honesty were to be bought with money, and if wisdom were hereditary."[23]

In my study I have encountered authors that said George III was not a tyrant; that Americans were too sensitive; and that America did not have a good enough reason to break up the British Empire.

Any who would claim that America did not have reason enough to declare independence, must tell us this: How could America ever expect to receive liberty and justice under such a corrupt system of government?

There was only one thing to do: declare independence.

Lost: the Consent of the Governed

THEME: "Governments . . . [Derive] Their Just Powers from the Consent of the Governed" (DI-2); Britain Lost America's Consent Through Arrogant Abuse of American Rights

February 13, 1766, while he was speaking before Parliament regarding the Stamp Act, the members asked Franklin many questions about America. One was, "What was the temper of America toward Great Britain before the year 1763?"

Franklin replied, in part, "The best in the world . . . They were governed by this country at the expense only of a little pen, ink, and paper; they were led by a thread. They had not only a respect, but an affection for Great Britain; for its laws, its customs and manners, and even a fondness for its fashions . . . "

And to the follow up question, "And what is their temper now?"

"Oh, very much altered."[24]

Thomas Jefferson said in a letter to John Randolph, written November 29, 1775: "Believe me, dear Sir, there is not in the British empire a man who more cordially loves a union with Great Britain than I do. But by the God that made me, I will cease to exist before I yield to a connection on such terms as the British Parliament propose; and in this, I think I speak the sentiments of America."[25]

Beyond these examples, little more need be said under this heading. The events of 1765 to 1776 give evidence enough. Appendix D, the Cross Reference, includes a section *Actions of the King and Royal Governors and Acts of Parliament Related to the Declaration of Independence.* This list justifies the bulk of Jefferson's list of complaints in the Declaration. The British had the affection of America; by their arrogant treatment of America, they lost that affection. They also lost America's consent to have any political connection with Great Britain.

Waging War Against Us

THEME: Britain Moved to Open Warfare Against America; the Legal Tie between Protection and Allegiance

When Franklin testified before Parliament on the Stamp Act, he was asked about Britain sending a military force to America to carry out the act. In his reply, he warned, "They will not find a rebellion; they may indeed make one."[26]

That warning was not heeded for long. British troops were sent to America. Parliament passed bills demanding that Americans quarter them. In April of 1775, open warfare broke out at Lexington and Concord, in Massachusetts, when British troops tried to seize American arms. This attempt to disarm Americans violated another principle from the English Bill of Rights of 1689. About the first of May, the Royal Governor of Virginia, Lord Dunmore, threatened to free the slaves and arm them. This after colonists had several times attempted to stop the slave trade, and the king had vetoed every such attempt.

No doubt this forms part of the background to the paragraph Jefferson wrote, which was stricken by Congress from the Declaration, wherein he said:

> . . . he is now exciting those very people [the slaves] to rise in arms among us, and to purchase that liberty of which he has deprived them, by murdering the people on whom he also obtruded them: thus paying off former crimes committed against the LIBERTIES of one people, with crimes which he urges them to commit against the LIVES of another.[27]

That fall, Jefferson wrote, "Lord Dunmore has commenced hostilities in Virginia. That people bore with everything, till he attempted to burn the town of Hampton."[28]

Also that fall, the king proclaimed the colonies in rebellion. We shall consider more of the circumstances below, when we discuss the Olive Branch Petition.

Months before Independence, Parliament passed an act, with the king's approval, declaring America out of the king's protection. [King George] "announced that if the colonies were attacked by foreign foes, Britain would furnish no help. American ships were declared . . . 'free booty,' which meant it would be legal to capture any American vessel on the high seas and take it over, cargo and all. As for the crew, they would be impressed into the British navy."[29] The king also hired Hessian troops to send against America.

In June of 1776, in debate in Congress, some pointed to "a certain position in law, that allegiance and protection are reciprocal, the one ceasing when the other is withdrawn."[30] Protection had been withdrawn. Thus *the colonies no longer owed any allegiance to the king.*

These and other facts can be summarized by reference to DI-25, 26, 27, and 28:

> He has abdicated government here by declaring us out of his protection, and waging war against us.
>
> He has plundered our seas, ravaged our coasts, burnt our towns, and destroyed the lives of our people.
>
> He is at this time transporting large armies of foreign mercenaries to complete the works of death, desolation and tyranny already begun with circumstances of cruelty and perfidy scarcely paralleled in the most barbarous ages, and totally unworthy the head of a civilized nation.
>
> He has constrained our fellow citizens taken captive on the high seas, to bear arms against their country, to become the executioners of their friends and brethren, or to fall themselves by their hands.[31]

Repeated Petitions, Repeated Injuries

THEME: America Sought Ways to Remain at Peace with England

Over a period of twelve years, Americans repeatedly sent petitions to England, striving to remain at peace, while at the same time still maintaining their rights.

In 1764 America learned of the plan of First Lord of the Treasury George Grenville, to have Parliament impose a stamp tax on America. Action on this tax was postponed for a year to allow time for the colonies to respond and to suggest alternatives. Virginia passed a petition opposing a stamp tax.[32] Pennsylvania and other colonies also passed resolutions against it.[33] The following year when the Stamp Act was considered, agents for some of the colonies tried to present these petitions against the bill. Parliament refused to receive them. Then they passed the bill, overwhelmingly.

In response, Virginia's House of Burgesses passed resolutions "declaring the independence of the people of Virginia of the Parliament of Great Britain, in matters of taxation."[34] The pattern was set, and would be followed without fail until the final break.

The controversy continued and became more intense. Although the Stamp Act was repealed in 1766, many other acts gave offense to America. When the Tea Act was passed in 1773, the British East India Company sent shiploads of tea to America. The colonists would not allow the tea to be unloaded. In most places, the ships returned to England. In Boston, when the ships refused to leave, some of the people there threw the tea overboard–the famous Boston Tea Party.

Parliament responded by voting to close the port of Boston, and to take various other repressive measures. These included changing the government of Massachusetts, quartering of troops there, etc. From then on, in any discussion of resolving the differences between Britain and America, the question arose: who would pay for the tea?

Initially Franklin urged Massachusetts to pay for the tea. He soon stopped urging this, and later commented that by closing the port of Boston, England had given "twenty times as much injury."[35] Later, in his discussions with Lord Howe, he offered to promise that Boston would pay for the tea, if the various offensive acts of Parliament were repealed. The ministry refused.[36]

Early in 1774, Franklin sought to present the petition of the Massachusetts Assembly to have the governor and lieutenant governor removed from office. Rather than consider the petition, the Privy Council allowed Franklin, who was only the agent or messenger, to be verbally abused by Alexander Wedderburn for over an hour.

That same year, the colonies agreed through their legislatures, to each send delegates to a Continental Congress. Thomas Jefferson wrote a paper called *A Summary View of the Rights of British America*, for use by Virginia's delegates. They chose to publish it as a pamphlet. Eventually, it was also published in England. A bill of attainder was introduced in Parliament naming about twenty Americans, presumably to be executed for treason. Because he had written this pamphlet, Jefferson's name was included.[37]

When the First Continental Congress met, it drew up a petition to submit to the British government. Parliament refused to receive or consider it, on the grounds that Congress was not a legal body. Not long after this, Lord North arose in Parliament, and during his remarks referred to the willingness of England's government to give America "every just and reasonable indulgence" on "proper application."[38]

And what might be "proper application"? Parliament refused to receive petitions of individual colonies through their legislatures; ignored the petitions of individuals or met them with threats against their lives; and refused to receive the petition of all the colonies through Congress. What was left?

The Olive Branch Petition

The Second Continental Congress also submitted a petition. Jefferson wrote the first draft, but "It was too strong for Mr. Dickinson." (John Dickinson, a year later, refused to sign the Declaration of Independence.) "He still retained the hope of reconciliation with the mother country, and was unwilling it should be lessened by offensive statements. He was so honest a man, and so able a one, that he was greatly indulged even by those who could not feel his scruples."[39]

This was the summer of 1775. In a remarkable example of patience and forbearance, they allowed Dickinson to rewrite the petition, and keeping only part of Jefferson's language, he produced the Olive Branch Petition. This document was extraordinary for its humility. Jefferson described the situation in his *Autobiography*.

> Congress gave a signal proof of their indulgence to Mr. Dickinson, and of their great desire not to go too fast for any respectable part of our body, in permitting him to draw their second petition to the King according to his own ideas, and passing it with scarcely any amendment. The disgust against this humility was general; and Mr. Dickinson's delight at its passage was the only circumstance which reconciled them to it. The vote being passed, although further observation on it was out of order, he could not refrain from rising and expressing his satisfaction, and concluded by saying, "There is but one word, Mr. President, in the paper which I disapprove, and that is the word *Congress*"; on which Ben Harrison [a delegate from Virginia] rose and said, "There is but one word in the paper, Mr. President, of which I approve, and that is the word *Congress*."[40]

In spite of their disgust with the humble nature of the petition, Congress passed it anyway. And in spite of the humble nature of the Olive Branch Petition, it was treated the same way as all the others. Parliament refused to receive it. The king refused to answer it.

The petition was signed on the 8th of July, 1775. Although the English government knew that this petition would soon be presented, on the 23rd of August the king signed the Proclamation of Rebellion. The Petition was presented on September the 1st. Without waiting to see what was in it, the king had declared the colonies in rebellion.[41]

What was in the petition?

It began "To the King's most excellent Majesty," and addressed George III as "Most gracious Sovereign." This to a man who had already shown himself as definitely not gracious, and whom Jefferson would describe as "the bitterest enemy we have."[42] It closed by wishing him a "long and prosperous reign," and that his "descendants may govern . . . with honor," as America's "sincere and fervent prayer." (OBP-14)

The first paragraph opens with a tone maintained throughout: "We your Majesty's faithful subjects . . . entreat your Majesty's gracious attention to this our humble petition." (OBP-1) After speaking of the glory and promise of the previous union (OBP-2), and the failed attempt of France to disrupt it (OBP-3,4), the petition reminds the king of the service the colonies gave in the French and Indian War (OBP-5). It then relates the growth of differences between England and America. The king's ministers "proceeding to open hostilities," have caused Americans "to arise in our own defense." Americans find the need to oppose the English "peculiarly abhorrent." Yet they assure the king they are "your still faithful colonists." (OBP-8) They declare themselves "Attached to your Majesty's person, family, and government with all the devotion that principle and affection can inspire." They "ardently desire the former harmony . . . may be restored." (OBP-11)

In reading the petition, one can feel the anguish not only of John Dickinson, but of other Americans who loved England. The eventual break was emotionally wrenching. One can see this in such words as "apprehensions that now oppress our hearts with unspeakable grief." (OBP-12) The writer knows the conflict will "inflame the contending parties" with "resentments and incurable animosities." (OBP-9) How can it be stopped? The king could do so, if he would. The petition not only pleads "for stopping the . . . effusion of blood," (OBP-9) but pleads with the king to "make the most favorable construction of our expressions on so uncommon an occasion." (OBP-10) All to no avail.

The Olive Branch Petition did not list the specific acts that violated American rights. There was no need. The Declaration and Resolves, passed by Congress on the 14th of October, 1774, had already identified many of them. Jefferson's *A Summary View of the Rights of British America* had thoroughly listed the acts and why they were wrong. The Olive Branch Petition requested their repeal. It also asked: that the taking of life be stopped; that arrangements be made "for collecting the united sense of your American people" [such as, by Congress?]; and that the king "direct some mode by which the united applications of your faithful colonists to the throne in pursuance of their common councils, [for example, through Congress?] may be improved into a happy and permanent reconciliation." (OBP-13)

A last great effort for peace. A last effort to reconcile England and America, even though written after the battles of Lexington and Concord. But it could not be done. England would not reply, except with army and navy.

Thus Jefferson said of America's numerous petitions, "to none of which, was ever even an answer condescended."[43] "In every stage of these oppressions we have petitioned for redress in the most humble terms: our repeated petitions have been answered only by repeated injuries." [Declaration of Independence, DI-30.]

In summary, considering the rights promised in the Virginia agreement and the colonial charters, the tradition of the common law, the required most favorable interpretation, the English Bill of Rights, and the removal of the king's protection, and hence of the obligation for allegiance, this conclusion seems inescapable:

America's resistance, and her Declaration of Independence, stood on a rock solid moral and legal foundation.

Questions

Question 1: How were the colonies financed?

Question 2: In contract law, one party to a contract cannot change the contract without the consent of the other party. Parliament felt free to change or take away colonial charters. Was a colonial charter a contract? What about the treaty between England and Virginia? Discuss.

Question 3: Did Americans have legal grounds to resist British troops? Explain.

Question 4: After seeing how Parliament operated, would this give Americans reason to include in the Constitution, Article I Section 6 Clause 2? Explain.

Question 5: What did the British government withdraw from America, that meant America no longer owed allegiance? Should these two things be connected? Why or why not?

Question 6: How long was action on the Stamp Act postponed before enactment? Why? Did the postponement serve its purpose?

Question 7: How many petitions from either colonial legislatures or the Continental Congress, did the king or Parliament receive and answer?

Concord Hymn

On April 19, 1775, British troops in Boston sought to capture American arms stored in Concord. On the way there they met American militia in Lexington, and again in Concord. The first battles of the War for Independence were fought that day.

At the 111th anniversary of the battles of Lexington and Concord, a monument was erected in Concord. Emerson wrote the following poem, which was set to music, and sung for the occasion. He did not live to see it.

CONCORD HYMN
Sung at the completion of the
Battle Monument, April 19, 1886
by Ralph Waldo Emerson (1803-1882)

By the rude bridge that arched the flood,
　　　Their flag to April's breeze unfurled,
Here once the embattled farmers stood,
　　　And fired the shot heard round the world.

The foe long since in silence slept;
　　　Alike the conqueror silent sleeps;
And Time the ruined bridge has swept
　　　Down the dark stream which seaward creeps.

On this green bank, by this soft stream,
　　　We set today a votive stone;
That memory may their deed redeem,
　　　When, like our sires, our sons are gone.

Spirit, that made their spirits dare
　　　To die, and leave their children free,
Bid Time and Nature gently spare
　　　The shaft we raise to them and thee.

CHAPTER THREE

The Constitution of the United States

Basic Principles

THEME: Principles of Freedom, of the Declaration of Independence and of the Constitution

As Jefferson said in the Declaration of Independence, the purpose of government is to protect the rights of mankind, rights with which they are "endowed by their Creator." [See DI-2.] What rights? Jefferson spoke of "life, liberty, and the pursuit of happiness." John Locke (in his *Essays on Civil Government*) and later Frederic Bastiat (in *The Law*, 1850) spoke of life (and person), liberty, and property. Bastiat said:

> . . . The Creator of life has entrusted us with the responsibility of preserving, developing, and perfecting it. In order that we may accomplish this, He has provided us with a collection of marvelous faculties. And he has put us in the midst of a variety of natural resources. By the application of our faculties to these natural resources we convert them into products, and use them. This process is necessary in order that life may run its appointed course.
>
> Life, faculties, production—in other words, individuality, liberty, property—this is man. . . .
>
> Life, liberty, and property do not exist because men have made laws. On the contrary, it was the fact that life, liberty, and property existed beforehand that caused men to make laws in the first place.
>
> What then, is law? It is the collective organization of the individual right to lawful defense.[1]

James Madison spoke of

> The diversity in the faculties of men[2], from which the rights of property originate . . . The protection of these faculties is the first object of government. From the protection of different and un-

equal faculties of acquiring property, the possession of different degrees and kinds of property immediately results.[3]

Supreme Court Justice George Sutherland speaking to the New York State
Bar Association, January 21, 1921, said,

It is not the right of property which is protected, but the right TO
property. Property, per se, has no rights; but the individual–the man–
has three great rights, equally sacred from arbitrary interference; the
RIGHT TO HIS LIFE, the RIGHT TO HIS LIBERTY, and the
RIGHT TO HIS PROPERTY. The three rights are so bound together as to be essentially ONE right. To give a man his life, but
deny him his liberty, is to take from him all that makes life worth living. To give him his liberty but take from him the property which is
the fruit and badge of his liberty, is to still leave him a slave.[4]

The Constitution was designed to create a free society, and to keep it free.
The other purposes listed in the Preamble were essential to that one which is
named last, and in the chief place: "to . . . secure the blessings of liberty to ourselves and our posterity." It is one thing for a people forming a new government
to begin free. It is quite another for them to remain free.

TABLE 2

Freedom can be lost in several ways:	Hence the Preamble says:
by crime.	"to . . . establish justice"
by anarchy, social chaos.	"to . . . insure domestic tranquility"
by conquest.	"to . . . provide for the common defense"
by disunion or foreign intrigues, setting the states against one another.	"to form a more perfect union"
by the growth of government	"to . . . secure the blessings of liberty to ourselves and our posterity"

But the most common way to lose freedom is by government itself. When
men have power, they often abuse it. As Jefferson said, "The natural progress
of things is for liberty to yield and government to gain ground."[5] With this in
mind, the delegates to the Convention in Philadelphia in 1787, tried to design

a government that would hold itself in check. James Madison put it this way, "In framing a government which is to be administered by men over men, the great difficulty lies in this: you must first enable the government to control the governed; and in the next place oblige it to control itself."[6]

To do that, the Founders tried to put these principles into our Constitution:

1. *Limited Government.* The powers of government were listed (or "enumerated"), and it was to exercise only those powers delegated to it. (See Article I Section 8.) In addition, government was prohibited from doing certain things. (See Article I Sections 9 and 10, and the Bill of Rights, the first ten Amendments.)

2. *"Government of laws, not of men."* Government should not act arbitrarily, but only in accordance with known, published law, that can be known by the people.

3. *Federalism.* Vertically separated power, divided between the national government and the states.

4. *Separation of Powers.* The division of the national government into three branches, the legislative (Congress) to make law, the executive (President, and those under him) to enforce and carry out the law, and the judicial (Supreme Court and other courts) to judge and interpret the law. Madison said, "The accumulation of all powers, legislative, executive, and judiciary, in the same hands, whether of one, a few, or many, and whether hereditary, self-appointed, or elective, may justly be pronounced the very definition of tyranny."[7]

In Lewis Carroll's *Alice In Wonderland,* there is a little story that I refer to as "the mouse's tail (or tale)." It's about a mouse and a cat named Fury, and goes like this:

Fury said to a mouse that he met in the house, "Let us both go to law: *I* will prosecute *you*–Come, I'll take no denial. We must have the trial; for really this morning I've nothing to do."

Said the mouse to the cur, "Such a trial, dear sir, with no jury or judge would be wasting our breath."

"I'll be judge, I'll be jury," said cunning old Fury; "I'll try the whole cause, and condemn you to death."

The cat wanted to be prosecutor, judge, jury, and executioner. That is the kind of liberty and justice you get without the separation of powers.

5. *Checks between departments.* For example, the President can veto an act of Congress, but they can override his veto by a two-thirds vote of each house. Jefferson said, "An *elective despotism* was not the government we fought for, but one which should not only be founded on free principles, but in which the powers of government should be so divided and balanced among several bodies of magistracy, as that no one could transcend [exceed] their legal limits, without being effectually checked and restrained by the others."[8]

6. *A Republic, using a system of elected representatives.* Power was to be derived from the People. However, the Founders did not establish a democracy, nor did they intend to. Their purpose was to PRESERVE LIBERTY. Hence they designed a system to make it difficult for one faction to gain control of all branches of the government and to oppress the people. Their hope was that if one branch tried to abuse its authority, another branch would stop it.

Madison said, "democracies have ever been spectacles of turbulence and contention; have ever been found incompatible with personal security or the rights of property; and have in general been as short in their lives as they have been violent in their deaths."[9]

Historian Alexander Tyler said, "A democracy cannot exist as a permanent form of government. It can only exist until [a majority of] the voters discover they can vote themselves largesse [gifts of money] from the public treasury. From that moment on the majority always votes for the candidate promising the most benefits from the public treasury, with the result that a democracy always collapses over loose fiscal policy [taxing and spending], always followed by a dictatorship."[10]

7. *Trial by Jury.* To be discussed more in its own section below.

8. *A bill of rights,* placing specific limitations on government, as mentioned under point 1., and intended to preserve certain rights essential to freedom, such as freedom of religion, speech, press, and assembly.

9. *A sound currency, based on gold and silver.* Such a currency cannot be arbitrarily inflated by unlimited printing of paper money, nor can it be arbitrarily deflated–gold and silver do not go out of existence. Thus Article I Section 8 Clause 5 gives Congress power "to coin money [and] regulate the value thereof." Article I Section 10 Clause 1 forbids the states from doing any of three things that could interfere with a sound currency. "No state shall . . . coin money; emit bills of credit; make anything but gold and silver coin a legal tender in payment of debts." The prohibition on states coining money was to assure a uniform currency for the United States. States were not to "emit bills of credit," that is, to print paper money. Finally, only gold and silver should serve as legal tender. States were not allowed to require a creditor to accept anything else as payment for a debt.

10. *An armed citizenry.* Only an armed citizenry can defend themselves from criminals, and only an armed citizenry can remain free. (See the section on the Second Amendment, below.)

11. *Equality before the law.* When the founders wrote the Constitution, black slavery still thrived in the South. While still legal in much of the North, the northern states soon acted to eradicate it within their own boundaries. However, at least for free citizens, the founders wrote into the Constitution the principle of equality before the law. This principle is not so much expressly stated as simply woven through the entire fabric. Certain passages relate to this principle.

Neither the United States, nor any individual state, may grant to anyone a title of nobility. [Article I Section 9 Clause 8, and Section 10

Clause 1] Also, "The citizens of each state shall be entitled to all privileges and immunities of citizens in the several states." [Article IV Section 2 Clause 1] Eventually, this principle was more explicitly stated in Section 1 of the Fourteenth Amendment: "No state shall make or enforce any law which shall abridge the privileges or immunities of citizens of the United States; nor shall any state deprive any person of life, liberty, or property, without due process of law; nor deny to any person within its jurisdiction the equal protection of the laws."

12. In order for any nation to remain free, the people must accept the principle of *individual responsibility*. To the extent possible, each person should take responsibility for his or her own actions and their consequences. They should take responsibility for their own support. There will always be a few who are physically or mentally incapable of doing so. However, when masses of people refuse responsibility and choose instead to depend on government for their support, then government can only support them by taking the earnings of others. The productive become the slaves of the unproductive. For both groups, freedom is lost. The productive lose freedom through the loss of the fruit of their labor and that part of their lives spent to produce what was taken. The unproductive lose freedom through their dependency.

Questions

Question 1: What are the basic rights of all humanity that government is intended to protect?

Question 2: What are enumerated powers, and what is their purpose?

Question 3: What purpose is served by the separation of powers and the checks between departments?

Question 4: Why did the founders not want a democracy? What are its failings?

The Structure of the Government of the United States of America

As mentioned earlier, the Constitution divided power among three branches: the legislative or law-making branch, Congress; the executive, or enforcement branch, the President and those under him; the judicial branch, the Supreme Court and other Federal courts. In addition to this separation of powers, the Constitution also provided for each branch, and even each house of Congress, to be chosen by a different method, and to have different terms of office.

HOUSE OF REPRESENTATIVES–DIRECT ELECTION BY THE PEOPLE

Members of the House of Representatives are elected directly by the people for a term of two years. They make up the lower house of Congress. Originally, this was the only branch of the national government that was elected directly by the people. Terms were kept short, so that this branch would reflect well the thinking of the people, and could be changed by them in a comparatively short time, if they needed to. They were also apportioned among the states according to population. States with more people were given more Representatives.

All bills for raising revenue, that is, all tax bills, must originate in the House of Representatives, as the house closest to the people.

SENATE–ELECTION BY STATE LEGISLATURES–LATER CHANGED

Each state elects two Senators, to serve in the upper house of Congress, the Senate. They serve for a term of six years. About one third of the Senate is elected each two years. This allows the Senate to give Congress stability. This helps to avoid problems if the people become caught up in some temporary passion. Senators were originally elected by the state legislatures, to give the states a voice in Congress. Because the people chose the members of the state legislatures, they still had a say in who was elected to the Senate, indirectly.

The Seventeenth Amendment changed this, and now the people of each state elect Senators directly.

As the Senate is made up of representatives of the States forming a kind of confederation, the Senate must ratify all treaties. Appointments made by the President, such as judges, executive department heads, ambassadors, etc., must also be confirmed by the Senate.

Questions

Question: One of the constitutional issues that has arisen in comparatively recent times, is that of "Federal mandates," requiring the states to pass certain kinds of laws, or to have certain programs. When these mandates come without any Federal money to support them, they are called "unfunded mandates." Are such mandates constitutional, or do they violate the Tenth Amendment? Would Congress have been less likely to enact these mandates if Senators were still elected by state legislatures?

PRESIDENT–THE ELECTORAL COLLEGE

The Constitution grants the executive power to the President. His term of office is four years. Originally, the President was eligible to be reelected without limit; however, the tradition was set by George Washington, and reinforced by Thomas Jefferson, James Madison, and James Monroe, that the President should not serve more than two terms. After that tradition was broken by Franklin Roosevelt, who was elected to four terms as President, the country chose to add the two term limit to the Constitution by means of the Twenty Second Amendment.

"Each state shall appoint, in such manner as the legislature thereof may direct, a number of electors, equal to the whole number of Senators and Representatives to which the state may be entitled in the Congress," and these electors vote to select the President.

The original idea behind the electoral college intended for the people to select well informed electors who would choose the President. While events have not developed along that line, there were still sound reasons for the choice of this method. The founders considered other methods, such as election by Congress, or directly by the people.

Election by Congress would tend to encourage conspiracy and intrigue within the Congress and between candidates and factions in Congress. It could also subvert the independence of the President, the separation of powers, and the checks between branches.

Direct election by the people at large presents other problems. First, it would make our country closer to a democracy, and the problems and instability of that form were described in an earlier section. [See Principle 6. in the summary list above, of principles included in our Constitution.] Second, it could aggravate the problems of vote fraud and recounts in close elections.

Certain parts of the country are notorious for vote fraud. People "vote" who are actually dead, or have moved away. Precincts report more total votes than were actually cast. The electoral college sometimes filters out such things. If the margin in a state is larger for either candidate than can be affected by the fraudulent votes, then the state's electoral votes go for the right person anyway. Then the effect of the fraud is stopped before it can cross the state line. Sometimes it may affect the outcome in a particular state, but not the national result. It may not always work out that way. Many believe that vote fraud in Illinois, Missouri, and Texas changed the outcome of the 1960 presidential election. However, if the President were elected by direct popular vote, then fraudulent votes would never be filtered out. They would go right into the total along with legitimate votes. Then in a close election, the winner might be the candidate whose party was most proficient in, or most committed to, cheating.

With the electoral college, if the vote is close in a particular state, there might be a recount of the votes in that state. If we used direct popular vote, then in a close election we might have to hold a *national* recount.

SUPREME COURT–APPOINTMENT AND CONSENT–TREASON

The President appoints members of the Supreme Court, and other Federal judges, with the "advice and consent of the Senate." They hold office "during good behavior." Hence, once appointed, they hold office for life, unless they resign or they are impeached and convicted. Any officer of the United States can be removed from office if impeached and convicted of, "treason, bribery, or other high crimes and misdemeanors."

History gives many examples of the misuse of the charge of treason. For this reason, Article III defines treason as making war against the United States, or helping their enemies, "giving them aid and comfort." To convict a person of treason requires "two witnesses to the same overt act," or "confession in open court."

PURPOSE OF DIFFERENT METHODS

Thus we see that each branch, and even each of the two houses of Congress, were intended to have different terms of office, and to be chosen by different methods. By dividing Congress into two such houses, and requiring the approval of both houses, the founders put a check on Congress' power to originate new law. They also made it difficult for any single faction to gain control of all the branches of government at the same time. This makes it harder for any faction to oppress the people.

CHECKS BETWEEN DEPARTMENTS

The purpose of the Founders was not to establish a democracy, but to preserve freedom, and to prevent government oppression. Hence they separated the various powers, and gave each branch checks upon the others.

Congress passes laws. The President can veto a law; however, this veto is not absolute. Congress can override a veto by a two thirds vote in each house. The Supreme Court, by judicial review, can declare a law or an action by the President, unconstitutional, and therefore null and void.

The President can appoint members of the judiciary, but only with the consent of the Senate. Hence, this gives the legislative and executive branches a check on each other, and on the judiciary. The President can also negotiate and sign treaties, but they only become law if ratified by the Senate with a two thirds vote. Any member of the executive or judicial branches can be impeached [accused] by the House of Representatives for "treason, bribery, or other high crimes and misdemeanors," and if convicted by a two thirds vote of the Senate, removed from office.

The checks on the judiciary include the manner of their appointment, possible impeachment, and the power of Congress to regulate those legal areas in which the Supreme Court can hear appeals [referred to as the "appellate jurisdiction" of the Supreme Court]. In response to a decision by the Supreme Court, Congress can also propose amendments to the Constitution, by a two thirds vote of each house. Amendments must then be submitted to the states and require ratification by the legislatures of three fourths of the states. This happened with the case of Chisholm v. Georgia (2 Dall. 419, 1793), which was quickly followed by the Eleventh Amendment [which, by the way, the author believes was a mistake].

The people, of course, have a check on the House of Representatives, by elections of the entire house every two years. Originally, the states also had a check on the Senate, through elections of one third of the Senate every two years by state legislatures. That was changed to direct election by the people with the Seventeenth Amendment, which removed a check by the states on Federal power. The people also have an indirect check on the President by election each four years through the Electoral College, chosen in such manner as the legislature in each state shall direct.

THE SUPREMACY CLAUSE AND THE OATH OF OFFICE

Article VI Section 2 makes the U. S. Constitution, and federal laws made "in pursuance thereof," the "supreme law of the land." Federal law, and the U. S. Constitution, take priority over any state law or state constitution. The term "in pursuance thereof," implies laws enacted in carrying out, or putting into effect, or according to, the Constitution. A law made in violation of the Constitution would not be "in pursuance thereof."

All members of Congress, members of state legislatures, and executive or judicial officers, "both of the United States and of the several states, shall be bound by oath or affirmation to support" the Constitution of the United States. (Article VI Section 3) In the case of the President, the Constitution specifies his oath of office in Article II Section 1 Clause 7. It calls for him to solemnly swear or affirm that he will "preserve, protect, and defend the Constitution of the United States." The framers put in the option to "affirm" because of certain religious groups who might have an objection to using the other language. This allows someone with that specific religious conviction, to still run for this or other offices, and still be able to take the "oath" and serve.

Why an "oath"? An oath is "a solemn appeal to God to witness to the truth of a statement or the sacredness of a promise." (Webster's Dictionary) The framers intended to bind the honor and conscience of the office holders, by covenant, to uphold the Constitution. The honor, honesty, integrity, and character of candidates for office matter. A candidate who lacks honesty, or who cannot or will not keep his word, cannot be trusted to abide by the oath of office. Among the most meaningful and important covenants or promises a person makes in life, stands that of marriage, the promise between husband and wife. Whether a candidate treats such a covenant with honor can give a clue about whether he or she will keep the oath of office. However, a candidate may make many other clues available, including advocating positions or programs that do or do not fit under the Constitution.

OUR CONSTITUTIONAL FORM VERSUS THE PARLIAMENTARY SYSTEM

Our Constitution provides for a government with power divided between three branches, having checks between departments. The Parliamentary system of England lacks such checks, or even such division. At one time the king or queen may have held executive power, but today it resides in the Prime Minister and his cabinet. Hence, a member of the legislature holds the executive power. As the court of last resort, Parliament also holds judicial power. Some Parliamentary systems have a separate President, as Germany did in the 1920s and early 1930s, until the death of Hindenburg. Then Hitler combined the offices of President and Chancellor.

These Parliamentary systems usually require the Prime Minister to "form a government," based on a majority in Parliament, or in one house thereof: thus, for England, based on a majority in the House of Commons; and in 1920s Germany, on a majority in the Reichstag. Where there are three or more parties represented, the Prime Minister's party may not have a majority. Then he or she must make an agreement with another party to obtain a majority.

Our Constitution provides for regular elections every two years, when the entire House of Representatives is up for election. One third of the Senate is elected each two years; hence each two years the Senate is subject to significant change. However, the remainder tend to lend stability. The President is elected each four years. The President's election by a majority of the electoral college does not require a majority of the popular vote. Thus, it does not require a runoff election in the case that no one has a majority of the popular vote. Nor does the President's election require a majority of Congress. As indicated above, the terms for the President and Congress are fixed.

In contrast, elections under a Parliamentary system can be long delayed, or ridiculously frequent. We noted above, that Franklin was in England for the elections of 1768 and 1774. The Long Parliament, elected in 1640, sat for at least eight years, twelve or thirteen if you count the time after the Presbyterians were ejected. They had made Presbyterianism the state church of England in 1645. Their persecution of other sects led to their ejection in 1648. The Parliament that was left deposed King Charles I in 1649, and was dissolved in 1653. Some systems do require elections after a certain time, as for instance, after at most five years. A new election can be called at any time if the members vote "no confidence" in the Prime Minister's government. If the members are more concerned about their own power and feathering their own nests, they will not call a new election even if the government is incompetent.

At the other extreme, Germany in the early 1930s held elections with absurd frequency, a formula for instability. In this case, chaos led to tyranny:

September 14, 1930 election of the Reichstag
(one house of the German Parliament).

March 13, 1932 election for President.
Hindenburg was just short of a majority.

April 10, 1932 election for President. Hindenburg won the runoff.

(May 30, 1932 Bruening resigns as Chancellor at
Hindenburg's insistence.)

(June 1, 1932 Papen appointed Chancellor,
the German equivalent of Prime Minister.)

(June 4, 1932 Papen dissolved the Reichstag.)

July 31, 1932 election of the Reichstag.

(September 12, 1932 the Reichstag voted Papen out of office. If they had not, Papen would have dissolved the Reichstag by means of Hindenburg's order.)

November 6, 1932 election of the Reichstag.

(December 2, 1932 Schleicher appointed Chancellor.)

(January 28, 1933 under pressure, Schleicher resigned as Chancellor.)

(January 30, 1933 Hitler appointed Chancellor. Almost immediately, he sought to have the Reichstag dissolved.)

(February 27, 1933 the Reichstag fire.)

March 5, 1933 election of the Reichstag.

Six elections in two and one half years; three legislative elections within about seven months. What a mess. It was all downhill after that.

In contrast, our Constitution does not allow either extreme. It demands regularly scheduled elections, at reasonable intervals. The times are fixed and orderly. The President's election does not come at a different time by months or years from a Congressional election, but concurrently with one. Nor does it require the jockeying between multiple parties to secure a majority with which to elect a Prime Minister, or to "form a government."

In 1930s Germany, the legislature had two houses: the Reichstag, elected by the people, and the Reichsrat, a sort of senate of seventy members representing the eighteen states that were part of Germany. The two houses were not equal, for the Reichstag could overrule the Reichsrat by a two thirds vote. The Chancellor and his government, the "ministers" over the various departments, were responsible to the Reichstag. If the Reichstag consented, the President could suspend many of the rules and constitutional guarantees, and allow the Chancellor to "rule by decree." This provision did not require the consent of the Reichsrat.

After the Reichstag fire, Hitler urged President Hindenburg to issue a decree that allowed restrictions on freedom of speech, press, and assembly, and giving additional powers to the government. Hindenburg complied. Even using the money and power of the state to spread his propaganda, and suppressing the free speech of his opponents, Hitler was only able to get 44 percent of the vote for his party in the March 5, 1933 election. Only with the help of the

Nationalist party, could the National Socialists exercise a bare majority in the Reichstag. However, with the arrest or detention of the Communist and some of the Social Democrat members, and the presence of Nazi storm troopers in the legislative hall to encourage the acquiescence of some of the other parties, the Reichstag gave the two thirds vote necessary to give all legislative powers to Hitler. Thus, without any involvement of the Reichsrat in the question, and without his party ever gaining a majority in the Reichstag or a majority vote of the people, Hitler became the dictator of Germany.

Questions

Question 1: Who were the members of the House of Representatives and the Senate intended to represent?

Question 2: What is the purpose of the oath of office?

Question 3: At what levels of government in the United States, and in what branches, are officers required to take an oath (or affirmation) to support the U.S. Constitution?

Question 4: Some of the instability shown in the historical events listed from Germany in the early 1930s relates to an officer (President or Chancellor) dissolving a house of the legislature. Under the U.S. Constitution, can the President dissolve Congress? (See Article II Section 3.)

Question 5: The Constitution of the Weimar Republic (Germany in the 1920s to 1933) had severe flaws. Contrast these with features of our Constitution.

The "General Welfare" Clause

Article I Section 8 of the Constitution is the primary section that defines the powers of Congress. We can find some Congressional powers defined in other parts of the Constitution, but most of them reside in this one section. Article I Section 8 contains 18 parts referred to as clauses, all part of one sentence. Each clause except the last ends with a semicolon, the last with a period. Clause 1 reads, "The Congress shall have Power to lay and collect Taxes, Duties, Imposts and Excises, to pay the Debts and provide for the common Defence and general Welfare of the United States; but all Duties, Imposts and Excises shall be uniform throughout the United States." Some refer to this as the "General Welfare Clause" of the Constitution.

General welfare is also mentioned in the Preamble, but that is not a grant of power, but an expression of purpose. Article I Section 8 Clause 1 is sometimes interpreted to mean that Congress has power to collect taxes and spend the money for any purpose that they consider to be for the general welfare. This would mean virtually unlimited power for Congress, but this interpretation distorts the Constitution.

During the debate over ratification, opponents of the Constitution charged that this clause conferred unlimited power on Congress. James Madison answered this objection in *The Federalist Papers*, No. 41, this way:

> But what color can the objection have, when a specification of the objects alluded to by these general terms immediately follows and is not even separated by a longer pause than a semicolon? If the different parts of the same instrument ought to be so expounded as to give meaning to every part . . . , shall one part of the same sentence be excluded altogether from a share in the meaning; and shall the more doubtful and indefinite terms be retained in their full extent, and the clear and precise expressions be denied any signification whatsoever? For what purpose could the enumeration of particular powers be inserted, if these and all others were meant to

be included in the preceding general power? Nothing is more natural nor common than first to use a general phrase, and then to explain and qualify it by a recital of particulars. But the idea of an enumeration of particulars which neither explain nor qualify the general meaning, and can have no other effect than to confound and mislead, is an absurdity . . .[11]

Madison affirms that Clauses 2 to 18 give the specifics that explain the general terms in Clause 1. All parts of the sentence should have meaning. Clauses 2 through 18 should then clarify and explain. However, if Clause 1 is not limited by the rest of the section, but includes the powers there listed, and beyond that, the power to do anything and everything else for which money can be spent, then the rest of the section has no meaning. The Founders intended Section 8 to limit the powers of Congress to those listed. If the section does not do that, then the list serves no purpose. The idea that the Convention would have written such a section with no meaning, and which explains nothing, is absurd.

Madison also points out similar wording in parts of the Articles of Confederation.

According to wording of this clause, the exercise of this power must be for the general welfare, not for the benefit of some at the expense of others. Examples of such general benefit include many of the particular powers enumerated in Section 8 after Clause 1; for instance, "to . . . fix the Standard of Weights and Measures" (Clause 5) makes commerce easier, helps prevent fraud, and benefits everyone. Similarly "To provide for the Punishment of counterfeiting the Securities and current Coin of the United States" (Clause 6) also prevents fraud and facilitates commerce. The provisions for raising and regulating army and navy, and when necessary, the militia, for our defense (Clauses 12 to 16) keep us free and independent.

The Constitution's Relationship to the Declaration of Independence

The Declaration and the Constitution were written in general by different groups of men (there were a few in common), and for different purposes, eleven years apart. The Bill of Rights was added to the Constitution shortly after, by yet another group of men. The Bill of Rights was passed by Congress in 1789, and ratified in 1791, becoming part of the Constitution, as the first ten amendments. Yet the correlation of the concepts in the two documents confirms that their ideas match.

For virtually every part of the Declaration, the Constitution contains parts that fit the Declaration's context. For almost every complaint in the lengthy list of complaints against the king and Parliament, the framers of the Constitution wrote passages in it to prevent a similar problem occurring in our government.

For example, the Declaration complains of Parliament's legislation "For quartering large bodies of armed troops among us." (DI-16) What provision do we have to prevent this? The third amendment, "No soldier shall, in time of peace be quartered in any house, without the consent of the owner, nor in time of war, but in a manner to be prescribed by law."

When the colonies became alarmed at various British measures aimed at them, they formed committees of correspondence. Massachusetts and Virginia were probably the first to adopt such committees. In Massachusetts in late 1772, these may at first have sought to keep the towns in the colony informed and to help bring about concerted action. Later, they served to keep the various colonies informed about British and American actions. Each colony wrote to the others about happenings there. Eventually, most of the colonies had such committees.

In 1773 in Virginia, when the legislature passed a resolution calling for committees of correspondence in each colony, the Governor dissolved the legislature. The following spring, the British Parliament passed a bill to close the port of Boston as of June 1, 1774. And so that May, the legislature in Virginia, in sympathy with the oppressions being suffered by Massachusetts, passed a resolution setting the day Boston was to be closed, June first, as a day of fasting, humiliation, and prayer. In Jefferson's words, "The Governor dissolved us, as usual."[12]

These and similar incidents in other colonies led Jefferson to write in the Declaration, the complaint against the king for dissolving legislatures. (DI-7, 8) He described the consequence of this dissolution as, "the state remaining in the meantime exposed to all the dangers of invasion from without, and convulsions within." These two concerns find an exact match in the words of the Preamble, "to . . . insure domestic tranquility, [and] provide for the common defense."

Do they only match on such matters of theory? No, the Declaration defines the problem for us, and the Constitution gives us a practical answer. For instance, we just mentioned the matter of colonial legislatures being dissolved by the King or his representative, the royal Governor. Can the President dissolve Congress? No. He can call them into special session when there is a need, and he can adjourn them IF the House and Senate disagree about the time of adjournment. (Article II Section 3)

The Declaration complains the king "has kept among us, in times of peace, standing armies, without the consent of our legislatures." (DI-13) In *A Summary View of the Rights of British America*, Jefferson says of this, "[If] his Majesty possess[ed] such a right as this, it might swallow up all our other rights, whenever he should think proper."[13] The Constitution's answer to the problem of standing armies, was to give Congress power "to raise and support armies, but no appropriation of money to that use shall be for a longer term than two years." (Art I Sect 8 Cl12) Each new Congress must make a new appropriation, that is, must consent, if the army or navy is to continue to exist. By the size of that appropriation, Congress can affect, even determine, what size army that it will allow. It also gives Congress the power "to make rules for the government and regulation of the land and naval forces." (Art I Sect 8 Cl 14)

So it continues on, point after point. The Declaration defines the problem; the Constitution gives us a practical answer.

The Commission on the Bicentennial of the United States Constitution said, "The Declaration of Independence was the promise; the Constitution was the fulfillment."

Questions

Question 1: Look at the complaints in the Declaration of Independence (DI-3 to DI-29). Choose two that have not been discussed above and find parts of the Constitution that attempt to answer the problem.

Question 2: The Preamble names one of the Constitution's purposes as "to form a more perfect union." The Declaration speaks of the people's right "to institute new government, laying its foundation on such principles, and organizing its powers in such form, as to them shall seem most likely to effect their safety and happiness." (DI-2) Did the Constitution accomplish this? By using what principles? Discuss.

After considering these questions, **study** the *Cross Reference between the Declaration of Independence and the Constitution*, in Appendix D, using the copies of those documents in Appendices B and C. **This cross reference is a key part of this book.**

To use this cross reference, the following may be helpful. First, acquaint yourself with the explanation with example, and the reference keys. Then by reference identification from the Declaration of Independence, for example, DI-5, you can look up the actions of the king, the royal governors, and the Parliament, that relate to that section of the Declaration. By looking in the Declaration, you can see what Jefferson said about these actions. Then by using the cross reference to the Constitution, you can find the parts of the Constitution that address the problem; that is, those parts that seek to prevent the problem from happening here. An explanation or discussion of the issue is offered in the section of the cross reference entitled *Exposition on the Cross Reference, with Principles from the Declaration of Independence and the Constitution.*

The Constitution and the Articles of Confederation

It has been said that the Constitutional Convention in 1787 was a runaway convention; that the delegates were only authorized to revise the Articles of Confederation, but instead scrapped the Articles and substituted an entirely separate document; and that this document used a different means of ratification than what the Articles specified as a means for amendment. This is only partly true.

The resolution of Congress on February 21, 1787, calling the convention to revise the Articles, had asked the convention to report "such alterations and provisions as shall . . . render the federal constitution adequate to the exigencies of Government and the preservation of the Union." That charge is quite broad. The convention was to make whatever changes were needed to keep the union, and to make the federal government work.

The convention did create a new document that was substantially different. The Articles of Confederation were so defective that a new document was essential. However, the Articles were not entirely scrapped; there was some good in them. I estimate that in principle about five eighths (5/8) of the Articles were kept, and incorporated into the Constitution, sometimes in the same words.

Although the Constitution specified in Article VII that it was to be ratified by conventions to be held in each state, the Convention did not submit it directly to the states. They sent it to Congress, who had given them charge to revise the Articles. Congress unanimously passed a resolution on September 28, 1787 to submit the Constitution to the states for ratification by the method specified.

Each state then had to call a convention to consider the Constitution. When enough states had ratified, on September 13, 1788, Congress passed a resolution by a vote of 9-0, setting dates for the appointment of electors, the assembly of the electors to vote for President, and the commencement of "proceedings under the said Constitution."

Thus the adoption of the Constitution was handled with great care, and every appropriate step was included. Congress was included three times: in calling the Convention, in sending the Constitution to the states for ratification, and in taking the initial step to put it into execution. The state governments were included in calling the state conventions. The people were included in selecting delegates to the state conventions, and of course, by their delegates ratifying the Constitution.

Should the people have been included by referring the Constitution for a direct vote of the people? No. The method used was better. A direct vote would probably have allowed only for yes or no. Nor would it have allowed for the kind of thorough discussion among those voting that a convention allowed for. Through their delegates, the people were able to say both yes, and amend it by including a bill of rights. Several of the conventions, while ratifying, urged a list of specific amendments to further protect the people's rights. The very first Congress under the Constitution drew from these concerns in drafting the Bill of Rights.

Judicial Review

The doctrine of judicial review, or the power or right of the Supreme Court to rule or declare an act of Congress or an action of the President to be unconstitutional, and therefore null and void, cannot be found in the Constitution. This idea was described in *The Federalist*, paper number 78, written by Alexander Hamilton. The line of argument set forth there was followed by Chief Justice John Marshall in Marbury v. Madison.

The line of argument is as follows: it often happens that two laws may be found to be in conflict. The courts, in interpreting the law, must decide which one to follow. In the absence of other evidence, a court will generally follow the later law, as the most current expression of the will of the legislature. In a similar way, if a law is in conflict with the Constitution, the court must decide which to follow, and should follow the Constitution, which is a higher, superior, or more fundamental, law.

Our Constitution contains limits placed upon the law-making power of Congress. As Hamilton explains in The Federalist, no. 78, for example, that

> . . . it shall pass no bills of attainder, no *ex post facto* laws . . . Limitations of this kind can be preserved in practice no other way than through the medium of courts of justice, whose duty it must be to declare all acts contrary to the . . . Constitution void. Without this, all the reservations of particular rights or privileges would amount to nothing . . .
>
> . . . No legislative act, therefore, contrary to the Constitution, can be valid. . . .
>
> . . . The interpretation of the laws is the proper and peculiar province of the courts. A constitution is, in fact, and must be regarded by the judges as, a fundamental law. . . . the Constitution ought to be preferred to the statute . . .[14]

Elbridge Gerry, Luther Martin, and George Mason, [three of the delegates to the Constitutional Convention, from Massachusetts, Maryland, and Virginia respectively, but none of whom signed the Constituion] all considered the judiciary to have the authority to "declare an unconstitutional law void."[15]

Thomas Jefferson, writing to James Madison from Paris, on March 15, 1789, said:

> In the arguments in favor of a declaration of rights, you omit one which has great weight with me; the legal check which it puts into the hands of the judiciary. This is a body, which, if rendered independent and kept strictly to their own department, merits great confidence for their learning and integrity. In fact, what degree of confidence would be too much, for a body composed of such men as Wythe, Blair and Pendleton? On characters like these, the "*civium ardor prava jubentium*" ["The wayward zeal of the ruling citizens"] would make no impression.[16]

In other words, they would decide according to appropriate principles regardless of political pressures. (Can we be sure that we will always have "such men" in the judiciary?)

How could a bill of rights serve as a legal check in the hands of the judiciary, unless this bill of rights were considered by the judiciary superior law, and unless the court had authority to act upon that belief? The challenge in designing the constitutional relationship between the Supreme Court and the other branches, is to "render [the court] independent" and yet to "keep it strictly to [its] own department." By the end of his life Jefferson had grave concerns for the future of our country, about the second half of that.

Questions

Question 1: Can the principle of judicial review be a correct Constitutional principle without being expressly written in the Constitution? In the Seventh Amendment, there is reference to the rules of the common law. These rules are not expressly stated in the Constitution, but must be drawn from other sources. If such rules can be "implied," can judicial review also be implied?

Question 2: How well did the convention succeed in creating an "independent judiciary"? What parts of the Constitution could give the Supreme Court some independence?

Question 3: How well did the convention succeed in keeping the judiciary "strictly to their own department"? Judicial review gives the Supreme Court a check on the acts of Congress; what are the checks on the Supreme Court? Are they adequate?

Trial by Jury

One answer in the Constitution to the problems presented by the Judiciary's independence, is trial by jury. This embodies the basic principle, John Adams said, that no person "can be condemned of life, or limb, or property, or reputation, without the concurrence of the voice of the people."[17]

Members of the jury hold no office; they are without power to be gained, enlarged, or protected by their decision. Here is independence without hope of power, reward, or continuance in office. If a judge makes a mistake, especially in one of the higher courts, it may be cited as precedent in hundreds of other courtrooms for generations. The judge remains in office, and tomorrow can make new mistakes or repeat the old ones. He or she can perpetuate systematic error. If a jury makes a mistake, it will affect that one case. Seldom will it be cited as precedent. Tomorrow that jury will be gone, returned to their regular daily lives, and for the next case, replaced by a new jury.

What is the jury to decide? In most cases there are two things to determine: the facts (that is, what happened?), and the law (that is, what laws, if any, apply, and how?). In civil cases, the law and the fact can sometimes, but not always, be separated. In criminal cases the two are generally intertwined, frequently so as to be inseparable. In such instances it is the province of the jury to decide both, in Hamilton's word, "complicatedly." They do so by a "general verdict," of guilty or not guilty.

Under the common law, the jury had the right and the power to give a verdict of not guilty, if they believed the law in question to be unjust, or unjust as applied to this particular case, or unconstitutional. Jefferson, in his *Notes on Virginia*, described the courts there in these words:

These magistrates have jurisdiction both criminal and civil. If the question before them be a question of law only, they decide on it themselves; but if it be of fact, or of fact and law combined, it must be referred to a jury. In the latter case, of a combination of law and fact, it is usual for the jurors to decide the fact, and to refer the law arising on it to the decision of the judges. But this division of the subject lies with their discretion only. And if the question relate to any point of public liberty, or if it be one of those in which the judges may be suspected of bias, the jury undertake to decide both law and fact.[18]

Not only Jefferson, but also John Adams, Alexander Hamilton, John Jay, and others among the Founding Fathers have left us their opinion that the jury have the right, power, and authority, to decide both law and fact.

In England in 1688, seven Anglican bishops wrote a petition against an action of King James II. The bishops were tried for criminal libel. The jury took the petition, the charges against the bishops, and the statute book into the jury room with them. They returned with a verdict of not guilty.[19]

Another example is the case of John Peter Zengger, a New York publisher. In 1732, he was tried for the same charge, for printing an article critical of the governor. The jury could have found the fact of publication and left the question of law to the judges. Instead, they found Zengger not guilty. This case has sometimes been referred to as "the day the press was freed."

In the case of Georgia v. Brailsford in 1794,[20] our first Chief Justice, John Jay, said this, in his instructions to the jury:

It may not be amiss, here, gentlemen, to remind you of the good old rule, that on questions of fact, it is the province of the jury, on questions of law it is the province of the court to decide. But it must be observed that by the same law, which recognizes this reasonable distribution of jurisdiction, you have nevertheless a right to take upon yourselves to judge of both, and to determine the law as well as the fact in controversy. On this, and on every other occasion, however, we have no doubt you will pay that respect which is due to the opinion of the court; for, as on the one hand, it is presumed that juries are the best judges of facts; it is, on the other hand, presumable that the courts are the best judges of law. But still, both objects are lawfully within your power of decision.

Thomas Jefferson said of trial by jury, "I consider that as the only anchor ever yet imagined by man, by which a government can be held to the principles of its constitution."[21]

Questions

Question 1: In 1895, in the case of Sparf v. U.S., the Supreme Court held that juries had to take the law from the judge. Should this always happen? Or should it be a general rule, with exceptions, as suggested by John Jay's remarks in Georgia v. Brailsford, and Thomas Jefferson's in *Notes On Virginia*? Discuss.

Question 2: Can trial by jury hold a government "to the principles of its constitution" if juries cannot find a defendant not guilty, when accused of breaking an unconstitutional law? Is there another way? Discuss.

Question 3: Can trial by jury act as a check on the Judiciary? If juries have lost the power to resolve both "law and fact complicatedly by a general verdict," can they act as a check on the judiciary?

Question 4: In the last hundred years Congress has created many agencies, bureaus, administrations, etc., to whom they have given "rule-making authority." These bodies create law, enforce it, and through their employees designated "administrative law judges," judge offenders. Proceeding against someone thought to be in violation of these "rules" is not considered a "civil suit" subject to the Seventh Amendment, nor a "criminal prosecution" subject to the Sixth Amendment. Yet even though it is not considered a criminal prosecution, the accused is subject to penalties, such as heavy fines. Has the accused been deprived of their right to trial by jury? Is this a violation of the Sixth Amendment? What about the principle spoken of by John Adams at the beginning of this section? By delegating "rule-making authority" to these agencies, has Congress violated Article I Section 1? What about the principle of Separation of Powers, as applied to these agencies?

Question 5: Some of the agencies described in Question 4 are considered "independent agencies." They are not subject to the President, nor to either of the other branches. In essence, they form a fourth branch, not mentioned in the Constitution. Is this constitutional? On what grounds?

Other Parts of the Bill of Rights
Freedom of Religion, Speech, Press, Assembly and Petition

The First Amendment reads, "Congress shall make no law respecting an establishment of religion, or prohibiting the free exercise thereof; or abridging the freedom of speech, or of the press; or the right of the people peaceably to assemble, and to petition the government for a redress of grievances."

The growth of freedom of religion, and the history of its absence, was described in an earlier section. Prior to the colonization of America, generally every state in Europe, and many other places, had an established state religion. These differed from place to place. Before the Reformation, government enforced religions might be Catholic, Greek Orthodox, Russian Orthodox, Muhammadanism, etc. After the Reformation, some countries adopted various forms of Protestantism as government enforced religions. A number of the English colonies in America had state religions: Anglican, in Virginia, for instance. Laws compelled attendance, doctrinal adherence, and payment by taxes to the decreed sect. Eventually in America this compulsion yielded to freedom, and spread from here to other countries.

Freedom of religion comprises a key part of freedom of conscience. Its importance to the moral health and survival of a free country can hardly be overstated. For religion without freedom yields hypocrisy, but with freedom it yields morality. George Washington said it well:

> Of all the dispositions and habits, which lead to political prosperity, Religion and Morality are indispensable supports. In vain would that man claim the tribute of Patriotism, who should labor to subvert these great pillars of human happiness, these firmest props of the duties of Men and Citizens. The mere Politician, equally with the pious man, ought to respect and to cherish them. A volume could not trace all their connections with private and public felicity. Let it simply be asked, Where is the security for property, for reputation, for life, if the sense of religious obligation

desert the oaths, which are the instruments of investigation in Courts of Justice? And let us with caution indulge the supposition, that morality can be maintained without religion. Whatever may be conceded to the influence of refined education on minds of peculiar structure, reason and experience both forbid us to expect, that national morality can prevail in exclusion of religious principle.

It is substantially true, that virtue or morality is a necessary spring of popular government. The rule indeed extends with more or less force to every species of free government. Who that is a sincere friend to it, can look with indifference upon attempts to shake the foundation of the fabric?[22]

Let us add to that the thoughts of Jefferson:

. . . can the liberties of a nation be thought secure when we have removed their only firm basis, a conviction in the minds of the people that these liberties are of the gift of God? That they are not to be violated but with His wrath?[23]

In 1991, government officials from Albania expressed regret for government actions in 1967 in banning all churches. They wanted churches and religion to return to Albania. "We need the help of churches to rebuild the moral base of our country, which was destroyed by communism."[24]

Freedom also cannot endure without freedom of speech and press. Only through the exercise of those freedoms can people thoroughly examine and debate political, religious, and other issues. Only through these freedoms can people even be adequately informed.

In England in 1688, seven Anglican bishops were tried for criminal libel for submitting a petition to King James II. The jury returned a verdict of "not guilty." The same year, James was deposed, and William of Orange and his wife Mary were invited by Parliament to become joint rulers of England. English history refers to this as the Glorious Revolution. The next year, Parliament passed the English Bill of Rights of 1689, which included a provision forbidding punishment for submitting a petition to the king.

The First Amendment in our Bill of Rights provides for the right to petition government "for a redress of grievances."

Jefferson affirmed his commitment to the principles of the First Amendment, in these words, which have since been carved in large letters around the rim of the rotunda of the Jefferson Memorial: ". . . I have sworn upon the altar of God, eternal hostility against every form of tyranny over the mind of man."[25]

THE RIGHT TO KEEP AND BEAR ARMS

As related above under Basic Principles, Bastiat said "What then, is law? It is the collective organization of the individual right to lawful defense."[26] Every person has a right to life. Each one has a right to protect their own person, their body. The "individual right to lawful defense" that Bastiat speaks of, is the right of self defense. The right to use force, if necessary, to defend yourself, is the origin of the force of law. It is the origin of government. As Bastiat said,

> If every person has the right to defend—even by force—his person, his liberty, and his property, then it follows that a group of men have the right to organize and support a common force to protect these rights constantly.[27]

The right of self defense is so basic, that the rights to life, liberty, and property, cannot exist without it. Essential to that right, is the right to keep and bear arms. Without this, the right to defend one's self becomes a barren right, a right in name only, but without effect.

Mankind forms governments to protect persons, liberty, and property. This common force, however, can only provide a supplement to, not a substitute for, individual force. No government can prevent all crime. Therefore, individuals still need to use force when necessary for self defense.

Government itself often becomes the enemy of the rights to life, liberty, and property. George Washington said, "Government is not reason, it is not eloquence—it is force! Like fire, it is a dangerous servant and a fearful master." The founders wrote the Constitution and the Bill of Rights to protect those rights, not only from crime or invasion, but from government.

A "standing army" is an army that continues in existence constantly, whether there is a need for it or not. The founders thought armies should be raised when needed for a war, or because of the threat of war, and then sent home, or at least reduced in size, during peace.

The founders feared "standing armies." Indeed, in the Declaration of Independence, one of the complaints against the king said, "He has kept among us in times of peace standing armies without the consent of our legislatures." (DI-13) In his *A Summary View of the Rights of British America*, Jefferson warned that if tolerated, this "might swallow up all our other rights, whenever [the king] should think proper."[28] He also pointed out that "fear [is] the only restraining motive which may hold the hand of a tyrant."[29] (That is, keep a tyrant from acting to carry out evil ideas.)

While there were other factors, in part America won her freedom and independence from Great Britain because so many of her citizens were armed. The British marched to Lexington and Concord in 1775 to take arms away from the Americans. When citizens have no arms, when only the police and the army are armed, not only are the citizens defenseless against criminals, but they are defenseless against tyranny.

Hence, in the Bill of Rights, the founders wrote the Second Amendment: "A well regulated militia being necessary to the security of a free state, the right of the people to keep and bear arms shall not be infringed." The first phrase about the militia is only a dependent clause (that is, a clause that cannot stand on its own), and is mentioned as a reason for what follows. It may be a sufficient reason, but it is not the only reason. The main part of the sentence is the independent clause, "the right of the people to keep and bear arms shall not be infringed."

Even in the dependent clause, in determining the meaning of the clause we should look at the whole clause, not just the mention of the militia. The militia's purpose as there stated, is to insure "the security of a free state." Hence, at least in part, it is to keep us free. The militia can only do that if its members are armed.

Some have argued that the right to keep and bear arms is not an individual right, but only a right of the militia. Those who so argue generally say that it applies to the National Guard. However, the National Guard is not the militia. The National Guard was created under Article I Section 8 Clause 12 (raising armies), not under Clause 15 or 16 (about the militia), and for different purposes, not subject to the restrictions found in Clauses 15 and 16.[30] Federal law includes in the militia all able bodied male citizens from 17 to 44 years of age.[31] At the time the Bill of Rights was written, the National Guard did not exist, and the militia was generally defined to include nearly all free, able bodied males. They were private citizens, and usually were required to provide their own arms.[32]

Tyrannical governments, such as the Nazis and the Communists, always disarm the people. So also, do governments that intend genocide, as happened in Sudan, where the Arab government disarmed the blacks in the southern and western parts of the country, including Darfur, in preparation for the murder of millions. It has been estimated that in the Sudan, over two million have been killed, and millions more driven from their homes.[33]

Questions

Question 1: The same wording used in the Second Amendment, "the right of the people," is used in both the First and Fourth Amendments. If the right to keep and bear arms is not an individual right, but only a right of the militia, would a consistent interpretation mean that the right of free assembly and the right to be secure from unreasonable search and seizure are not individual rights? Or that if the rights in the First and Fourth Amendments are individual rights, so are the rights in the Second Amendment? What about the wording of the Ninth and Tenth Amendments?

Question 2: The militia is mentioned only in a dependent clause, while the right is stated without restriction in an independent clause. Should the meaning of the independent clause be restricted by the dependent clause?

Question 3: In interpreting the Second Amendment, should we go by the current definition of the militia, or by how it was defined at the time it was written? Which is more likely to preserve our freedom?

The Third to Sixth and Eighth Amendments

These amendments generally protect the security of Americans from arbitrary action by government. The Third Amendment prevents the quartering of soldiers "in any house without the consent of the owner," at least in peacetime. During a war, it could be done "in a manner to be prescribed by law," but since Independence, it never has. The Fourth Amendment also protects the security of people in their homes, by forbidding "unreasonable searches and seizures." A search requires a warrant, based on "probable cause, supported by oath or affirmation, and particularly describing the place to be searched, and the persons or things to be seized." The Fifth Amendment also seeks to protect people and their property, by specifying that no person shall "be deprived of life, liberty, or property, without due process of law; nor shall private property be taken for public use without just compensation." (Unfortunately, that last phrase has been gutted by the Supreme Court. See the section on Kelo v. New London.)

The Fifth and Eighth Amendments also seek to protect the procedural rights of persons accused of crime, and to protect them from cruelty. The Fifth Amendment requires that persons accused of major crimes, unless in military service during war, cannot be held or tried unless first indicted by a grand jury. This means that the prosecution must present evidence to a grand jury, generally of twenty four members, and a majority of them must conclude that there is enough evidence to justify holding the person for trial. This amendment also forbids trying the same person twice for the same offence, or forcing him "to be a witness against himself." (This is often referred to as the privilege against "self incrimination.") The Eighth Amendment says that "Excessive bail shall not be required, nor excessive fines imposed, nor cruel and unusual punishment inflicted."

We discussed above, the Sixth Amendment requirement for trial by an impartial jury in all criminal cases. That amendment also calls for a speedy and public trial. Hence, the accused cannot be held indefinitely without trial, nor tried in secret. The accused also has the right "to be informed of the nature and cause of the accusation; to be confronted with the witnesses against him; to have compulsory process for obtaining witnesses in his favor, and to have the assistance of counsel for his defence." That the author of the amendment felt the need to mention these rights indicates that they have not always been honored. For instance, consider the trial of Nicholas Throckmorton in England in 1554. The judges allowed into evidence the written statements attributed to certain men who were living, or even present. Yet these men were not brought forward to testify. Throckmorton did not have counsel, or an attorney to assist him. When he tried to call a witness in his behalf, the court refused to allow that witness to testify. The court even sought to destroy the impartiality of juries. When the jury acquitted Throckmorton because of a lack of sufficient evidence against him, the judges imprisoned and fined the jury.

THE NINTH AND TENTH AMENDMENTS

The first eight amendments list various individual rights. The ninth and tenth are different. While they do not list individual rights, they seek to limit the power of the national government. One of the concerns expressed by some of the founders about a bill of rights, was that no matter how carefully it was written, something would get left out. Then whatever should be a right of the people that was not written in the bill of rights, would be denied, because it was not included. On the other hand, Jefferson said that "a bill of rights is what the people are entitled to against every government on earth, . . . and what no just government should refuse, or rest on inference."[34] Many of the states agreed with him. They insisted that a bill of rights be added. Yet the problem of completeness remained. Hence, when the first Congress under the Constitution wrote the Bill of Rights, they included the Ninth Amendment:

> The enumeration in the Constitution of certain rights shall not be construed to deny or disparage others retained by the people.

In other words, just because we didn't list it, doesn't mean that you can deny the people a genuine right. How can we judge a genuine "right"? Can this language be used to invent unjust "rights"? We must return to the basic principles described earlier, such as defense of life, liberty, and property.

The Tenth Amendment is similar to the ninth, but flipped over. The ninth says, if there is a specific limitation on government power that we didn't mention, but should have, it still applies. The tenth says, if there is a specific government power that we didn't mention, then the national government does NOT have it.

"The powers not delegated to the United States by the Constitution, nor prohibited by it to the states, are reserved to the states respectively, or to the people."

Article I Section 10, and parts of Article IV, place specific limits on the states. Aside from those limits, the Tenth Amendment reserves any powers not delegated to the national government for the states or the people. Why doesn't it just say to the states? Because each state constitution determines what powers the people in that state delegate to their state government. This amendment to our national Constitution does not change that relationship.

Interstate Commerce—
Gibbons v. Ogden, 22 U.S. 1 (1824)

THEME: Principles of the Constitution; Limited and Enumerated Powers;
Federalism

In 1824 the U.S. Supreme Court decided the case of Gibbons versus Ogden, in an opinion written by Chief Justice John Marshall. This case and opinion justly enjoyed preeminence in Constitutional law on the subject of the interstate commerce clause for over 100 years, until it came in conflict with the New Deal. Some recent texts have attempted to change the meaning of the case, by omitting a key part of the decision.

Article I Section 8 Clause 3 of the Constitution indicates "The Congress shall have Power . . . To regulate Commerce with foreign Nations, and among the several States, and with the Indian Tribes."

Ogden held an "exclusive right" given by New York, to operate steamboats between New York City and parts of New Jersey. Gibbons was operating steamboats in the same area by license under an act of Congress, the Coasting Act.

The U.S. Supreme Court ruled that the state monopoly was invalid, because the Constitution had given power to regulate interstate commerce to Congress. The "acts of New York must yield to the law of Congress." To reach this decision, the court had to define "commerce," and "among the several states."

Some recent history books ignore the part of the decision about "among the several states." This allows them to distort the meaning of the decision, and claim that it meant Congress had complete power over all commerce.

"Among" has basically the same meaning as "between," except that "between" relates to two things, while "among" relates to more than two. In his opinion for the court, Chief Justice John Marshall said, "The word 'among' means intermingled with. . . . it may very properly be restricted to that commerce which concerns more states than one." It did not cover commerce that was "completely internal [to one state], which is carried on between man and man in a state, or between different parts of the same state, and which does not extend to or affect other states."[35] [Such commerce is sometimes called "intrastate commerce."] "Such a power would be inconvenient and certainly unnecessary."

"The enumeration of the particular classes of commerce to which the power was to be extended . . . presupposes something not enumerated; and that something, if we regard the language or the subject of the sentence, must be the exclusively internal commerce of a state." In other words, if the Constitution meant to give Congress power over all commerce, there would be no need to identify three specific types of commerce to which its power applies. The fact that it lists those three types can only mean that there is another type of commerce not subject to the power of Congress–namely, intrastate commerce. Marshall continued to say that the national government's "action is to be applied to all the external concerns of the nation, and to those internal concerns which affect the states generally; but not to those which are completely within a particular state, which do not affect other states, and with which it is not necessary to interfere for the purpose of executing some of the general powers of the government."

Review this case, when you study the later decisions related to interstate commerce; this became a hot issue during the "New Deal" of Franklin Roosevelt.

Questions

Question 1: Give examples of "intrastate" commerce, and "interstate" commerce.

Question 2: How would the distinction between all commerce and commerce among the several states affect the power of the Federal government?

July 4, 1826

THEME: A Remarkable Event; Did It Have Meaning for Liberty and Independence?

The remarkable event of July 4, 1826 is seldom mentioned in the history books. I mention it here so that you may judge for yourself as to its significance.

John Adams and Thomas Jefferson played prominent roles in securing American Freedom and Independence, and in the early years of our republic. After the friendship of Adams and Jefferson had been interrupted by political problems for some years, through the help of a mutual friend, Benjamin Rush, their friendship was renewed, and grew ever stronger until their deaths. On the Fourth of July, 1826, John Adams died. His last words were, "Thomas Jefferson still survives!" But Jefferson had died earlier, on the afternoon of the same day. Adams and Jefferson were 90 and 83, respectively. These two passed away precisely on the fiftieth anniversary of the Declaration of Independence.

Some may consider this to be mere coincidence, but that is not how it was viewed then. Historian David McCullough said of this, "People at the time saw it as the clearest sign imaginable that the hand of God was involved with the destiny of the United States."[36]

Five years later, James Monroe died, on July 4, 1831, on the 55th anniversary. Hence, the second, third, and fifth Presidents, all died on the Fourth of July.

CHAPTER FOUR

Prelude and Postlude to the Civil War; Lincoln; Emancipation

American Patriotic Songs

Knowledge of these songs may be diminishing. For instance, most Americans know the first verse of our national anthem, but many know *only* the first verse. The four songs listed here were all written in the 1800s: the *Star Spangled Banner* in 1814, *America* in 1831, the *Battle Hymn of the Republic* in 1861, and *America the Beautiful* in 1893.

E. D. Hirsch chose to include three of them in his preliminary list of the things he believes Americans should know, given in his book *Cultural Literacy*. All four are included in the *Core Knowledge Sequence* published by the Core Knowledge Foundation. They are included here for essentially the same reasons that they were included there–they are considered part of the body of "core knowledge" of our nation.

THE STAR SPANGLED BANNER - OUR NATIONAL ANTHEM

During the War of 1812, Dr. William Beanes was captured by the British, and taken aboard a British warship. A lawyer named Francis Scott Key (1779-1843) went to negotiate with the British for the release of Dr. Beanes. The British agreed, but held both men over the night of September 13 to 14, 1814, during a battle. The British fleet bombarded Fort McHenry, near Baltimore. Dr. Beanes was without his glasses, and asked Mr. Key, "Can you see the flag?" That the American flag still flew over the fort on the morning of the fourteenth, evidenced that the Americans still held the fort. The British retreated. Key wrote the words to *The Star Spangled Banner* in the early morning of September 14. Numerous versions exist, with slight variations in the wording.

> O say can you see by the dawn's early light
> What so proudly we hailed at the twilight's last gleaming,
> Whose broad stripes and bright stars through the perilous fight,
> O'er the ramparts we watched, were so gallantly streaming?
> And the rockets' red glare, the bombs bursting in air,
> Gave proof through the night that our flag was still there.
> O say does that star spangled banner yet wave
> O'er the land of the free and the home of the brave?
>
> On the shore dimly seen through the mists of the deep,
> Where the foe's haughty host in dread silence reposes,
> What is that which the breeze, o'er the towering steep,
> As it fitfully blows, half conceals, half discloses?
> Now it catches the gleam of the morning's first beam,
> In full glory reflected now shines in the stream;
> 'Tis the star spangled banner, O long may it wave
> O'er the land of the free and the home of the brave!
>
> And where is that band who so vauntingly swore,
> That the havoc of war and the battle's confusion
> A home and a country should leave us no more?
> Their blood has washed out their foul footstep's pollution,
> No refuge could save the hireling and slave

From the terror of flight, or the gloom of the grave,
And the star spangled banner in triumph doth wave
O'er the land of the free and the home of the brave!

O thus be it ever when freemen shall stand
Between their loved home and the war's desolation!
Blest with victory and peace, may the heaven rescued land
Praise the Power that hath made and preserved us a nation!
Then conquer we must, when our cause it is just,
And this be our motto: "In God is our trust!"
And the star spangled banner in triumph shall wave
O'er the land of the free and the home of the brave!

AMERICA

The words to this song were written by Samuel Francis Smith (1808-1895)
about February of 1831. He was translating some German songs, when he became intrigued with one of the tunes. (It is the same tune used by the British
for *God Save the King*.) Smith felt to write a patriotic poem to go with that tune.

My country! 'tis of thee,
Sweet land of liberty,
Of thee I sing;
Land where my fathers died,
Land of the pilgrim's pride,
From every mountain side,
Let freedom ring!

My native country, thee,
Land of the noble free,
Thy name I love;
I love thy rocks and rills,
Thy woods and templed hills,
My heart with rapture thrills
Like that above.

Let music swell the breeze,
And ring from all the trees,
Sweet freedom's song;
Let mortal tongues awake;
Let all that breathe partake;
Let rocks their silence break,
The sound prolong.

Our fathers' God! to Thee,
Author of liberty,
to Thee we sing;
Long may our land be bright
With freedom's holy light;
Protect us by Thy might,
Great God, our King!

BATTLE HYMN OF THE REPUBLIC

Julia Ward Howe (1819-1910) wrote the words to this song late in 1861, during the Civil War. She had just visited a camp of Union soldiers in Washington, D.C. Although written several months before Lincoln's Emancipation Proclamation, it refers to freeing of the slaves. It expresses a firm belief in the righteousness of the cause of the Union, and a commitment to that cause. That commitment is expressed in the last verse as a willingness to "die to make men free." Today that verse is usually sung as "live to make men free."

In the original, the last line of the chorus changes with each verse. It may be more common today to use the same chorus throughout. The entire poem contains six verses, but the third and sixth are commonly omitted, as shown here. (Hence, below are the first, second, fourth, and fifth verses. Those are the ones most commonly sung.)

Mine eyes have seen the glory of the coming of the Lord;
He is trampling out the vintage where the grapes of wrath are stored.
He hath loosed the fateful lightning of his terrible swift sword;
His truth is marching on.

Chorus
Glory, glory, hallelujah! Glory, glory, hallelujah! Glory, glory, hallelujah!
His truth is marching on.

He has sounded forth the trumpet that shall never call retreat;
He is sifting out the hearts of men before his judgement seat.
Oh, be swift my soul to answer him; be jubilant my feet!
His day is marching on.

Chorus

I have seen him in the watch fires of a hundred circling camps;
They have builded him an altar in the evening dews and damps.
I can read his righteous sentence by the dim and flaring lamps,
For God is marching on.

Chorus

In the beauty of the lilies, Christ was born across the sea,
With a glory in his bosom that transfigures you and me.
As he died to make men holy, let us die to make men free,
While God is marching on.

Chorus

AMERICA THE BEAUTIFUL

Katherine Lee Bates (1859-1929) wrote this song about the summer of 1893.
The first sentence refers to the view she had from the top of Pikes Peak (14,110
feet) in Colorado. "Alabaster cities" apparently refers to her visit to an exposition in Chicago. The song carries a number of important concepts, including
freedom, mercy, heroism, love of country, her plea for nobleness and brotherhood, and a recognition that self control is essential to "liberty in law."

Oh beautiful for spacious skies,
For amber waves of grain,
For purple mountain majesties
Above the fruited plain!
America! America!
God shed his grace on thee
And crown thy good with brotherhood
From sea to shining sea.

Oh beautiful for pilgrim feet,
Whose stern impassioned stress
A thoroughfare of freedom beat
Across the wilderness!
America! America!
God mend thine every flaw,
Confirm thy soul in self control,
Thy liberty in law.

Oh beautiful for heroes proved
In liberating strife,
Who more than self their country loved,
And mercy more than life!
America! America!
May God thy gold refine
Till all success be nobleness,
And every gain divine.

Oh beautiful for patriot dream
That sees beyond the years.
Thine alabaster cities gleam
Undimmed by human tears.
America! America!
God shed his grace on thee
And crown thy good with brotherhood
From sea to shining sea.

Texas' War for Independence and the War with Mexico

THEME: Seeking Truth through a Fuller Account of the Facts; True History Is Not the Enemy Nor the Captive of One Race or Ethnic Group

With American Independence came governance over the territory east of the Mississippi River. The Northwest Ordinance provided for future government of that part north of the Ohio River, not already part of one of the original thirteen states. Under the Constitution, in both north and south the territory began to be divided into new states, admitted into the Union on an equal footing with the first thirteen.

Mexico gained independence from Spain in 1821. By 1823, or earlier, settlers from the United States moved into Texas under a land grant given Steven Austin through Mexican land law. Some from the southern states brought slaves with them, although Mexico officially abolished slavery in 1829.

Mexico's government was unstable. For instance, between 1833 and 1855 the presidency changed on average every seven months. Mexico in the period leading up to 1846 has been described as "in a chronic state of revolution." In 1835, Santa Anna changed the Mexican Constitution, and became a dictator.[1] In essence, he abolished the Constitution of 1824, divided Mexico into several regions, and appointed a military governor over each, subject to himself. Rebellions broke out in several areas of Mexico. Santa Anna suppressed them. At first, Texans wanted the 1824 Constitution restored. Perhaps seeing this as impossible, they decided to seek independence from Mexico.

Many textbooks have mentioned that after the United States annexed Texas, the United States considered the boundary with Mexico to be the Rio Grande, while Mexico considered the Nueces River to be the boundary. This author has never seen one that told the reader why, and which boundary, if either, had actually been honored. Hence, most students have little knowledge by which to judge who was right. Some textbooks also use certain facts about relations with Mexico and omit others, apparently to make Texas and America look bad.

The Nueces River "once formed the boundary between the Spanish provinces of Texas and Nuevo Santander."[2]

In 1836, Texas sought independence from Mexico. When Mexican dictator Santa Anna brought an army of 7,000 to Texas, he besieged about 180 Texans in the Alamo, an old mission in San Antonio. The Texans withstood the siege for almost two weeks, but in the end they were all, or nearly all, killed. Santa Anna's army suffered reported casualties of over 1,500 killed or wounded. Santa Anna had a policy of "no quarter," meaning he would not take or spare prisoners. Any captured would be killed.

The siege of the Alamo is typically described in classes on American History; less commonly mentioned is the massacre at Goliad. At the Battle of Coleto, James Fannin and his men numbering about 300 to 400 surrendered to Mexican troops, a part of Santa Anna's army. They were taken to the presidio at Goliad. After several days the Mexicans executed Fannin. They spared a few Texans with some medical training. They marched the rest out into the countryside, and shot nearly all of them. (One man is known to have escaped.)[3]

April 21, 1836, (with battle cries of "Remember the Alamo! Remember Goliad!") Texans under Sam Houston defeated forces of Santa Anna at the Battle of San Jacinto. Most of the Mexican soldiers that were killed that day died during the battle. There were some who tried to surrender or who were taken prisoner that some of the Texans also killed. However, the Texans also captured about 600 whom they spared.[4]

Those captured included Santa Anna, and he signed a treaty. The terms of the treaty included Mexico's recognition of Texas' independence, and the Rio Grande as the boundary between them.[5] Mexico's Congress refused to ratify this treaty. Santa Anna himself disregarded it, and repeatedly sent Mexican troops into Texas. About 1842, on at least two occasions, Mexican troops penetrated Texas as far as San Antonio, having crossed both the Rio Grande and the Nueces River. After some fighting, they withdrew or were driven out.[6]

In March of 1845, the United States annexed Texas. President Polk sent a U.S. ambassador to Mexico to negotiate a settlement of the boundary question, the claims of American citizens against Mexico, and to offer to buy California and New Mexico. When Mexico refused to negotiate, President Polk sent U.S.

troops into the disputed area between the Nueces River and the Rio Grande. Mexican troops crossed the Rio Grande and fought the U.S. troops. This led to war.

Questions

Question 1: Mexico did not recognize Texas independence. How then could they determine a boundary, if they still considered Texas to be part of Mexico? Was the old boundary between provinces of Mexico still valid?

Question 2: Of the two rivers considered to be the boundary by the two parties, the Rio Grande, and the Nueces, which one had been honored, or observed, as the boundary?

Question 3: Mexico did not recognize the treaty signed by Santa Anna. To undue the effects of the treaty, they could seek to negotiate a new one, or they could go to war. Was there any other way? What did they choose?

Question 4: Abraham Lincoln served one term in Congress, during 1847 to 1849. He opposed the war with Mexico, but always voted for bills to support the troops with equipment, rations, pay, etc. He introduced what were called the Spot Resolutions, questioning President Polk about whether the spot where the President said that American blood was shed on American soil, was actually American soil. What do you think? To whom did the land between the Nueces and Rio Grande rivers belong? Why?

Question 5: At the end of the Mexican War, Mexico ceded to the United States a large area of new territory, for which America paid Mexico $15 million. What do you think the nation should have done with that territory with regard to slavery? Why?

The Constitution and the Doctrines of Nullification and Secession

THEME: Principles of the Constitution; Ideas and Actions Leading to Civil War

After the War with Mexico, the question of what to do about slavery in the new territory was settled by the Compromise of 1850. Only four years later, the slavery issue was reopened by the Kansas-Nebraska Act. That led to the formation of the Republican Party, and in 1860, to the election of the first President from the new party, Abraham Lincoln. Eleven states from the South then tried to secede from the Union. This was not the first time that secession, or the issue of state nullification of federal law, had arisen. In 1832, questions of nullification or secession were raised, especially in South Carolina, over tariffs. Even earlier, during the administration of John Adams, issues over whether states had to abide by "unconstitutional" federal laws arose with the Kentucky Resolution in 1798 over the Alien and Sedition Acts.

The Alien Act allowed the President to expel from the country anyone not yet a citizen, that he considered "dangerous to the peace and safety of the United States." The Sedition Act led to the prosecution of some Republican (the party of Jefferson and Madison, also sometimes called Democratic-Republican) newspaper editors. Under the act, it was a crime to criticize the President or Congress in a way considered "false, scandalous, and malicious." Republicans considered the act an attack on freedom of speech and press. (The Alien and Sedition Acts were allowed to expire after Republicans won the 1800 elections.) The Kentucky Resolution asserted that these acts should be null and void. In essence, the resolution attempted to make the states able to void national laws.

How can we keep the national government within its constitutional limits? The checks and balances among the three branches built into the Constitution were intended to do that, but have not always succeeded. Some advanced the doctrine that the Constitution was a compact of the states, and a state could nullify federal law within its borders. Others (and some of the same people) have said that a state could withdraw from that compact. That is, a state could secede from the Union. Even since the Civil War there have been advocates of that theory.

Since the writing of the Constitution, some people have advocated a "broad construction" of the Constitution, and some have advocated a "strict construction." A broad construction tends to interpret the Constitution in favor of greater power to the federal government. Such a view can allow the government to run roughshod over the states and to trample the rights of the people. A strict construction would interpret the Constitution to limit the power of the federal government; to stick closely to the meaning of the bare words of the Constitution. It's possible to be too strict. For instance, because the Constitution makes no mention of acquiring territory, would that make the Louisiana Purchase unconstitutional? Or, as the Congress at the time believed, was the power to make such a purchase inherent in the power to make treaties?

Returning to the questions of nullification and secession, some advocates of a "broad construction" have brought the accusation that a "strict construction" of the Constitution would have allowed the South to secede. Let's look at the Constitution.

Is the Constitution a compact of the states? Consider the ratification process. The Constitution was ratified by each of the original thirteen states, but not by their legislatures. It was ratified by conventions called for that purpose. The legislatures participated by calling the conventions, and setting the rules by which delegates to those conventions would be elected. The Preamble reads "We the People of the United States . . . do ordain and establish this Constitution for the United States of America."

Should a state be able to nullify a federal law? Or are there other ways for states to affect federal constitutional questions? Remember that before the Seventeenth Amendment (adopted in 1913) the states were represented in Congress. The state legislatures elected the members of the U.S. Senate. So the states had a voice in making federal law. Article V requires Congress to call a Convention for proposing amendments to the Constitution "on the Application of the Legislatures of two thirds of the several States." These were some of the means for the states to deal with federal issues. Article VI Section 2 states "This Constitution, and the Laws of the United States which shall be made in

Pursuance thereof . . . shall be the supreme Law of the Land." Federal law and Constitution are superior to, or take precedence over, state laws and state constitutions.

Secession? Does the Constitution have anything to say about what the southern states did, or tried to do? Article I Section 10 Clause 1: "No State shall enter into any Treaty, Alliance, or Confederation; . . . coin Money; emit Bills of Credit . . . " Clause 3: "No State shall, without the Consent of Congress, . . . keep Troops, or Ships of War in time of Peace, enter into any Agreement or Compact with another State, or with a foreign Power, or engage in War, unless actually invaded . . . " Article III Section 3 Clause 1: "Treason against the United States, shall consist . . . in levying war against them . . . " Finally, Article VI Clauses 2 and 3, require members of Congress and the state legislatures and every executive and judicial officer both of the states and of the United States, to take an "Oath or Affirmation, to support [the U.S.] Constitution." Every officer of any southern state who participated in secession broke his oath of office.

Questions

Question 1: Do the use of conventions for ratification, and the words of the Preamble, invalidate the state-compact theory? Why or why not?

Question 2: If a federal law is enacted in conflict with the Constitution, is it still "in Pursuance thereof"? Are the states bound by it? What recourse does a state have?

Question 3: Can the state-compact theory take precedence over the express words of the Constitution to justify secession?

Question 4: When the men of South Carolina fired on Fort Sumter, was that treason?

The Growth of Lawlessness and Mob Violence

THEMES: Freedom Requires Law, Not Anarchy Nor Mob Rule; Illegal or Immoral Orders Must Not Be Obeyed; Combining Lawlessness With Government Portended the Civil War

This trend can be considered a precursor or forerunner of the Civil War. It indicated a willingness on the part of some to resort to violence, rather than wait for the processes of the law. In that way, it resembles the actions of the South, in refusing to submit to the ordinary process of the lawful election of a President of the United States. In 1861, eleven states chose war rather than accept the election of Lincoln. Twenty-three years before that, Lincoln spoke out against the growth of lawlessness and mob violence. On January 27, 1838, he addressed the Young Men's Lyceum of Springfield, Illinois. We shall refer to parts of this speech in this section, and more below in another section.

At the time, Lincoln was serving in the Illinois state House of Representatives. This was the first great speech of his career of which we still have record. In many ways, it was prophetic.

MOB ACTIONS IN MISSISSIPPI, ILLINOIS, AND OHIO

He speaks of "outrages committed by mobs . . . from New England to Louisiana." He does not want to talk about all of them, but he does describe some:

> In the Mississippi case they first commenced by hanging the regular gamblers–a set of men certainly not following for a livelihood a very useful or very honest occupation, but one which, so far from being forbidden by the laws, was actually licensed by an act of the Legislature passed but a single year before. Next, Negroes suspected of conspiring to raise an insurrection were caught up and hanged in all parts of the State; then, white men supposed to be leagued

with the Negroes; and finally, strangers from neighboring States, going thither on business, were in many instances subjected to the same fate.[7]

He goes on to refer to the murder of Elijah Lovejoy on November 7, 1837. Lovejoy was the editor of the *Alton Observer*, an abolitionist newspaper. A pro-slavery mob shot him when he tried to defend his last printing press, which they were bent on throwing into the river.[8]

A similar incident, not mentioned by Lincoln, occurred in Cincinnati, Ohio, in the summer of 1836. A mob sought to destroy the office and equipment of the *Philanthropist*, an abolitionist paper published by James G. Birney. They dumped the printing press into the Ohio River, and then decided to tar and feather Mr. Birney. They went to the hotel where they expected to find him. Salmon P. Chase, later a member of Lincoln's cabinet and still later the Chief Justice of the Supreme Court, blocked the door to the hotel. He was a large man who stood six feet two, and the mob backed off.[9]

Lincoln observed, "whenever the vicious portion of population shall be permitted to gather in bands of hundreds and thousands, and burn churches, ravage and rob provision-stores, throw printing presses into rivers, shoot editors, and hang and burn obnoxious persons at pleasure and with impunity [that is, without punishment], depend on it, this government cannot last." [10]

When good citizens see that their lives and property have no defense from mob violence, then government loses its best friends, who now want better protection. Thus in the mid 1960s, when riots occurred in several major cities in the United States, with widespread looting, violence and destruction, there were some who said we needed to turn the government over to a dictator for a while. When order was restored, he could turn it back to us. As Kenneth McFarland pointed out, however, there are no instances known in all history of a dictator doing that.

MOB ACTIONS AND GOVERNMENT LAWLESSNESS IN MISSOURI

Just as ominous are instances where lawlessness and government are combined; this also foreshadowed the Civil War. Such instances occurred in Missouri in the 1830s.

In 1831 members of the Church of Jesus Christ of Latter Day Saints, commonly called "Mormons," began moving into Independence, Missouri, and the surrounding area in Jackson County. The previous occupants of the county were mostly pro-slavery, while Mormons were opposed to slavery (though not abolitionists). In addition, the Mormons spoke of the area of Jackson County as their future "Zion," and anticipated that at some time that land would all be theirs. However, they did nothing illegal to try to gain it. As the number of Mormons moving into the area grew, the old residents became alarmed, for they realized that they could soon be outvoted. Political offices might be held by Mormons. The friction between the two groups grew.

In July 1833, a large meeting was held by those determined to drive the Mormons out of Jackson County. They adopted a document which included this passage, ". . . believing as we do, that the arm of the civil law does not afford us a guarantee, or at least a sufficient one, against the evils which are now inflicted upon us . . ."[11] Signers included a judge, justices of the peace, the county clerk, a constable, a colonel and a captain of the militia. On July 20, again declaring that "The evil is one that no one could have foreseen, and is therefore unprovided for by the laws; and the delays incident to legislation would put the mischief beyond remedy,"[12] they gathered as a mob, and with the Lieutenant Governor of Missouri, Lilburn W. Boggs, watching, they destroyed the Mormon printing office, and tarred and feathered two men. Soon the Mormons were driven from the county on threat of death.[13]

Over the course of time, they settled in mostly uninhabited Caldwell and Daviess counties, to the north of Independence. Their principle city was called Far West.

In 1838, the year of Lincoln's speech, an anti-Mormon mob led by Samuel Bogart, kidnaped three men, apparently with plans to kill them. Judge Elias Higbee in Far West, ordered the militia from Far West to disperse the mob and free their prisoners. This was done, at a cost of several lives. But Bogart was a captain in the militia of another county, and in some reports sent to the governor, the mob was referred to as Bogart's militia company, and it was falsely claimed that almost the entire company had been wiped out, and that the Mormons were planning to attack the town of Richmond.[14]

On October 27, without any investigation, Lilburn W. Boggs, now Governor, issued an order to General Clark, saying that "The Mormons must be treated as enemies and must be exterminated or driven from the state."[15] This order was unconstitutional. The U. S. Constitution forbids any state from engaging in war, unless actually invaded. [Article I Section 10 Clause 3] The order was what the law calls a bill of attainder, that decrees a punishment on someone without a trial. [Forbidden: Article I Section 10 Clause 1] (A bill of attainder is generally a legislative action, but the fact that this was the action of the executive still cannot make it constitutional.) If there were some among the Mormons who were guilty of wrongdoing, the governor's order made no attempt to distinguish between the guilty and the innocent.

FROM GOVERNOR BOGGS' EXTERMINATING ORDER
Headquarters Militia, City of Jefferson, October 27, 1838.

Sir: –Since the order of the morning to you, directing you to cause four hundred mounted men to be raised within your division, I have received by Amos Rees, Esq., and Wiley C. Williams, Esq., one of my aids, information of the most appalling character, which changes the whole face of things, and places the Mormons in the attitude of open and avowed defiance of the laws, and of having made open war upon the people of this state. Your orders are, therefore, to hasten your operations and endeavor to reach Richmond, in Ray county, with all possible speed. The Mormons must be treated as enemies and *must be exterminated* or driven from the state, if necessary for the public good. . . .

L. W. Boggs,
Governor and Commander-in-Chief.
To General Clark[16]

On October 30, a body of two to three hundred armed men entered the small Mormon town of Haun's Mill, and despite pleas for peace, and mercy, killed between 17 and 19 men and boys.[17] The next day an army of about two thousand militia surrounded Far West. General Lucas sent a party to Far West under a flag of truce, and after consultation, several of the Mormon church leaders were escorted into the camp of the army, expecting to negotiate a peaceful settlement. They were taken prisoner. Thousands of Mormons were then driven from the state under threat of death. Meanwhile, the commanding officers began proceedings against the Mormon leaders.

THE COURAGE AND INTEGRITY OF ALEXANDER DONIPHAN TO DEFY AN ILLEGAL ORDER

On November first, the commanding officers held what they called a court martial to try the prisoners, apparently now about twenty in number. The prisoners were civilians, who could not legally be tried by court martial. They were not present in this "court," nor informed of charges against them, nor represented by counsel, nor allowed to call witnesses in their behalf. This court martial was held in secret at night. The prisoners were not aware that it was being conducted until afterward.[18]

The "court" sentenced the prisoners to death. Near midnight, Samuel D. Lucas, who had played a prominent part in the mob actions in Jackson County in 1833, issued the following order.

GENERAL LUCAS ORDER TO ALEXANDER W. DONIPHAN
Brigadier-General Doniphan:

Sir:—You will take Joseph Smith and the other prisoners into the public square of Far West, and shoot them at 9 o'clock to-morrow morning.

Samuel D. Lucas,
Major-General Commanding.

GENERAL DONIPHAN'S REPLY TO THE ORDER OF GENERAL LUCAS
> It is cold-blooded murder. I will not obey your order. My brigade
> shall march for Liberty tomorrow morning, at 8 o'clock; and if you
> execute these men, I will hold you responsible before an earthly
> tribunal, so help me God.
>
> A. W. Doniphan,
Brigadier-General[19]

By his refusal to obey the order, Doniphan saved the lives of the prisoners. No action was ever taken against him. Today in Liberty, Missouri, there is a plaque erected in Doniphan's honor; there is a school named after him; there is an Alexander Doniphan Memorial Highway.

Many a Nazi officer before and during World War II justified his actions on the ground that he was "just following orders." Had there been enough officers and men in the German and Japanese Armies like Alexander Doniphan, there would have been no holocaust, and no World War II. Had Lt. William Calley and those with him been men like Doniphan, there would have been no My Lai Massacre during the Vietnam War.

(One of the myths sometimes perpetuated about this period is that the treatment of the Mormons was because of polygamy. However, they did not begin to practice polygamy until they had gone to Illinois, after being driven out of Missouri. They abandoned the practice about 1890.)

LAWLESSNESS IN KANSAS, ON THE FLOOR OF CONGRESS, AND IN ATTITUDES

In May of 1856 this trend toward lawlessness manifested itself in two parts of the country, almost at the same time. First, in the warfare and murders committed in "Bleeding Kansas," when pro-slavery and anti-slavery factions fought over whether Kansas would become a slave or free state. Second, on the floor of the United States Senate. Charles Sumner of Massachusetts made an inflammatory speech against slavery, with stinging criticism of Senators Butler of South Carolina and Stephen Douglas of Illinois.

A southern senator said far worse things about Senator Seward of New York (calling him "an infidel and a traitor") without violence following.[20] However, for Sumner, violence followed. Preston Brooks, a Congressman from South Carolina and a relative of Butler, entered the Senate chamber and beat Sumner on the head with a cane. Brooks injured Sumner so severely, that he was unable to attend to his duties in the Senate for three years.

Many in the South treated Brooks as a hero and commended his criminal action. Some even sent him canes. Equally reprehensible, was the reaction of some in the North to the execution of John Brown. Brown is generally considered responsible for several murders in "Bleeding Kansas." In October, 1859, he led a group to seize the federal arsenal at Harpers Ferry, Virginia (now West Virginia). He intended to trigger a slave rebellion. He was captured, tried, and sentenced to death. Many in the North mourned his execution. In the case of both Preston Brooks and John Brown, people were sympathizing with lawlessness and violence.

This included the abolitionist William Lloyd Garrison and probably his followers. Garrison condemned the Constitution, and advocated violating the Constitution in order to end slavery.

Lincoln's attitude stands in stark contrast. He recognized that lawlessness is incompatible with freedom, and that the Constitution protected the free men and women of America. He also wanted the end of slavery, but not at the expense of law and the Constitution. He saw that their destruction would threaten the freedom of *all* Americans.

FROM ABRAHAM LINCOLN'S ADDRESS BEFORE THE YOUNG MEN'S LYCEUM OF SPRINGFIELD
January 27, 1838 (On the subject, "The perpetuation of our political institutions"):

Shall we expect some transatlantic military giant to step the ocean and crush us at a blow? Never! All the armies of Europe, Asia, and Africa combined, with all the treasure of the earth (our own excepted) in their military chest, with a Bonaparte for a commander, could not by force take a drink from the Ohio or make a track on the Blue Ridge in a trial of a thousand years.

At what point, then, is the approach of danger to be expected? I answer, If it ever reach us it must spring up amongst us; it cannot reach us from abroad. If destruction be our lot we must ourselves be its author and finisher. As a nation of freemen we must live through all time, or die by suicide.

. . . there is even now something of ill omen amongst us. I mean the increasing disregard for law which pervades the country–the growing disposition to substitute the wild and furious passions in lieu of the sober judgement of courts, and the worse than savage mobs for the executive ministers of justice. . . . Accounts of outrages committed by mobs form the every-day news of the times. They have pervaded the country from New England to Louisiana.[21]

. . . "How shall we fortify against it?" The answer is simple. Let every American, every lover of liberty, every well-wisher to his posterity swear by the blood of the Revolution never to violate in the least particular the laws of the country, and never to tolerate their violation by others. As the patriots of seventy-six did to the support of the Declaration of Independence, so to the support of the Constitution and laws let every American pledge his life, his property, and his sacred honor–let every man remember that to violate the law is to trample on the blood of his father, and to tear the charter of his own and his children's liberty.[22]

. . . There is no grievance that is a fit object of redress by mob law.[23]

[*Continuing on the dangers that may come from men of ambition and talent.*]

. . . Towering genius disdains a beaten path. . . . It sees no distinction in adding story to story upon the monuments of fame erected to the memory of others. . . . It thirsts and burns for distinction; and if possible, it will have it, whether at the expense of emancipating slaves or enslaving freemen.[24]

Questions

Question 1: In what ways does mob action break down regard for law?

Question 2: How do the actions of the mobs described above compare to the Boston Tea Party? In Jackson County, Missouri, the mob first held a meeting and adopted a "declaration." How does this compare or contrast with Congress and the Declaration of Independence?

Question 3: Regarding Lincoln's reference to "some transatlantic military giant" that could "step the ocean and crush us at a blow," Lincoln's speech was given long before intercontinental ballistic missiles were developed during the Cold War with Communist Russia. Yet, so far, he has been correct. Will he continue to be?

Question 4: Is a soldier obligated to follow an illegal or immoral order?

Question 5: Suppose the Mormons, in 1839, then living in Illinois, filed suit in federal court against Missouri. Given the Eleventh Amendment, what would be the likely outcome? Would it be different since the adoption of the Fourteenth Amendment?

Literary connection: Mobs in the South are described in Mark Twain's *Huckleberry Finn*.

Lincoln's Speech at Peoria, Illinois, in Reply to Senator Douglas.
October 16, 1854

THEME: Principles of Freedom and of the Declaration of Independence and Constitution

[*Lincoln's comparative inactivity in politics, since 1848, ended when Stephen A. Douglas pushed through Congress his Kansas-Nebraska Act on May 30, 1854. This Act repealed the Missouri Compromise of 1820, opening to slavery territory where it had previously been forbidden to go. The Act provided for the people of the territory to decide for themselves whether or not to allow slavery. Douglas called this "popular sovereignty." The following are excerpts from Lincoln's speech.*]

In order to [have? gain?] a clear understanding of what the Missouri Compromise is, a short history of the preceding kindred subjects will perhaps be proper.

When we established our independence, we did not own or claim the country to which this compromise applies. Indeed, strictly speaking, the Confederacy then owned no country at all; the States respectively owned the country within their limits, and some of them owned territory beyond their strict State limits. Virginia thus owned the Northwestern Territory–the country out of which the principal part of Ohio, all Indiana, all Illinois, all Michigan, and all Wisconsin have since been formed. [*He describes which States owned what other territory.*]

. . . We were then living under the Articles of Confederation, which were superseded by the Constitution several years afterward. The question of ceding the territories to the General Government was set on foot. Mr. Jefferson, the author of the Declaration of Independence, . . . then a delegate in Congress; afterward, twice President; who was, is, and perhaps will continue to be, the most distinguished politician of our history; a Virginian by birth and . . . a slaveholder–conceived the idea of taking that occasion to prevent slavery ever going into the Northwestern Territory. He prevailed on the Virginia legislature to adopt his views, and to cede the Territory . . . Congress accepted the cession . . . and the first ordinance [of Congress] for the government of the Territory provided that slavery should never be permitted therein. This is the famed "Ordinance of '87" . . .

[This territory] is now what Jefferson foresaw and intended–the happy home of free . . . people, and no slave among them.

Thus, with the author of the Declaration of Independence, the policy of prohibiting slavery in new territory originated. Thus, away back to the Constitution, in the pure, fresh, free breath of the Revolution, . . . Congress put that policy into practice . . . And thus, in those five States, and in five millions of free, enterprising people, we have before us the rich fruits of this policy.

But now new light breaks upon us. Now Congress declares this ought never to have been, and the like of it must never be again. The sacred right of self-government is grossly violated by it. We even find some men who drew their first breath–and every other breath of their lives–under this very restriction, now live in dread of absolute suffocation if they should be restricted in the "sacred right" of taking slaves to Nebraska. That perfect liberty they sigh for–the liberty of making slaves of other people–Jefferson never thought of, their own fathers never thought of, they never thought of themselves, a year ago . . .

But to return to history. In 1803 we purchased what was then called Louisiana, of France. It included the present States of Louisiana, Arkansas, Missouri, and Iowa; also the present Territory of Minnesota, and the present bone of contention, Kansas and Nebraska. Slavery already existed among the French at New Orleans, and to some extent at St. Louis. In 1812 Louisiana came into the Union as a slave state, without controversy. In 1818 or '19, Missouri showed . . . a wish to come in with slavery. This was resisted by Northern members of Congress. . . This controversy lasted several months . . . At length a compromise was made . . . It was a law, passed on the Sixth of March, 1820, providing that Missouri might come into the Union with slavery, but that in all the remaining part of the territory purchased of France, which lies north of thirty-six degrees and thirty minutes north latitude, slavery should never be permitted. This . . . is the "Missouri Compromise." In excluding slavery north of the line, the same language is employed as in the ordinance of 1787. It directly applied to Iowa, Minnesota, and to . . . Kansas and Nebraska.[25]

[*He goes on to describe other states coming into the Union, and the compromise of 1850. He thus shows that until 1854, the principle of the Northwest Ordinance and the Missouri Compromise had been a fixed principle. Namely, to not allow slavery into any area unless it was already there, or could not be avoided. Then he takes up its repeal through Douglas' bill, and Douglas' expressed indifference as to whether slavery were "voted up or voted down in the territories . . ."*]

This declared indifference, but, as I must think, covert real zeal, for the spread of slavery, I cannot but hate. I hate it because of the monstrous injustice of slavery itself. I hate it because it deprives our republican example of its just influence in the world; enables the enemies of free institutions. . . to taunt us as hypocrites; causes the real friends of freedom to doubt our sincerity; and especially because it forces so many good men among ourselves into an open war with the very fundamental principles of civil liberty, criticizing the Declaration of Independence, and insisting that there is no right principle of action but self-interest.[26]

. . . But if the Negro is a man, is it not to that extent a total destruction of self-government to say that he too shall not govern himself? When the white man governs himself, that is self-government; but when he governs himself and also governs another man . . . that is despotism. If the Negro is a man, why then my ancient faith teaches me that "all men are created equal," and that there can be no moral right in . . . one man's making a slave of another.[27]

. . . Slavery is founded in the selfishness of man's nature–opposition to it in his love of justice. . . . Repeal the Missouri Compromise, repeal all compromises, repeal the Declaration of Independence, repeal all past history, you still cannot repeal human nature. It still will be the abundance of man's heart that slavery extension is wrong, and out of the abundance of his heart his mouth will continue to speak.[28]

. . . Near eighty years ago we began by declaring that all men are created equal; but now from that beginning we have run down to the other declaration, that for some men to enslave others is a "sacred right of self-government." . . . When Pettit, [Senator from Indiana] in . . . his support of the Nebraska bill, called the Declaration of Independence "a self-evident lie," he only did what consistency and candor require all other Nebraska men to do. Of the forty-odd Nebraska senators [that is, supporters of the bill] who sat present and heard him, no one rebuked him. Nor am I apprised that any Nebraska newspaper, or any Nebraska orator, in the whole nation has ever yet rebuked him.[29]

. . . Let us turn slavery from its claims of "moral right" back upon its existing legal rights and its argument of "necessity." Let us return it to the position our fathers gave it, and there let it rest in peace.[30]

[*Lincoln believed that if the spread of slavery were stopped and it were restricted to the areas where it existed, that it would eventually die out.*]

Questions

Background for the question that will follow:

Frederic Bastiat said, "The safest way to make laws respected is to make them respectable. When law and morality contradict each other, the citizen has the cruel alternative of either losing his moral sense or losing his respect for the law."[31]

At the time America became a nation, most people recognized that slavery was wrong, but could not be "abolished overnight." By 1854, southerners argued that slavery was a positive good. In doing so they defended a system that allowed the forced concubinage of black women. Senator Pettit of Indiana called the Declaration of Independence a self evident lie. At the other extreme, abolitionists such as William Lloyd Garrison wanted slavery abolished in defiance of the Constitution. He called the Constitution "a covenant with death, an agreement with hell," and according to one source, publicly burned it.[32] By 1860, many people in both North and South were condoning violence: the North, John Brown; the South, Preston Brooks.

Question 1: What does all this say about the change in the moral climate in the United States from 1776 to 1860 because of the presence of slavery?

Lincoln's Reply at Alton, in the Seventh Debate with Douglas,

October 15, 1858. (Excerpts)

THEME: Principles of Freedom and of the Declaration of Independence and Constitution

I have intimated that I thought the agitation would not cease until a crisis should have been reached and passed. . . . We might, by arresting the further spread of it [slavery], and placing it where the fathers originally placed it, put it where the public mind should rest in the belief that it was in the course of ultimate extinction. . . .[33]

The Democratic policy in regard to that institution will not tolerate the merest breath, the slightest hint, of the least degree of wrong about it. Try it by some of Judge Douglas's arguments. He says he "don't care whether it is voted up or voted down" in the Territories. . . . Any man can say that who does not see anything wrong in slavery, but no man can logically say it who does see a wrong in it. . . . He contends that whatever community wants slaves has a right to have them. So they have if it is not a wrong. But if it is a wrong, he cannot say people have a right to do wrong.

. . .You may turn over everything in the Democratic policy from beginning to end, whether in the shape it takes on the statute-book, in the shape it takes in the Dred Scott decision, in the shape it takes in conversation, or the shape it takes in short maxim-like arguments—it everywhere carefully excludes the idea that there is anything wrong in it.

That is the real issue. That is the issue that will continue in this country when these poor tongues of Judge Douglas and myself shall be silent. It is the eternal struggle between these two principles—right and wrong—throughout the world. They are the two principles that have stood face to face from the beginning of time; and will ever continue to struggle. The one is the common right of humanity, and the other the divine right of kings. It is the same principle in whatever shape it develops itself. It is the same spirit that says, "You toil and work and earn bread, and I'll eat it." No matter in what shape it comes, whether from the mouth of a king who seeks to bestride the people of his own nation and live by the fruit of their labor, or from one race of men as an apology for enslaving another race, it is the same tyrannical principle. I was glad to express my gratitude at Quincy, and I reexpress it here to Judge Douglas—that he looks to no end of the institution of slavery. That will help the people to see where the struggle really is. It will hereafter place with us all men who really do wish the wrong may have an end.[34]

Questions

Question 1: What principle does Lincoln identify as the essence of slavery?

Lincoln's Address at Cooper Institute, New York,
February 27, 1860. (Excerpts)

THEME: Principles of Freedom and of the Declaration of Independence and Constitution

. . . In his speech last autumn at Columbus, Ohio, as reported in *The New York Times*, Senator Douglas said:

> Our fathers, when they framed the government under which we live, understood this question just as well, and even better, than we do now.

I fully indorse this, and I adopt it as a text for this discourse. I so adopt it because it furnishes a precise and an agreed starting-point for a discussion between Republicans and that wing of the Democracy headed by Senator Douglas. It simply leaves the inquiry: What was the understanding those fathers had of the question mentioned?

What is the frame of government under which we live? The answer must be, "The Constitution of the United States." That Constitution consists of the original, framed in 1787, and under which the present government first went into operation, and twelve subsequently framed amendments, the first ten of which were framed in 1789.

Who were our fathers that framed the Constitution? I suppose the "thirty-nine" who signed the original instrument may be fairly called our fathers who framed that part of the present government. . . .

What is the question which, according to the text, those fathers understood "just as well, and even better, than we do now"?

It is this: Does the proper division of local from Federal authority, or anything in the Constitution, forbid our Federal Government to control as to slavery in our Federal Territories?

Upon this, Senator Douglas holds the affirmative, and Republicans the negative. . . . Let us now inquire whether the "thirty-nine," or any of them, ever acted upon this question; and if they did, how they acted upon it–how they expressed that better understanding. . . .[35]

In 1789, by the first Congress which sat under the Constitution, an act was passed to enforce the ordinance of '87, including the prohibition of slavery in the Northwestern Territory. The bill for this act was reported by one of the "thirty-nine"–Thomas Fitzsimmons, then a member of the House of Representatives from Pennsylvania. It went through all its stages without a word of opposition, and finally passed both branches without ayes and nays, which is equivalent to a unanimous passage. In this Congress there were sixteen of the thirty-nine fathers who framed the original Constitution. They were John Langdon, Nicholas Gilman, Wm. S. Johnson, Roger Sherman, Robert Morris, Thos. Fitzsimmons, William Few, Abraham Baldwin, Rufus King, William Paterson, George Clymer, Richard Bassett, George Read, Pierce Butler, Daniel Carroll and James Madison.

This shows that, in their understanding, no line dividing local from Federal authority, nor anything in the Constitution, properly forbade Congress to prohibit slavery in the Federal territory; else both their fidelity to correct principle, and their oath to support the Constitution, would have constrained them to oppose the prohibition.

Again, George Washington, another of the "thirty-nine," was then President of the United States and as such approved and signed the bill. . . .[36]

[*Lincoln examines actions of Congress in 1784, 1787, 1789, 1798, 1803, 1804, and 1819-20, that placed restrictions upon slavery in U.S. territory and the way members of the "thirty-nine" voted.*]

Here, then, we have twenty-three out of our thirty-nine fathers "who framed the government under which we live," who have, upon their official responsibility and their corporal oaths, acted upon the very question which the text affirms they "understood just as well, and even better, than we do now". . .[37]

The sum of the whole is that of our thirty-nine fathers who framed the original Constitution, twenty-one–a clear majority of the whole–certainly understood that no proper division of local from Federal authority, nor any part of the Constitution, forbade the Federal Government to control slavery in the Federal Territories.[38]

[*Lincoln now considers the amendments in the Bill of Rights. The Dred Scott decision cited the Fifth Amendment, and Senator Douglas cited the Tenth Amendment.*]

Now, it so happens that these amendments were framed by the first Congress which sat under the Constitution–the identical Congress which passed the act, already mentioned, enforcing the prohibition of slavery in the Northwestern Territory. Not only was it the same Congress, but they were the identical, same individual men who, at the same session, and at the same time within the session, had under consideration, and in progress toward maturity, these constitutional amendments, and this act prohibiting slavery in all the territory the nation then owned. The constitutional amendments were introduced before, and passed after, the act enforcing the ordinance of '87; so that, during the whole pendency of the act to enforce the ordinance, the constitutional amendments were also pending.[39]

The Emancipation Proclamation

THEME: Principles of Freedom and the Constitution

Lincoln said many times before his election, that he would not disturb slavery in those states where it already existed. Yet eleven slave states chose civil war rather than submit to his election. It was only through their rebellion that the southern states gave him both reason and authority to deal with slavery within their confines. When the Civil War began, the nation split over the issue of Union and state obedience to Federal law under the Constitution, versus the "right" of a state to secede. Slavery remained the underlying cause of the war. Without it, the war would not have happened. Lincoln eventually concluded that as a necessary war measure, he should put an end to slavery in those states in rebellion.

The Emancipation Proclamation applied only to slaves in those states or parts of states that were in rebellion against the Federal government as of January 1, 1863. Some have erroneously said, that because it applied only to areas that were not under Union control, that it did not actually free *any* slaves. This, of course, is hokum. Practically, it did not free them *immediately*. It meant, however, that as soon as such an area came under Union control, or as soon as any slave from such an area could make it to the Union lines, they were free.

Lincoln wrote the Proclamation in this way for the following reasons:

- He recognized that the Constitution did not authorize him to do anything about slavery in those areas not in rebellion.
- He could only act against slavery as a measure necessary to win the war.
- By issuing a preliminary Proclamation, September 22, 1862, and specifying that slaves would be freed in those areas in rebellion as of January 1, 1863, he gave the states in the Confederacy a chance to stop the war and return without the loss of their slaves. He warned them. By continuing their rebellion after the warning, they were left without excuse.

Roots of the Sioux War of 1876

THEMES: Complexity of Race Relations; True History Is Not the Enemy Nor the Captive of One Race or Ethnic Group; Pursue Truth Wherever It Leads.

Before the Civil War, Indian Agent Thomas Fitzpatrick tried to establish peace between whites and Amerindians, and between the tribes of Amerindians. With the coming of the Civil War, the U.S. government could not enforce the peace. Some of the Sioux and their allies took the opportunity to prey upon people traveling West, especially along the Platte, and to take land belonging to other tribes. After the Civil War, these trends led to war with the Sioux.

Most books on American history perpetuate myths about this war. In many cases some things are related as fact that are actually false, and often many facts are omitted or suppressed. By not mentioning key facts, the readers are left with erroneous impressions. Many newspaper articles on the subject perpetuate similar or the same myths. *The Plainsmen of the Yellowstone* by Mark H. Brown is an excellent source, which will be cited below. A summary of much of the relevant facts follows. For anyone who wants the full story, this author recommends Mr. Brown's book. Mr. Brown gives relevant facts regardless of what side they fall on. Moreover, he cites facts ignored by other authors. Having read the relevant treaties, and having copies of them, I can state that Mr. Brown relates treaty terms and boundaries accurately. Other authors ignore them.

MYTHS OF THE SIOUX WAR

Myth 1: The Bozeman Trail went through Sioux land. *Fact*: The Sioux claimed it, but by the treaty of 1851, it was Crow land.

Myth 2: The Sioux left the reservation and went to war because of white intrusion into the Black Hills in search of gold. *Facts*: The causes of the war began before gold was found. They will be discussed below. Part of the Sioux had never stayed on the reservation, had never abided by any treaty, and had made war on anyone they wanted to for many years.

Myth 3: The Sioux wiped out the entire Seventh Cavalry at the Battle of the Little Bighorn. (Big Horn or Bighorn, see note.)[40] *Fact*: Custer divided his command into three groups just before entering that battle. These groups were commanded by himself, Major Reno, and Captain Benteen. The group with Custer was wiped out, but the other two survived.

Those are probably the most common myths. Others encountered from time to time include the following ideas:

Myth 4: Sitting Bull left the reservation because of the Black Hills intrusion. *Fact*: He was one of the renegades who never stayed there.

Myth 5: The surveyors for the Northern Pacific went through Sioux land. *Fact*: They never came closer than about 40 miles from the reservation.

Myth 6: Amerindians had no concept of land ownership. *Fact*: They did, but it was a concept of tribal ownership.

Myth 7: One text says that at the Battle of the Little Bighorn, Custer attacked a Sioux camp that was hunting according to treaty. *Fact*: Actually, those Sioux were on the Crow Reservation, where they did not belong.

Myth 8: From the way some histories are written it might be inferred that the war was caused by the destruction of the buffalo herds, which brought the tribes to the brink of starvation. *Fact*: The northern herds in Montana and Wyoming were still plentiful until 1881.[41]

While the author thought that was near the full range of myths, he has recently encountered yet two more:

Myth 9: The Army agreed to the Treaty of 1868 with the Sioux in order to gain more land. *Facts*: It is true that compared to the 1851 Treaty, the Sioux lost a sizable chunk of the Nebraska panhandle north of the North Platte River, and some land in North Dakota between the Heart River and the 46th parallel of north latitude. However, they gained considerably more, at the expense of other tribes. This included a lot of land in Wyoming, plus some in Montana, South Dakota, and a bit in North Dakota. The Army had to surrender the Montana Road and three forts along it. It seems pretty clear that the purpose was to make peace with the Sioux. As an attempt to appease aggressors, it was unsuccessful.

Myth 10: The gathering of the Sioux and their allies on the Little Bighorn was in preparation to drive the miners and prospectors out of the Black Hills. *Fact*: Considering simple geography makes this assertion seem preposterous. The site of the Battle of the Little Bighorn was at least 150 miles from the Black Hills. In addition, the renegades had been roaming that far from their reservation, or farther, for years.

In 1851, at the urging of Indian Agent Thomas Fitzpatrick, a conference was held at Fort Laramie to draft a treaty. This was intended to settle matters not only between Amerindians and whites, but between tribes. Amerindians variously estimated from 10,000 to 60,000 in number gathered for this conference, including Arapahoes, Arickaras, Assiniboines, Cheyennes, Crows (or Absaroka), Minnetaries, Shoshones, and Sioux.[42]

The resulting treaty had several features, including obligations for peace between the different parties, provisions for the payment of damages caused by either side, and the boundaries of tribal territories.

See Map No. 1 (pages 138–39) for the approximate boundaries of Crow land under this treaty. The eastern boundary for the Crows was the Powder River. At this latitude, the western boundary for the Sioux was the Black Hills, which was also the eastern boundary for the Gros Ventre, Mandans, and Arickaras, part of whose land lay between the Crows and the Sioux.

In the treaty of 1851, the Amerindians had recognized the right of the U.S. to establish roads and military posts on Amerindian lands. "Article 2. The aforesaid Indian nations do hereby recognize the right of the United States Government to establish roads, military and other posts, within their respective territories."[43] The Bozeman Trail, also called the Montana Road, ran through what the 1851 treaty recognized as Crow land. It was a route from the North Platte to the settlements in western Montana, such as Virginia City. Establishment of this road and of forts along it was within the terms of the 1851 treaty. But the Sioux, led particularly by Red Cloud, with their allies among the Cheyenne and Arapaho, were determined to stop travel on this trail, to destroy Fort Philip Kearny,[44] and to claim this land for themselves. They also took part of the land belonging to the Gros Ventre, Mandans, and Arickaras.

In 1866 some Sioux and Cheyennes came to Fort Laramie for negotiation. When troops arrived, intending to fortify the Montana Road, "Red Cloud and other Sioux leaders left the council in disgust and anger." One Sioux put it this way:

> Great Father sends us presents and wants new road, but white chief
> goes with soldiers to steal road before Indian say yes or no![45]

In mid July 1866, the Army commenced building Fort Philip Kearny. This fort was one of four on the Bozeman Trail. Although Crow land by treaty, the Sioux now claimed this land. By December 21st, the troops at this fort had fought the Sioux in fifty one skirmishes.[46] On that day, the "wood train" was in danger, and Colonel Carrington sent a detachment of eighty-one under the command of Captain Fetterman to relieve the wood train. Fetterman apparently violated his orders by crossing a ridge, and the entire detachment was massacred.[47]

In 1868 a new treaty was signed with the Sioux, and a new one with the Crows. New boundaries were established, giving the Sioux some of the land that previously belonged to the Crows and the Gros Ventre. The Sioux agreed "not to oppose railroad construction, except on the reserved lands, and not to molest white people or to steal stock belonging to them."[48] The Montana Road was closed, and the forts (Kearny and Reno) along it in the new territory of the Sioux were abandoned.

There were basically three groups of Sioux—one that usually stayed within the reservation and hunting grounds and may have abided by the treaty; a group of renegades, led by Sitting Bull, Crazy Horse, Gall, Spotted Eagle, etc., who "roamed where they pleased and made war on anyone whom they thought they could attack successfully";[49] and a third group that stayed on the reservation in the winter and joined the renegades in the summer.[50]

Some have suggested that the renegades such as Sitting Bull and his group, were not subject to the treaty. When the treaty was first signed at Fort Laramie, none of this group were present. That was a problem. At great personal risk, a Catholic priest named Father De Smet led a party in search of the camp of the hostiles, and found them. Sitting Bull was there. A council was held to discuss the matter, and a delegation was sent to Fort Rice, where they signed. Both Gall and Red Cloud eventually signed the treaty.[51] Others were parties to it by representation. If not, then the standard for an Amerindian tribe to be subject to a treaty becomes one that in most cases would be impossible to meet; namely, that every single member personally agree to and sign the treaty. Such a standard would mean only in rare instances could any treaty be binding on any tribe. Then on whom is it binding? On whites only, or on no one? To hold to such a standard can only have one of two meanings: either the hypocritical position that treaties were binding only on whites, or that treaties were binding on no one, and were mere fictions, exercises in futility.

Sitting Bull told trader Charles Larpentaur in 1867, "I have killed, robbed, and injured too many white men to believe in a good peace. . . . I would rather have my skin pierced with bullet holes."[52]

Over the next eight years the renegade Sioux

- attacked the Crows on the Crow Reservation, taking effective control of part of it; at times the Crows appeared to be in danger of being driven off their reservation. (Repeatedly.)[53]
- raided the Crow Indian Agency. (Repeatedly in 1875. Probably earlier also.)[54]
- raided Fort Ellis, and nearby. (1873, 1874)[55]
- raided settlements in the Gallatin valley. (Repeatedly, 1874 and probably earlier.)[56]
- attacked railroad survey parties (planning for the future building of the Northern Pacific) north of the Yellowstone, in 1872 and 1873.[57] (See Map No. 2, engagements labeled Baker, 1872, and Custer, 1873.)
- attacked trappers, wagon trains, etc., that were NOT on Sioux land.[58]

Many of these offenses were committed anywhere from 70 to over 150 miles from Sioux territory. (See Map No. 2, pages 140–41) Of this period, General Crook wrote,

. . . it was well known that the treaty of 1868 has been regarded by the Indians as an instrument binding upon us but not binding on them.

It is notorious that, from the date of the treaty to the present, there has been no time that the settlers were free from the very offences laid down in the sentences quoted.

Indians have without interruption, attacked persons at home, murdered and scalped them, stolen their stock, in fact violated every leading feature of the treaty.[59]

In 1874, Custer reported finding gold in the Black Hills. Soon many prospectors headed for this area, even though it was on the Sioux Reservation. The U.S. government tried to prevent prospectors from going there, and to expel those who did.

For example, consider the following letter:

St. Paul, Minnesota, Aug. 18, 1874
Commanding Officer, Fort Ellis:

It is reported that a mining party is about to leave or has left Bozeman for the Black Hills. If this is true, prevent its departure; or if it has already gone, overtake it, burn its wagons and outfit, disarm the men, arrest the leaders and confine them at your Post. If necessary use your whole force in execution of these orders, leaving only a small infantry guard at the Post. Acknowledge receipt and report the present situation and any action you may take.

s/O. D. Greens, A.A.G.
(From the Headquarters of the Department of Dakota)[60]

The effort to keep prospectors out of the Black Hills, or to expel them, was not successful; but the government tried to comply with the treaty. That could not be said for the renegade Sioux. Many of the hostile acts of the Sioux occurred before the discovery of gold in the Black Hills; hence, that was not the cause. It probably did make the situation worse. Finally the government decided that the concessions for peace made in 1868 had not achieved peace; the Sioux aggression had continued and it was time to put a stop to it.

When the Sioux War began in 1876, and Custer attacked Sitting Bull's camp on the Little Bighorn, this band of Sioux were on the Crow Reservation.[61]

Explanation of Maps
Map No. 1:

As shown, most of the Bozeman Trail, or the Montana Road, ran through what was Crow Land by the Treaty of 1851. The numerous fights with the Sioux near Fort Philip Kearny, including the Fetterman Massacre and the Wagon Box Fight, as well as the engagement with Connor and the Hayfield Fight, were all within this Crow Land.

The northern of the engagements with Cole in 1865, was within the territory of the Gros Ventre, Mandans, and Arickaras. With regard to the southern Cole engagement, it is not clear from the boundary descriptions in the 1851 treaty whether this was within anyone's territory. If so, it was also within the territory of the Gros Ventre, et. al.

Map No. 2:

This map shows a much smaller Crow Reservation after the treaties of 1868. The Sioux Reservation after 1868 included all of South Dakota west of the Missouri River, and a sliver of North Dakota. The Sioux also had rights from their 1868 treaty to the Unceded Hunting Grounds that included approximately the southeast corner of Montana, and that part of Wyoming east of the Bighorn Mountains and north of the North Platte River. That is certainly more than one quarter, perhaps one third, of Wyoming.

The Sioux engagements with Baker in 1872 and Custer in 1873 involved the survey parties planning for the Northern Pacific Railroad. They were far from Sioux territory. Even farther from Sioux land were the Sioux raids on the Crow Indian Agency, on Fort Ellis, and in the valley of the Gallatin River.

The battle between Custer and the Sioux on the Little Bighorn, June 25, 1876, was well within the Crow Reservation. Other engagements shown on this map that are not marked with a name or date, were part of the war of 1876 to 1877. The one marked as within the boundaries of the Sioux Reservation occurred in September 1876, as General Crook followed the trail of some of the hostiles, which had led there from outside the reservation.

MAP NO. 1: Crow Land by the Treaty of 1851, the Montana Road, and Actions of the Sioux

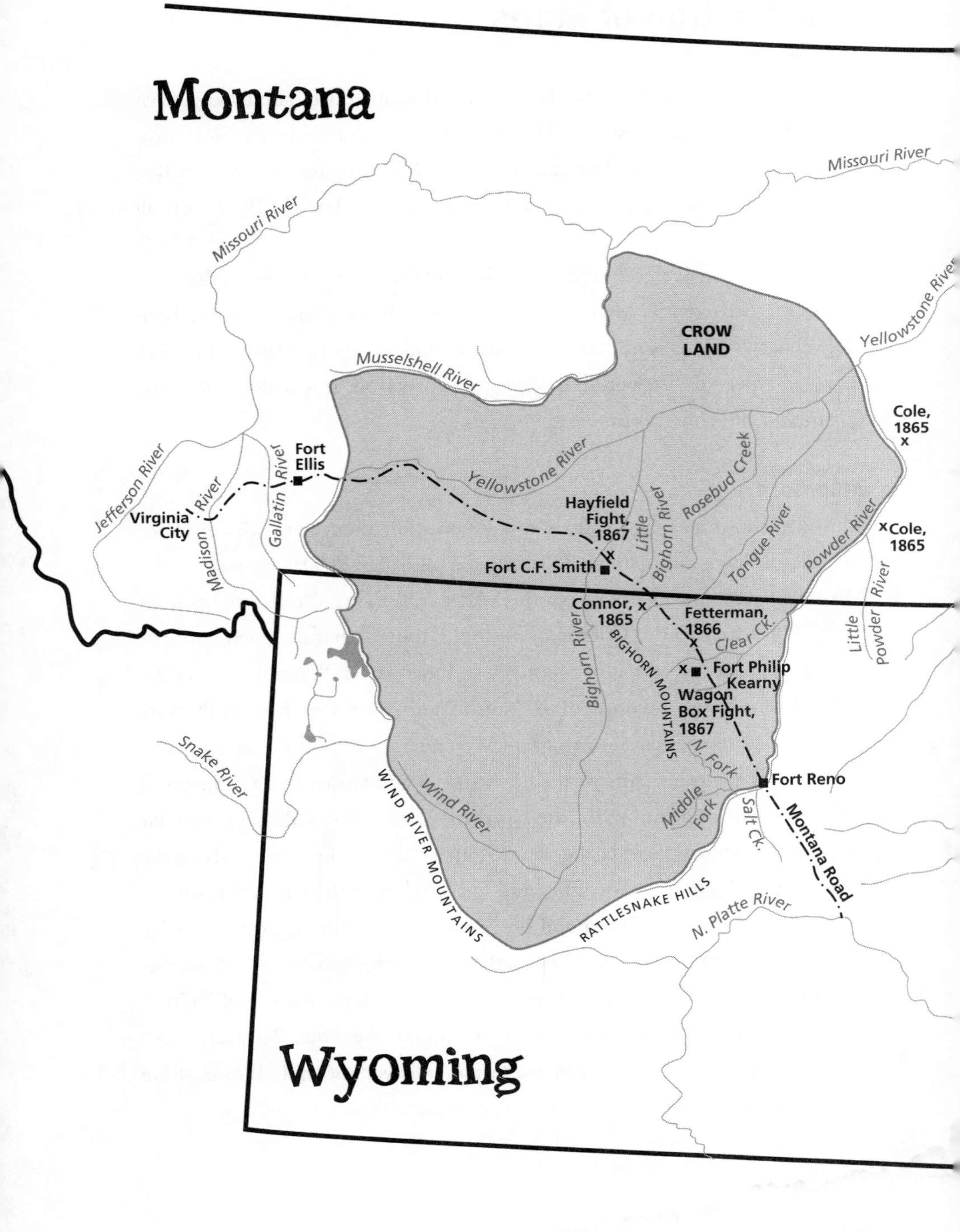

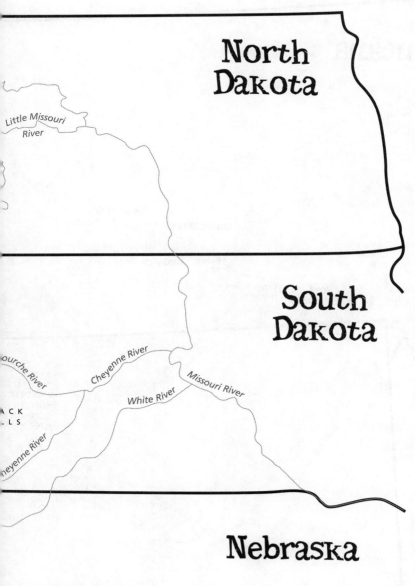

North
Dakota

*Little Missouri
River*

South
Dakota

ourche River   *Cheyenne River*

White River   *Missouri River*

A C K
L S

heyenne River

Nebraska

x **Engagements with Sioux**

MAP NO. 2: Boundaries from 1868 Treaties and Actions of the Sioux

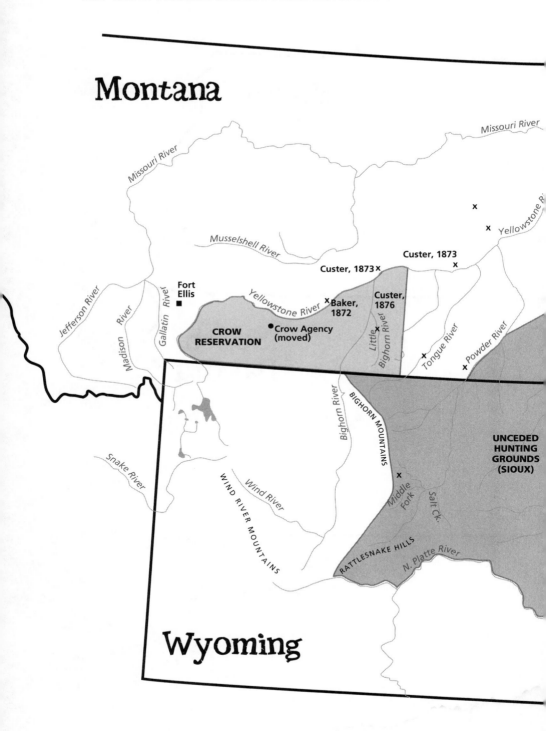

North Dakota

Little Missouri River

South Dakota

SIOUX RESERVATION

x

Cheyenne River

Fourche River

Missouri River

White River

C K
L S

Cheyenne River

Nebraska

x Engagements with Sioux

CHAPTER FIVE

An Economics Primer

In order to understand and evaluate parts of our history, we need to first understand Economics and the free market. The Twentieth Century brought events causing much debate over these principles.

Adam Smith

In 1776, the same year America declared Independence, a British subject named Adam Smith published his monumental treatise on Economics. The title was *An Inquiry into the Nature and Causes of The Wealth of Nations*. The book is usually referred to by the last four words of the title. In *The Wealth of Nations*, Adam Smith put forth a case for the free market. Each individual has the right to choose his or her own profession; the right to choose what he or she will produce; the right to choose what trades to enter, voluntarily. The role of government in such a free market is to prevent or punish theft by force or fraud; to see that people do not hurt one another. That is, to protect persons, liberty, and property.

When trades or exchanges are voluntary, then they will only happen when both parties believe that they will benefit. Government should not force exchanges, nor set the terms of the trade by force. The free actions of individual people will promote the public good, and improve the standard of living, by increasing production. Each person acting freely, although acting only in his own self interest, is "led by an invisible hand to promote an end which was no part of his intention. . . . By pursuing his own interest he frequently promotes that of the society."[1] Because he freely seeks his own interest, he can choose what to produce based on his own talents, interests, abilities, resources, and his judgement of what the market will buy. As a result, he will produce more of what the market finds useful, than if his choices were controlled. Because he freely seeks his own interest, he has *incentive*. He has a desire to produce because he benefits from it. Under socialism, a people see no benefit from their own production. Therefore, they lose incentive.

Say's Law

French economist Jean-Baptiste Say wrote *A Treatise on Political Economy*, first published in 1803. One of Say's major advances in Economics was his "law of markets," or what is commonly called "Say's Law."

Before describing this law, we need to describe common terms used in Economics. The first two are "supply" and "demand." Supply means the products available, or the amount of a product that is available. Demand means how much of a product people are willing and *able* to buy; or that they want and *have the means or ability* to buy.

The essence of Say's Law is that supply, or production, is what creates demand.[2] To illustrate this, let us imagine a farmer who grows food, a carpenter who builds things, and a smith who makes tools. It is the food that the farmer grows that allows him to buy tools from the smith, or to pay the carpenter to build a shed for him. In other words, it is the farmer's production, or supply, that creates his demand for other products. What you produce gives you the ability to buy, *if* others want what you produce. If the others want wheat, but the farmer grows soy beans, he may suffer for that decision. He may have no demand with which to buy other products. Similarly, the carpenter and the smith can only buy food from the farmer if they make things that others want. It is their production that gives them the ability (demand) to buy wheat from the farmer.

More production then, or a greater supply of more products, will generally mean more demand for those products.

Other common terms in Economics include the "factors of production," namely, land, labor, capital, and one introduced by Jean-Baptiste Say, entrepreneurship. Each of these factors has its appropriate return: for land, rent; for labor, wages; for capital, interest; and for entrepreneurship, profit. An entrepreneur is one who starts or runs a business. The word as used by Say implied that the entrepreneur was willing to take a risk. To succeed, he or she must have knowledge and judgement, must manage the problems of hiring others to work for him or her, of buying supplies or raw materials, of arranging financing for the enterprise, and of finding buyers for the end product. The business may involve bringing a new product to market.[3]

Frederic Bastiat:

What Is Seen and What Is Not Seen

French author and statesman Frederic Bastiat was mentioned earlier, in the section on the Constitution and Basic Principles, with quotation from his work, *The Law*. In another work, *What Is Seen and What Is Not Seen*, he analyzed a number of economic fallacies, or false ideas. In doing so, he gave us a valuable tool to use when considering many economic ideas. To illustrate this, we will first talk about the *fallacy of the broken window*.[4]

Someone throws a rock through a window belonging to James Goodfellow. A few of the neighbors gather round and begin to talk about this unhappy event. But then one of them gets the happy thought that this may be good for the economy. James will have to replace the window. The money he spends will benefit the glass maker, who will then spend it on something else, and thus it will go out in ever widening circles, bringing great benefit. This is the fallacious argument.

What is seen is that James must buy a new window. What is not seen is what James would have done with that money if the window had not been broken. In the France of 1850, in Bastiat's example, James must spend six francs for a new window. To put it more in our terms, let us suppose that the new window will cost $100. Perhaps James needs a new pair of shoes, that now he cannot buy. Or perhaps he would have bought a new suit, or a book, or a new tool with which he could be more productive. What becomes clear is that the change in what James will do because of the broken window does not benefit the economy, it *diverts* it–that is, it causes it to go in a different direction–and James has suffered a loss. He replaces the window. Then, instead of having a new suit, or a new pair of shoes, or a new tool, and a window, he only has a window. The money that would have gone to the shoe maker, or the tailor, or the tool maker, has gone to the glass maker instead. The idea that the broken window helps the economy is false. See Table 3, next page.

In spite of the fact that this false idea was refuted over 150 years ago, we still hear it today. After a hail storm broke many car windshields, and damaged roofs of both cars and houses, a television newsman said that all the repair work would be good for the region's economy.

One of the variations of this fallacy, is that war is good for the economy. War

TABLE 3: **James Goodfellow–His experience and the economy.**

The window is broken.	The window is not broken.	The window is not broken.
$100 "goes into the economy."	$100 "goes into the economy."	$100 "goes into the economy."
he replaces the window	he buys a new suit	he buys a new tool that makes him more productive
Results	**Results**	**Results**
James has a window.	James has a window and a new suit.	James has a window and a new tool.
James has suffered a loss.		By investment James hopes to produce more, therefore, to earn more.
The economy receives $100.	The economy receives $100.	The economy receives $100.
The glass maker receives $100.	The tailor receives $100.	The tool maker receives $100.
The economy is diverted.	The economy takes its course undisturbed	James will produce more in the future. There is a net gain.

may benefit certain people, or certain industries, but the principle is the same as that of the broken window, only worse, because war causes the death of many people. There are times when a free people may need to fight to defend themselves and their freedom, but war cannot be justified on economic grounds.

Destruction is not profitable.

Then there is the fallacy of restraint of trade, or protectionism. Let us suppose either a tariff or an import quota restricting the importation of cars. A tariff raises the price that a person must pay for a foreign car, thus allowing makers of cars here to charge more for their cars. An import quota prevents any more than a limited number of foreign cars from entering the country, and thus allows makers of cars here to charge more. Let us suppose John wants to purchase a car that would cost $7,000, but because of tariffs or quotas, it will cost $10,000. The auto makers will argue that these trade restrictions help them, and so by helping American manufacturing, help the American economy. The benefit to the car makers, their employees and suppliers, is what is seen.

What is not seen? Without these restrictions, if left free, John would pay

$7,000 for a car, and with the other $3,000, perhaps he would buy computers for his business. Because John gains only a car, instead of a car and computers, he has suffered a loss. The computer company, its employees and suppliers, have also suffered a loss. The purchase of the computers is not seen, because it is prevented. The economy is not helped; it is diverted.

To accurately use this approach, we must trace all consequences. Hence we must ask, what if John buys a foreign car with that $7,000 instead of one made here? Does not this cause a loss for our economy? The answer is no. The country from which John's new car comes will not be willing to sell it to him unless they can use that money. After all, in their country they use a different currency. What good is our money to them? International trade and exchange can be a complex subject. The simple form of the answer is that they will only want our money if they can use it, if they can get something they want in exchange for it. Hence, they will only sell the car to John if someone in that country either will purchase something from us, or from another country where they will use it to buy from us. (Or someone elsewhere will use the money to invest in American business.)

We will use this approach of "what is seen and what is not seen" to look at other fallacies.

The Errors of Thomas Malthus, David Ricardo and Paul Erlich

Thomas Robert Malthus published his *Essay on Population* in 1798. Malthus asserted that population tends to grow geometrically or exponentially, while food supply only grows arithmetically. Hence, population would inevitably outgrow food supply, leading to war, famine, disease and death. One result would be what Malthus and his friend David Ricardo called the "iron law of wages." According to this "law," wages could never grow beyond a level of bare subsistence living–in other words, wages would be barely enough to live on, and for most people it would never get any better.[5]

The ideas of Malthus had a major effect on the thinking of Charles Darwin, and formed part of the foundation of the theory of evolution.[6] However, at least where humans are concerned, events have proven Malthus wrong. They have also proven wrong one Paul R. Erlich, whose book *The Population Bomb*, was published in 1968. Like Malthus, Erlich predicted famine and mass starvation, because of "overpopulation." He predicted that hundreds of millions would starve to death in the 1970s. It did not happen.[7]

Have there been famines? Yes, occasionally, in a few places. It has not been because of overpopulation, but because of drought and government interference, as in Ethiopia, or because of tyrannical government, as in Cambodia. In Ethiopia, the government even interfered with the distribution of relief supplies sent from America and elsewhere.

In October 1980, economist Julian Simon made a bet with Paul Erlich that the combined prices of five metals, namely chrome, copper, nickel, tin and tungsten, would be lower in ten years. Erlich, as an advocate of scarcity and overpopulation, expected prices to be higher. Simon won the bet by a wide margin.[8]

Neither Malthus nor Erlich understood the power of freedom to bring about invention, technological advance and economic growth. The United States of America has been the great catalyst for the growth of freedom and production around the world. Standards of living have risen dramatically. Food supply has increased faster than population.[9] Many parts of the world that in former times needed food imports in order to sustain life, now raise enough to be self-sustaining, or have become exporters. The "iron law of wages" applies only to countries where government interferes with the market and deprives people of freedom. It does not resemble modern America. Nor does it resemble many other countries where the people are sufficiently free to make the economy grow.

The Errors of John Maynard Keynes

In 1936, during the Great Depression, the book *The General Theory of Employment, Interest and Money*, by Englishman John Maynard Keynes was published. Keynes called for government to actively intervene in the economy, and to promote full employment through large amounts of government spending in general, and deficit spending in particular. [deficit spending: spending more than the government receives in taxes.] He claimed that free market economies were inherently unstable, and must be managed by government fiscal policy. [fiscal policy: how much the government should tax and how much it should spend.][10]

One of the most significant efforts of Keynes in his book, was trying to refute Say's Law [that is, to prove it wrong]. In order to do so, he twisted, or misstated, or misinterpreted Say's Law into something different. Keynes gave Say's Law as "supply creates its own demand." That, of course, is false–and it is not Say's Law. Just because a business creates and produces a product does not mean that anyone will buy it. If they don't, the business will suffer a loss. Say would have called that misdirected production. The followers of Keynes may want to say that "demand creates its own supply," but that is also false.[11] Imagine a group of people marooned on an island, as in the old television show *Gilligan's Island*, and one or more of them could have a lot of money, such as Thurston Howell III from that show. Suppose they wanted to watch television. However much they might want and have the means to pay for it, their "demand" will not call into being a supply of the necessary equipment. Only production can do so. If they do not have the abilities and means to produce it, they will have to go without it, regardless of their demand.

Keynes believed the cause of the Great Depression, and of recessions generally, was a shortage of demand. His answer to this problem was increased government spending, including deficit spending, to create more demand. He even said that pyramid building could be good for the economy, by creating demand. While he admitted that spending government money on something more useful would be better, he claimed that just the act of spending it would benefit the economy.[12] During the depression, there were government sponsored activities on a par with pyramid building. Men hired to rake leaves from point A to point B, and back again. Men hired to dig holes, and then fill them up.

Before looking at this more closely, let us recognize that some of what government does benefits the economy. When government acts to suppress crime, to provide standards of weights and measures, to prevent fraud, to protect persons, liberty, and property, it helps the economy. These things are necessary for a free society. Without them, there is anarchy.

Now let's consider the ideas of Keynes. Let us apply Bastiat's technique to these proposals. Take pyramid building, for example. What is seen is the new pyramid, an object essentially worthless, and the employment and wages given the workers. What is not seen? Several things: what these workers would have been doing if they had not been working on the pyramid; what the government could have done with the money had it not chosen to build the pyramid; or what those from whom the government took the money would have done with it, had they been left free to use it. The actions of these private individuals who are taxed to pay for this pyramid are not seen—indeed, they do not happen—because these persons are prevented from taking those actions.

It is the same with all taxes, and all government spending. The followers of Keynes may claim that the government helps the economy by what it spends. This spending is what is seen. What the citizens would have done with the same money, if it had been left in their hands, is not seen, because it is prevented. The economy is not helped, it is diverted.

We shall examine this more, below.

Keynes also advocated using inflation as a way to reach full employment. According to Keynes, inflation and recession could not happen at the same time. Inflation refers to rising prices. When prices rise, money loses part of its value. As prices rise, it takes more money to buy the same amounts of the same products. For instance, if inflation is 2% per year, then next year it will cost $102 to buy the same things that $100 will buy this year. If inflation is 10% per year, then a year from now it will cost $110 to buy the same things that $100 will buy this year. Hence, products cost more, and money is worth less.

In his book, Keynes asserted that while workers and trade unions would resist a loss of money wages, they would not resist a loss of real wages due to inflation. In this, as in much else, events have proven that he was wrong. For decades now, many labor contracts have included a provision for automatic "cost of living" increases.

Keynes and the "Phillips Curve" Exposed by History

One of Keynes' followers named A. W. Phillips proposed the "Phillips Curve," which claimed to show in a graph, that higher inflation led to lower unemployment, and vice versa. As time went on, the data from real life refused to fit the curve. Plotting the data from the 1970s and 1980s, it not only did not fit the curve, it bore no resemblance.[13] High inflation led to high unemployment. Keynes had said this could not happen. Keynesian economists sought to explain the difference by referring to "supply shocks" related to increases in the price of oil, from the actions of OPEC. This cartel tried to hold down production. [OPEC: an organization of "Oil Producing and Exporting Countries." cartel: a group of businesses acting together.] (Clearly, "supply shocks" did not explain what happened in Germany in the early 1920s. See below, in the section on the beginning of World War II.) This explanation fails for several reasons. First, the high inflation had other causes besides OPEC trying to drive up oil prices, primarily related to the actions of government. Second, inflation had been growing worse in the United States before such actions of OPEC. Third, high inflation, regardless of the cause, forces up interest rates.

Interest is the cost of money. For example, if you get a loan of $100 at 5% interest for a year, then at the end of the year you must pay back $105. The $5 of interest is the cost for the use of the $100.

What bank would want to loan money at 5% if inflation is at 10%? The bank would be paid back in money that was not worth as much as what they had loaned. Furthermore, a bank must attract depositors: people who deposit money in the bank. That is how the bank gets the money to lend to others. Depositors do not want to put money in the bank, if inflation is high, knowing that later, when they take their money out of the bank, it will be worth less. To encourage people to deposit, banks pay interest on the money that is deposited. If the bank can pay depositors 3%, but loan money at 8%, the bank makes a profit. The higher inflation goes, the higher the interest that the bank must pay to attract depositors. Then the bank must charge a higher interest rate to stay in business. So the higher inflation goes, the higher it forces interest rates. High interest rates are generally bad for the economy. Many businesses borrow money to help pay for the costs of starting or expanding a business. The business must be able to pay back that money with interest. The higher interest rates go, the more difficult it becomes for a business to do that. Therefore, as interest rates rise, fewer new businesses will be started, and fewer businesses will expand. Because most people borrow money in order to buy a home, high interest rates also hurt the housing market.

In the 1970s, especially toward the end of that period and in 1980, rising inflation and interest rates brought economic recession and higher unemployment. After 1982, falling inflation and interest rates occurred with prolonged economic growth, prosperity, and lower unemployment.

The "Multiplier"

Among the most common arguments made by the followers of Keynes about government spending are those about what some economists call "the multiplier." The idea of the multiplier is this: if you receive an extra $100, you will probably spend most of it, say $80. Those who receive that $80 spend most of it, say $64, and so on. The total effect can be calculated by multiplying the $100 by a factor that depends on how much of each additional dollar people are inclined to spend. In the example I just gave, the "marginal propensity to consume," or MPC, is 0.8, and the multiplier is 1 divided by 1 minus MPC, or 1 divided by 1 minus 0.8, which equals 5.

Let's consider how they apply this idea to government spending. First, they say that the "balanced budget multiplier" is 1; that is, for each additional dollar the government takes in taxes and spends, the economy is one dollar better off. So if government raises taxes by another $100 billion and spends it, the economy will grow by $100 billion, or it would be $100 billion better off. Essentially, that's because when the government runs a balanced budget, it spends all the money that it takes in. If it uses deficit spending, that's even better, because then the full multiplier of say 5, would take effect, and the economy would be $500 billion bigger.

The government spends the money, and the recipients spend most of it, etc. This is what is seen. What is not seen?

First, let's consider the case where the government raised this $100 billion through taxes. If left with the people, they would have spent part of it, say $80 billion, and saved the other $20 billion. Even the Keynesian economists have to admit that there is just as much benefit from the $80 billion spent by the people, as if spent by government. But they say, the government would spend the other $20 billion, while the people would save it. What would the people do with that $20 billion? Invest in stocks and bonds, put it in banks, where it is loaned to businesses or loaned for home building, etc. Hence it also goes into the economy, and likely does far more good that way than if government spent it. It should have at least the same "multiplier" effect as the other $80 billion. Actually, it should help the economy more than the other $80 billion. Investment in inventions or in machinery and equipment to improve productivity creates growth. Such investment foregoes current consumption, in order to increase production and thereby make possible greater future consumption.

If savings should have the same multiplying effect as consumption, if as economist Mark Skousen says, "both components of income–consumption and savings–are spent," then what happens to the "multiplier"? It should be 1 divided by 1 minus the propensity to spend (in either form, consumption or saving). That would mean 1 divided by 1 minus 1, which is 1 divided by 0. Therefore, the entire concept is fatally flawed.[14]

What if government runs a deficit? Either it borrows the money, or it prints it. If it borrows the money by selling bonds, then what is not seen, is what other investments would have been made in the economy with that money. If they print it, then by putting more money in pursuit of the available goods the government causes prices to rise. Everyone suffers a loss from all of their money being worth less. This is inflation used as a hidden tax.

In either of these cases, there is no reason to believe that the economy is helped. Rather, it is diverted.

The fallacy of the "balanced budget multiplier" was caused by defining national output, usually called GDP or Gross Domestic Product, as C + I + G (Consumption + Investment + Government), and treating them as if G can be changed without affecting C and I. The fallacy implies that the higher government raises taxes, and the more it spends, the more the economy will grow and the more the country will prosper. If that were true, then communism should have produced the fastest growing and most prosperous countries in the world. Instead, the Communist countries were among the poorest, until in the late 1980s and early 1990s the Communist system in Russia and Eastern Europe collapsed. The higher government raises taxes, the less people have to keep, to use, or to invest, from what they earn. This destroys *incentive*. If laws protect persons, liberty and property, as described earlier, then people are free to save, to grow, to improve, to invest, to invent, to risk. If laws and government regulations are not based on these principles, they interfere with the market and people are less free to grow, to invest, etc. This destroys *initiative*. Incentive and initiative are critical for progress and economic growth.

If G=0, that is, no government, then C and I will be adversely affected. The lawlessness of anarchy will not allow maximum production. At that point, adding government that respects and protects freedom and basic rights will lead to greater production through higher C and I. When G becomes too large, a reduction in G will leave people with greater freedom and will enhance C and I; but when G is already too large, an increase in G will diminish C and I, resulting in lower output.

Savings and Growth

Associated with the Keynesian fallacy of the multiplier, is what Keynesians call "the paradox of thrift." This paradox says that while saving may benefit an individual, that for a nation, an increase in saving harms the economy; that an increased attempt to save can even result in a decrease in actual saving, and recession for the country.

We shall consider the reasoning behind this "paradox," as found in an Economics text of Paul Samuelson's. We begin with the assertions "that saving and investment are dependent on quite different factors"; that they can each be represented by a curve or line, or "schedule" on a graph of saving or investment versus national product; and that the intersection of the saving and investment schedules determines the amount of national product. Each "schedule," for example the saving schedule, shows how much saving (or investment) will increase with an increase in national product. Samuelson shows both lines sloping upward to the right on the graph (the direction of higher national product), but with savings having a steeper upward slope than investment, and investment starting higher than savings. See Figure 1 (page 158).

The point where saving and investment intersect is referred to as the point of equilibrium. At this ideal point, "everyone will be content to go on doing just what he has been doing."[15] Companies produce just the right amount of product so that they can sell it all, but there are no shortages. The amount families want to save is the same as the amount businesses want to invest.

If people try to save more, then the line or curve for saving shifts upward, which makes the intersection with the investment line move down and to the left on the graph, which means less saving and investment, and lower national product.

The entire presentation of these ideas is theoretical. No data is given to support them. Indeed, as we will see below, data from the real world is contrary to this theory.

Let's consider these ideas in sequence.

First, saving and investment are not completely independent variables. Investment is dependent upon saving. Production for current consumption cannot be invested. Savings actually has two sources, not one; that is, not just families. Businesses may choose to save, by not spending all their revenue on wages, rent, interest, dividends and taxes, all put toward producing for current consumption. They may accumulate reserves. Or they may spend out of current revenue on research and development, or on new equipment, which are forms of investment.

Businesses can also go into debt in order to invest. If they choose to borrow money to invest in new plant and equipment, someone else must have first saved that money, so it can be loaned to these businesses. Hence, savings is the only source of investment.

That part of investment that is made with borrowed money, depends on savings in another way. When more savings are available, interest rates will be lower. That means business will not pay as much for the use of the money they borrow. Then some businesses will make investments that they would not make if the interest rate were higher. Hence, more savings leads to more investment.

Second, there is no reason to believe that the intersection of the two imaginary curves determines the size of the national product. Nor is there any data provided as evidence. In some cases that assertion is clearly not possible. Consider the case of a country living close to a bare subsistence level. The "marginal propensity to consume" could be close to 1, for instance, 0.98. Such a subsistence level does not allow for much investment. Samuelson continually refers to desired investment, or investment opportunities. Let's suppose an economy of $100 billion, and investment opportunities of $10 billion. With an MPC of .98, Saving could not exceed $2 billion. The theory says that the MPC will multiply output to get to the "intersection" where saving would equal desired investment; that plainly will not happen. If the MPC remains at 0.98, the "multiplier" would be 50, and the economy would have to expand to $500 billion virtually overnight to reach equilibrium. (Additional investment of $8 billion

Figure 1: The So-called "Paradox of Thrift"

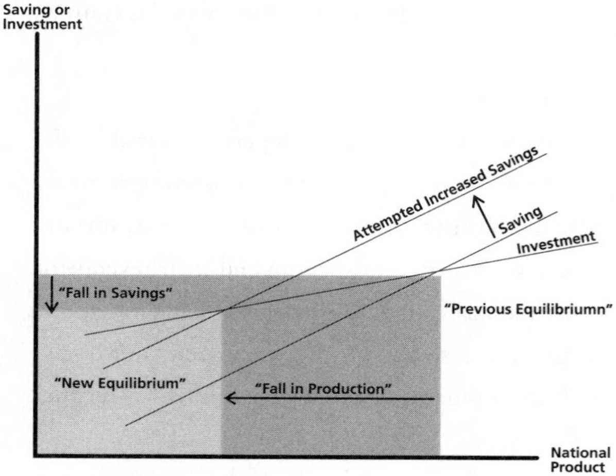

times 50 = $400 billion + the original $100 billion.) The MPC would shrink somewhat if output were higher. Still, to get savings to $10 billion would require an enormous leap in output such as no country has ever made. Nor is an investment of that size likely to increase production to such a level.

The following example is not mythical, but is based on actual events. Picture a village in Africa. Life is hard, and near the subsistence level. Either the women or their children must frequently make long trips to carry back water. If the women do it, they're not available for other work, and if the children do it they're not available for school. Missionaries from America see the need, are provided by their church with appropriate equipment, and dig a new well. A burden is lifted from the people, the standard of living improves. Children can now go to school, and education will make for a better future. The need was there. The investment opportunity was there. The MPC did not make it happen. In this case, an outside party provided the investment through their savings.

How strange to think of some particular amount of desired investment, or investment opportunities, independent of available savings. There are always more investment opportunities than anyone can actually fund, especially in a free market.

In a free market no such "equilibrium" as described (where we're all content and just continue to do what we're doing) ever exists. The dreams, ambitions, inventions, new products and new ways of doing things, devised by free people make for constant change.

Finally, suppose people become more frugal, and try to save more. As implied above, the additional savings will cause interest rates to drop, and investment will increase. Now is there data to support this, or does the data support the "paradox of thrift"?

This so called paradox has no resemblance to reality. Historical evidence shows that in general, higher rates of saving lead to higher rates of growth. In a paper for which he won a Nobel Prize, economist Franco Modigliani produced a graph of the savings rate of various countries, plotted against the rate of growth of their economies.[16] Statistically, the correlation is far from perfect. However, there are many other factors that this simple graph does not account for, such as the laws in each country. How high are the taxes? How free are the people? How much does the law or government regulation interfere with the workings of the market, or with the incentive to invest? Are there other unusual local circumstances? But while the correlation is not perfect, it is clear from the graph and from other data, that savings and growth are closely related in a positive way, not in the negative way described by the Keynesians.

Government and Business

There are also clear lessons in how various business enterprises were built, and what happened to them. In the late 1800s, American companies built five transcontinental railroads. The Union Pacific and the Central Pacific met in Utah, May 10, 1869, to complete the first one. It ran from Omaha to San Francisco. This line was built with large subsidies from Congress, including large grants of land on either side of the track. The two companies had incentive to build quickly, for their subsidies or land grants increased with each mile. In addition, each wanted to build faster than the other; the effort would push the point where they would meet further west, or east, increasing the distance, and hence the subsidy, for their company rather than the other.

The Northern Pacific, between Minneapolis and Portland, Oregon; the Southern Pacific, between San Francisco and New Orleans and St. Louis; and the Atchison, Topeka and Santa Fe, from Kansas to San Diego, were also built with government subsidies.

In contrast, James J. Hill built the Great Northern from Minnesota to Seattle without any government subsidies. He built it with different priorities–the kind of priorities that such an enterprise must have to survive and be profitable in the long run. He had to; the government was not going to save him from incompetence. Railroad companies should care about such things as the condition of the road bed, the quality and durability of the steel rails, how steep the route is, and how direct. They must try to avoid sharp curves, which cause wear on the track and increased risk of accidents. Of course, they must also link areas with people and enterprise. That's not just trying to build faster or farther, for governments to give you money or land. Some of the other lines were not as careful about such things as Mr. Hill.

In the Panic of 1893, all four of the transcontinental railroads built with government subsidy went into receivership. But not the Great Northern.

In our time some prominent people have asked why business should not welcome competition from government. Answer: It is not the purpose of Government to compete with private businesses. Government serves as the referee; it's not supposed to be in the game. Imagine yourself as a business owner. How would you like to compete with someone who:

• Can set the regulations you must abide by.
• Does not need to be efficient.
• Does not need to give good service, nor a good product.
• Does not need to make a profit.
• Because they don't need to make a profit, they can set their prices arbitrarily low.
• Can tax away your profit to make up for their own shortfall.
• Does not need to raise start up money in the capital market, but can raise it through taxes.

These facets taken together mean that government can compete in what is basically a dishonest way. The prices set may not represent the real cost of the product or service. The balance may be hidden in taxes. Regulations can be written to force consumers to use the government product or service, or to drive competitors out of business.

Freedom and Prosperity

In the May 2002 issue of *Ideas on Liberty*, the magazine of the Foundation for Economic Education, an article by Mark Skousen compares freedom to per capita income:

> Each nation is scored and ranked according to its degree of economic freedom, based on ten factors, such as level of taxation, trade restrictions, labor regulations, inflation, property rights, and government intervention in the economy.

Based on these factors, he grouped countries into four groups. The freest countries included the "United States, Ireland, Britain, Switzerland, Australia, New Zealand, . . . Hong Kong," and a few others. (Skousen actually called these the "free" countries. However, because many laws interfere with freedom even in such places as the United States, Britain, and Australia, "freest" may be a more appropriate term.) Canada, Japan, most of Europe, several countries in Latin America, and various others scattered about the globe, totaling about 60, were in the next category of "mostly free." The rest (81 of 155 surveyed) fell into the groups of "mostly unfree," or "repressed." In 1998, the average per capita income in the freest group was the equivalent of more than $20,000 per year. For the "mostly free" group it was about half of that. For the other two groups the average was not more than about $3,000 per year.[17]

The United States has led the world in inventions, in technological advance, in production. As of the early 1960s, with only six percent of the world's population, the United States produced about one half of all the world's goods. As educational levels gradually rose in many other countries, and as the effects of our technological advances and our technological aid to other countries have grown, that has changed. Yet we are still the world's leader.

The lesson is clear. Freedom brings prosperity.

Questions

Question 1: Name at least three key economic principles.

Question 2: On what does strong economic growth depend?

Question 3: What principles did Keynes ignore or mistake?

CHAPTER SIX

From the Great Depression to World War II

THEME: Freedom and the Interstate Commerce Clause; Principles of the Free Market and the Constitution

Hoover, Roosevelt, the Federal Reserve and the Great Depression

From 1929 until World War II America suffered economically from what we call the Great Depression, that brought severe unemployment. America's entry into World War II in 1941 brought full employment, but not prosperity.

Much of the blame for the Great Depression has fallen on Herbert Hoover. While he made some mistakes in dealing with it, for reasons that will follow, most of that blame does not belong to him. Typically, people think that the depression began with the "stock market crash" of October 24, 1929. In *Free to Choose*, economists Milton and Rose Friedman point out that "Business activity reached its peak in August 1929, two months before the stock market crashed, and had already fallen appreciably by then."[1] (Nor did all the stocks begin their decline at the same time. Many stocks had gone into decline as much as a year earlier, in 1928. Many others began to decline in 1929, but months before the October crash.[2]) The stock market's decline did not, by itself, bring on the Great Depression.

The Federal Reserve System was created in 1913 specifically to prevent recessions and particularly banking crises. That system failed utterly in dealing with the crisis of the Great Depression, and by their actions helped to bring it about. From 1929 to 1933, the Federal Reserve failed in dealing with a series of banking crises and allowed the money supply to shrink by one third. In September 1931, "after two years of severe depression—[the Federal Reserve *raised*] the rate of interest (the discount rate) that it charged banks for loans more sharply than ever before in its history. . . . The effect . . . was highly deflationary—putting further pressure on both commercial banks and business enterprises."[3] ". . . roughly 10,000 out of 25,000 banks disappeared during those four years . . . The total stock of money showed an equally drastic decline. . . . a monetary collapse without precedent."[4]

The Great Depression has been viewed by many as a failure of the free market economy, and a reason for massive government intervention and interference in our economy. Actually, as a failure by the Federal Reserve System, it was more a failure of government. The depression was worsened and prolonged by the Federal Reserve, and may also have been prolonged by other government actions. The worst economic record of any Presidency in American history, was that of Franklin Roosevelt; he held the office for twelve years, and prosperity never returned during his tenure.

It has often been said that America did not come out of the depression until World War II. While the country's production increased, and may have reached "full employment" during the war, it was not prosperity. Numerous things were rationed, such as meat, gasoline, etc. Obviously, much of the production was solely for the war. "National product statistic[s] . . . showed real private sector spending declining slightly during World War II and rising sharply in 1946."[5] That is, the recovery was not complete until after the war.

Franklin Roosevelt, the Supreme Court and the Interstate Commerce Clause

When Franklin Roosevelt took office as President in 1933, at his bidding the Congress passed numerous bills intended to take government control of the United States economy. Many of these measures claimed the interstate commerce clause as their constitutional justification. The Supreme Court did not see it that way, and during the first few years of Roosevelt's presidency, the court ruled several of these acts unconstitutional in eight different cases. The court overturned the Agricultural Adjustment Act of 1933, the Bituminous Coal Conservation Act of 1935, the National Recovery Administration (N.R.A.), part of the National Industrial Recovery Act, and other laws.

SCHECHTER POULTRY CORP. V. UNITED STATES, CARTER V. CARTER COAL CO., UNITED STATES V. BUTLER, ETC.

Congress created the National Recovery Administration in 1933, and the Administration created a system of codes that businesses were required to follow.

In many cases these codes were "old trade-association agreements [rewritten] into new N.R.A. codes. Some codes were almost word for word the same as the agreements."[6] For the most part, these codes were written by people from each industry to which the codes applied. Many of these codes sought to limit production, and to control relations between employers and employees, fixing minimum wages and maximum hours by industry. What Congress had done, was to give legislative power to the N.R.A., and the N.R.A. had, in part, given it to others. Schechter Poultry Corp. v. United States, 295 U.S. 495 (1935), sometimes called the "sick chicken case," involved a wholesale poultry business accused of violating the N.R.A.'s code. The Supreme Court ruled that Schechter was not engaged in interstate commerce, and therefore was outside the power of Congress under Article I Section 8 Clause 3. They also ruled that it was unconstitutional for Congress to delegate its legislative power to the executive branch, or to private persons.

In a similar way to the N.R.A. codes, the Bituminous Coal Conservation Act of 1935 allowed the executive branch to establish a Bituminous Coal Code. Through this code, it was to regulate maximum hours and minimum wages in coal mining. The Act imposed a 13.5% tax on any coal mined without compliance to the code. In Carter v. Carter Coal Co., 298 U.S. 238 (1936), the Supreme Court once again ruled unconstitutional the delegation of legislative power, and the extension of Congress power under the commerce clause to activities of a local character. Justice Sutherland, in writing the opinion of the Court, said, "Extraction of coal from the mine is the aim and the completed result of local activities. . . . The relation of employer and employee is a local relation. At common law, it is one of the domestic relations." Hence, the "employment of men, the fixing of their wages, hours of labor," were outside the realm of Congress' authority. He quoted the Court's opinion in the Schechter case, as follows:

> If the commerce clause were construed to reach all enterprises and transactions which could be said to have an indirect effect upon interstate commerce, the federal authority would embrace practically all the activities of the people, and the authority of the state over its domestic concerns would exist only by sufferance of the federal government.

I would add, that if so construed, the freedom of the people would exist only by sufferance of the federal government.

The Agricultural Adjustment Act of 1933 imposed a "processing tax" on processors of various farm commodities. The money from the tax was used to pay farmers to reduce the acreage planted in such commodities, and thereby to reduce production. Such a system, of course, takes money from the processors and gives it to the farmers. In the case of United States v. Butler, 297 U.S. 1 (1936), the Supreme Court ruled that Congress did not have authority to control agricultural production. The Court also ruled that such an action invaded the rights reserved to the states under the Tenth Amendment. It held further, that if

> Congress could invoke the taxing and spending power as a means to accomplish [this] end, Clause 1 of Section 8 of Article 1 [of the Constitution] would become the instrument for total subversion of the governmental powers reserved to the individual states.

I would add, it could be the instrument for total subversion of freedom.

ROOSEVELT'S PLAN TO CHANGE THE SUPREME COURT

With several "New Deal" programs having been ruled unconstitutional by the Supreme Court, after the 1936 election, in February 1937 President Roosevelt proposed a plan to change the court. He claimed that because of their age, that the justices were falling behind in their work, and the court needed younger men. Six of the justices were at least 70 years old. Roosevelt wanted Congress to allow him to appoint an additional justice to the Supreme Court for each one of that age.

In effect, FDR wanted to expand the court from 9 justices to 15, so that he could appoint six new justices. Many of the decisions against his programs had been by rulings of 5-4 or 6-3. This would allow him to change the balance to at least 9-6 in favor of his plans.

A storm of controversy arose over his plan. Many said he wanted to "pack the court." Chief Justice Hughes denied that the court was falling behind in its work. To many Americans, the President's plan appeared to be a direct assault on the independence of the judiciary. To others, the court's actions were based on "antiquated" or "reactionary" views.

THE "SWITCH IN TIME THAT SAVED NINE"

Before Congress could take up the President's "court packing plan," Chief Justice Hughes and Justice Roberts began voting with the three on the court who had previously been in the minority. New Deal legislation was now being upheld by the court by 5-4 votes. An old proverb says that "A stitch in time saves nine." (That is, mending a piece of clothing early saves time compared to the much more extensive mending needed if you wait too long.) This change in position by the Supreme Court was now called the "Switch in time that saved nine," meaning of course, the nine justices.

WICKARD V. FILBURN (1942)–THE AFTERMATH OF THE "SWITCH IN TIME"

In *A Summary View of the Rights of British America,* Jefferson says of the Hat Act, "By an act passed in the fifth year of the reign of his late Majesty, King George the second, an American subject is forbidden to make a hat for himself, of the fur which he has taken, perhaps, on his own soil; an instance of despotism, to which no parallel can be produced in the most arbitrary ages of British history."[7] We can however produce a modern parallel with the case of Wickard v. Filburn,[8] wherein an American farmer was forbidden to grow grain on his own land to eat and to feed to his own livestock.

Under the Agricultural Adjustment Act of 1938, the government had assigned a marketing quota to Filburn that set a limit on his 1941 wheat crop. The government sought to impose a penalty on Filburn for having grown wheat for consumption on his farm, in excess of this marketing quota.

The case went to the U.S. Supreme Court, where Justice Jackson speaking for the court reasoned that if Filburn had not grown the wheat, he might have purchased wheat, that might have moved in interstate commerce, and that Congress therefore had the authority to prevent him from "producing to meet his own needs. That [his] own contribution to the demand for wheat may be trivial by itself is not enough to remove him from the scope of federal regulation where, as here, his contribution, taken together with that of many others similarly situated, is far from trivial."

Thus the court ruled that Congress had the authority to regulate not just interstate commerce, or even commerce between different parts of the same state, but even activities where there was no transaction.

Questions

Question 1. Can this case be reconciled with Gibbons v. Ogden? Why and how, or why not?

Question 2. The opinion of the court assumed the existence "of many others similarly situated." How many others were there? How many would justify the conclusion that their demand for wheat, taken together, would not be trivial?

Question 3. The courts have consistently ruled that taxpayers do not have judicial standing to sue the government over the part of their taxes which may go to a program they consider unconstitutional. It is said to be a bad rule of law that does not apply to both parties; for instance, that allows party A to sue B, but does not allow B to sue A. Considering the reasoning of Wickard v. Filburn, what about the taxes not only of those who may want to challenge a program, but "of many others similarly situated," that taken together, "is far from trivial"? Should such a consideration give taxpayers standing to sue? Or is Justice Jackson's argument flawed?

Question 4. Senator Sam Ervin of North Carolina once said of Wickard v. Filburn that insofar as the application of the law to the facts was concerned, the case was a judicial oddity that belonged in a legal Smithsonian Institution. On the other hand, Chief Justice Roberts, during his confirmation hearings in 2006, mentioned the case, apparently with approval. Who's right and why?

Economic Errors in Dealing with the Depression

The recession of 1907 was sharp, but comparatively short. "The recession lasted only thirteen months in all, and its severe phase only about half that long."[9] Congress in 1913 created the Federal Reserve to prevent such events in the future. However, in 1929 to 1938, the Federal Reserve neither followed the banking methods that resolved the banking crisis in 1907, nor other methods available to them that might have ameliorated the Great Depression.

As the money supply shrank and production declined in the United States, for the economy to regain its balance, prices would have to fall. With less money available, Americans would tend to buy fewer imports. Falling prices would encourage other countries to buy more American goods, hence encouraging exports. These effects should result in an inflow of money into the United States, particularly gold. (Much of the world, including the U.S., was on the gold standard.) The Friedmans report the following:

> The facts are clear. The U.S. gold stock *rose* from August 1929 to August 1931, the first two years of the contraction . . . Had the Federal Reserve System followed the rules of the gold standard, it should have reacted to the inflow of gold by increasing the quantity of money. Instead, it actually let the quantity of money decline.[10]

Severe inflation or deflation are both bad. Inflation hurts creditors, people on fixed incomes, such as those on pensions, and anyone holding the currency or certain assets measured in terms of the currency. We will talk more about inflation in a later section. Deflation hurts debtors. The deflation at the time of the great depression was so severe, that fairness would dictate that loans be renegotiated.

The decline in the quantity of money meant that the only way production could be maintained was to significantly reduce prices, unless the money supply could be increased. Production is the only means to prosperity. Many of the actions of government during this period were wrong-headed. The Federal government and some of the state governments tried to force the economy to go where they wanted it to go. It did not work. These governments sought to mandate minimum prices, minimum wages, maximum hours, and in some cases to force reduction in production. The mandated prices, hours, and wages, would have the same effect, that is, to drive down production. In some industries where the decline in prices was comparatively small, the fall in production was enormous (e.g., 80% or more). Prosperity could not be achieved by such means.

In contrast, in some industries in which prices fell significantly (e.g., 45-65%), the drop in production was much less.[11]

Increased bureaucracy and regulation and higher tax rates also hurt the economy, including a top income tax rate of 75%. Such a rate reduces incentive, and prevents those affected from investing in ventures that they would try otherwise. With such a high tax rate, the return on many potential businesses would simply not be enough to justify the risk and the effort.

In 1933 to 1934, the United States went off the gold standard, and the government forced citizens to surrender their gold and gold certificates (certificates redeemable in gold, that is, able to be exchanged for gold). The federal government took the gold and gave the citizens paper money in its place at the rate of about $21 per ounce. The government then raised the price of gold to $35 per ounce. This is called "devaluing the currency." The dollar's value was reduced, with the expectation that prices would rise. It also meant that, eventually, the money supply could be greatly expanded.

However, this certainly did not help the people generally. The money they had was now worth less than previously, at least in terms of gold, which they were now forbidden to own. While the government wanted to force prices up, the people did not have anything more than they had before with which to purchase the goods they needed. Had the gold and gold certificates remained in the hands of those who owned them, and the price of gold been raised, there would have been an immediate expansion in the money supply. Those who previously held $21 in gold, would then have held $35 in gold.

The question should also be raised: Was this a violation of the fifth amendment, by taking private property for government use without just compensation?

The Beginning of World War II

THEMES: Defense of Freedom by Strength or by Appeasement? The Harsh Peace; Evils of Inflation.

A summary of events leading up to World War II, and into the early years of the war follows:

1. Japan invaded Manchuria (part of China) in 1931.
2. Hitler announced Germany was rearming in defiance of the Treaty of Versailles in March 1935.
3. Italy invaded Ethiopia in 1935.
4. Germany sent troops into the Rhineland in March 1936 (also against the treaty).
5. Japan invaded China proper in 1937.
6. Germany annexed Austria in March 1938 (also against the treaty).
7. Germany took the Sudetenland from Czechoslovakia in October 1938 (Munich Agreement).
8. Germany took most of the balance of Czechoslovakia by March 1939.
9. Germany took Memel from Lithuania in March 1939.
10. Italy invaded Albania in April 1939.
11. Germany invaded Poland, September 1, 1939.
12. In response, France and Britain declared war on Germany.
13. Russia (U.S.S.R.) invaded Poland, September 17, 1939, dividing it with Germany.
14. Russia invaded Finland, November 30, 1939.
15. Germany invaded Denmark and Norway in April 1940.
16. Germany invaded Belgium, Netherlands, Luxembourg, and France in May 1940.
17. Italy declared war on France and Britain, June 10, 1940.
18. Russia annexed Bessarabia and northern Bucovina in June 1940, and in August took over Estonia, Latvia, and Lithuania.

19. Italy invaded Egypt from Libya in September 1940.

20. Germany sent troops into Romania in October 1940.

21. Italy invaded Greece from Albania, October 28, 1940 (unsuccessfully).

22. Japan invaded French Indochina in 1940.

23. Japan invaded Thailand in 1941.

24. German troops arrived in North Africa in February 1941.

25. Germany invaded Yugoslavia and Greece in April 1941.

26. Germany invaded Russia in June 1941.

27. Japan attacked the United States at Pearl Harbor, Hawaii, December 7, 1941.

28. In response, the United States declared war on Japan on December 8.

29. Germany declared war on the United States on December 11.

30. Japan invaded Burma, Sumatra, Java, Borneo, Celebes, New Guinea, and the Philippines in 1942.

31. Japan attacked the United States base at Midway, June 4, 1942. This battle was a turning point in the war: the United States lost a destroyer and an aircraft carrier, while Japan lost a heavy cruiser and four aircraft carriers.

Events 11 and 12 mark the beginning of World War II, and events 27 to 29 mark the entry of the United States into that war. Most of the events in this list were acts of aggression committed by the Axis Powers, Germany, Italy, and Japan, or by the U.S.S.R. (Russia). In spite of events 2, 4, and 6 violating the Treaty of Versailles, signed at the end of World War I, Britain and France did nothing. In particular, at the rearming of the Rhineland, France was unwilling with one hundred divisions to confront three German battalions. Britain and France were even complicit in events 7 and 8, as we will discuss below. Even their own declaration of war on Germany failed to goad them into action. This failure to act appears more surprising when we consider the events of 1923.

The Treaty of Versailles, signed in 1919, and two other treaties, placed the blame for World War I on Germany and Austria, and required that they pay reparation for damages. The treaty took Germany's colonies from her and gave them to Britain, France, and Japan. The treaty also placed limits on Germany's armed forces, and forbid her from maintaining any armed presence in the

Rhineland. Germany surrendered coal, chemicals, farm animals, machinery, ships, etc. in payment. She still owed billions of dollars more in reparations; far more than some economists believed she could pay.

To pay these reparations, and to pay the German war debt (money borrowed by her government during the war), Germany chose to simply print more paper money. In 1914 the German Mark was worth about twenty four cents. One could exchange it for gold. However, after the war, the printing of paper money and the accompanying inflation continued to accelerate until the chaos of November 1923. What a mark could buy before the war, soon required hundreds (1922), then thousands (January 1923), then millions (August 1923) of marks to purchase. By November 1923, a loaf of bread cost hundreds of billions of marks. Later that month even trillions of marks could scarcely equal one dollar. Workers were paid twice a day (one source says some were paid three times a day). The workers or their wives would immediately rush to the stores to try to buy whatever they could before prices jumped again and the pay they had just received lost all value. Unemployment soared. Farmers did not want to bring produce into the cities, to be paid in worthless paper. For millions of people, their life savings were wiped out. Such savings lost all value, because the money in which it was measured lost all value. Anyone trying to live on a pension or a fixed income became destitute.

This shows how inflation acts as a hidden tax, silently stealing from everyone who holds the inflated currency.

In January of 1923, France, considering Germany in default on her reparations payments, sent in troops to occupy the Ruhr, Germany's main industrial area. Workers there declared a general strike. Resistance to the French occupation continued until late September. France withdrew her troops in 1925.

Surely we must note the striking irony. France invaded Germany over these reparations in 1923; but when Germany under Hitler in defiance of the treaty: rearmed; armed the Rhineland; annexed Austria; and swallowed France's ally, Czechoslovakia, France did nothing.

Much of the information that follows is drawn from William L. Shirer's *The Rise and Fall of the Third Reich.* Some comes from *Winston Churchill: The Valiant Years* by Jack LeVien and John Lord.

Hitler and National Socialism compared with other forms of socialism

The term "Nazi" comes from the first two syllables in the first word in the name of Hitler's political party, the National Socialist German Workers Party.

What is socialism? One definition is *government control of the means of production*. This definition, however, is too narrow. It recognizes only one means or method used by socialists to bring about their ends. They seek power and to *control the results of production*[12] –to control the distribution of wealth. In socialist doctrine, they seek *equality of economic outcome*. To do this, socialists take the earning of some and bestow it on others who have not earned it. This results in the destruction of incentive, initiative, and freedom. The most productive will often seek to escape by leaving the country. In practice, no socialist regime has ever brought about equality of economic outcome; and while the doctrine calls for sharing the wealth, in practice it generally results in the sharing of poverty. In practice, in most cases it also means more for those in power. In many cases, socialists are less concerned with the equal outcome called for by their doctrine, than they are with power and control over other people's lives.

When law, or government, takes that which belongs to one person and gives it to another to whom it does not belong, that is what Bastiat called "legal plunder." Such legal plunder can take any of a seemingly infinite number of forms. He named many of these, such as tariffs, subsidies, guaranteed jobs, minimum wages, a right to relief, progressive taxation, etc. "All these plans as a whole–with their common aim of legal plunder–constitute socialism."[13] Or put another way, socialism is massive legal plunder on a broad scale. As Bastiat would put it, "Universal plunder," or "Everybody plunders everybody."[14]

Communism, Nazism or National Socialism, Fascism, Fabian Socialism, or the Socialism of "social democrats," are variations of the same philosophy.[15] They have differences–for instance, Communists or Nazis, if in power, will likely kill you if you oppose their plans—but they are all rooted in the desire for government power to control other peoples lives and their economic activities and outcomes. Communists seek to create a Socialist society by violent or subversive overthrow of governments; to gain power by force or subversion. Social democrats seek to create a Socialist society by democratic means. Benito Mussolini was a Socialist. He was prominent in the Italian Socialist Party, before differences arose between him and others in that party over whether Italy should enter World War I. So he formed his own Fascist Party, joining Socialist ideology with an aggressive nationalism that sought for conquest.[16] Hitler's National Socialism was similar. Communism also sought for conquest. Both sought for world domination.

Both Communism in Russia and Nazism in Germany sought to destroy freedom of religion, and persecuted churches. They both sought to control the education of youth, to indoctrinate them in the philosophy of "the Party." They controlled the press, and suppressed freedom of speech. Both used secret police, arrested and killed people without trial, or with only a "show trial" with the outcome predetermined. Both sent millions to concentration camps or slave labor camps. Both imposed massive bureaucracy, regulations and "red tape" on production. Both restricted people's choice of profession.

Nazism had particular hatred for Jews and sought to exterminate them. Had Hitler remained in power, other groups would have followed the Jews as targets of his hatred. He also hated Poles, Slavs, Christians (not just one flavor of Christians: Catholics, Protestants and Latter Day Saints (Mormons)), and they all felt Nazi wrath, although not as heavily as the Jews. Indeed, the Nazis planned to stop the publication of the Bible; to take control of all churches; to substitute Hitler's book *Mein Kampf* for the Bible; and to replace priests and pastors with Nazi speakers.[17]

Communism suppressed the churches in Russia, except for a very few. Some church buildings were used for other purposes, such as for storing grain.[18]

Communism exerted economic control by means of government ownership of farms and factories; setting wages and prices; limiting choice of profession; deciding what should be produced and setting production goals. Workers of every kind could not change jobs or professions without government permission. One result was economic privation. Economically, freedom and incentive work, Socialism does not. For instance, in Communist Russia, when small private farming plots were allowed, they were far more productive than the big collective farms.

Nazism used some of the same means of economic control, but did not take government ownership of farms and factories. However, government set wage and price controls. They also set limits on dividends, and controls on what and how much businesses could produce. Businesses were forced to join cartels. All small corporations below a certain size were dissolved and new ones forbidden. Farmers were bound to the land by law. The state controlled "who could be hired for what."[19] Hence, as with the Communists, they sought to control production and distribution. Some of their methods were the same, some were different. While they did not take ownership of the means of production, they did exert control over them. National Socialism was, indeed, Socialism.

Freedom and any variety of Socialism are incompatible.

The Munich Agreement;
Neville Chamberlain's Assertion;
Churchill's Response

THEME: The Failure of Appeasement; Peace and Freedom Require Strength in Opposing Tyranny

In 1938, after taking over Austria, Hitler demanded that the Sudetenland, part of Czechoslovakia, be turned over to Germany. He insisted that this be done by October 1, or Germany would invade Czechoslovakia. France had a treaty of alliance with Czechoslovakia, that required her to come to the Czechs' aid if attacked by Germany. In such an event, both Britain and Russia would likely have aided France. Russia was obligated by treaty to do so.[20]

It is probable that in such a war, if France and Britain had acted, which they did not in 1938 nor in 1939-40, Germany would have lost quickly. Czechoslovakia had mountains near the border with Germany, which they had fortified, and an army of 800,000. It would have been difficult even for the bulk of Germany's forces to break through. Meanwhile, the German army had only twelve divisions, five regular and seven reserve, on the western border, to hold off 100 French divisions. The Czech and French armies together at that time outnumbered the German by nearly two to one. Czechoslovakia was a valuable ally with a defensible border.[21] Had the West challenged Hitler at this point, it would have saved billions in resources and millions of lives.

France and Britain, through the French Premier, Daladier, and the British Prime Minister, Neville Chamberlain, sought to negotiate with Hitler for a peaceful solution. Chamberlain met with Hitler at Godesberg on September 22-23. Preceding this meeting, Hitler was so agitated and so out of control that he would sometimes throw himself on the floor and chew on the edge of the carpet.[22] Chamberlain was ready to appease Hitler and give him what he demanded. But, at Godesberg, Hitler raised his demands. Chamberlain, at that time, rejected them.[23]

On September 29, Chamberlain, Daladier, Mussolini, and Hitler, met in Munich, Germany. Mussolini brought forth a proposal for a "compromise." It was similar to Hitler's Godesberg demands; it was actually written in Berlin. Yet Chamberlain and Daladier accepted it.[24]

On his triumphant return to England, Chamberlain called it "peace with honor. I believe it is peace in our time."[25] England was delirious with joy.

Winston Churchill, however, saw things differently. In what must be considered one of the defining moments of his leadership, he took a very unpopular stand; but it was a stand for truth, freedom, and right. On October 5, in the House of Commons, he said:

> We have sustained a total and unmitigated defeat. . . . We are in the midst of a disaster of the first magnitude. The road down the Danube . . . the road to the Black Sea has been opened . . . All the countries of Mittel Europa and the Danube valley, one after another, will be drawn in the vast system of Nazi politics . . . radiating from Berlin . . . And do not suppose that this is the end. It is only the beginning of the reckoning. This is only the first sip, the first foretaste of a bitter cup which will be proffered to us year by year unless, by a supreme recovery of moral health and martial vigor, we arise again and take our stand for freedom.[26]

The Czech Foreign Minister, Dr. Krofta, said, "We have been forced into this situation; . . . today it is our turn, tomorrow it will be the turn of others."[27] The Munich Agreement was just the beginning of the betrayal of Czechoslovakia by its western allies, and its subjugation by the Nazis. In spite of the "guarantees" given of the country's new boundaries, by mid to late March of 1939, Germany had taken over most of it, except for a piece taken by Hungary, and a piece taken by Poland[28] –another astonishing lack of foresight, this time by Poland. Her turn was coming, in less than a year.

Hitler had assured Chamberlain that the Sudetenland was the "last territorial demand that he had to make in Europe."[29] Yet in less than a year, he had taken the rest of Czechoslovakia, Memel from Lithuania, and Europe was on the brink of war over his demands in Poland.

Churchill warned,

> If you will not fight for the right when you can easily win without bloodshed; if you will not fight when your victory will be sure and not too costly, you may come to the moment when you will have to fight with all the odds against you and only a precarious chance of survival. There may even be a worse case. You may have to fight when there is no hope of victory, because it is better to perish than to live as slaves.[30]

The "Miracle at Dunkirk"[31]; Churchill's Resolve

On September 1, 1939, Germany attacked Poland, and on September 17 Russia also invaded Poland. This time France and Britain declared war on Germany. But while Germany overran Poland, they did nothing. With "approximately 110 French and British divisions" facing about "23 German divisions" on the border between France and Germany, the allies did not attack.[32] Over the fall, winter, and into the spring of 1940, the two sides watched one another.[33] The Allies would not act against three German *battalions* in 1936, nor against 12 German divisions in 1938, nor against 23 in 1939. In May of 1940, they faced 136.[34]

On May 10, the day Winston Churchill replaced Neville Chamberlain as Prime Minister, the Germans struck on the western end of the front, through the Netherlands and Belgium, whose neutrality they had recently promised they would not violate.[35] The British and French had expected this, and rushed in to meet them. On May 14th, through the Argonne forest across a pontoon bridge built over the Meuse River, near Sedan, France, about forty miles west of where France, Belgium, and Luxembourg meet, the Germans sent two tank divisions. They broke through the Allied lines, and by nightfall held an area of fifteen by thirty miles. Two more tank divisions crossed the Meuse near Dinant, Belgium, and two more near Montherme, France. Soon they turned to the west, and began driving toward the sea. "On May 20," they "reached. . . the mouth of the Somme." By that time, the German force between Sedan and the English Channel included seven tank divisions reinforced with divisions of mechanized infantry. The entire British Expeditionary Force and over 100,000 French troops were cut off. They were surrounded, and in danger of being crushed, or driven into the sea. The tanks turned north.[36]

Then a strange thing happened. On May 24, at the Aa canal, they stopped. Hitler had ordered the halt, for several reasons, including the urging of Rundstedt, and the assurance of Goering that the Luftwaffe [the German air force] would destroy the enemy.[37] For two days the tanks sat. Finally the order was changed, but the delay gave the Allies precious time to organize their defense, including the placement of heavy artillery. Now the German tanks "found it hard going."[38]

Meanwhile, Britain was a seafaring land, and they decided to try a rescue. They hoped to evacuate up to 45,000 troops across the English Channel.[39] "More and more boats swarm across the Channel which, many think by an act of God, is calm enough for a rowboat."[40] It was not that calm for the entire evacuation, as you will see below, but it was for a time. Over 850 vessels of all kinds were used, both public and private, "from cruisers . . . to . . . sailboats. . . [On] May 27, they took off 7,669 troops; the next day, 17,804; the following day, 47,310."[41]

"Not until [the] fourth day" of the evacuation did the Germans fully realize what was happening. For the first few days, the Luftwaffe were "grounded by bad weather." Heavy rain began on May 26. There were clouds and scattered rain on the 29th and 30th, and where it wasn't raining sometimes there was mist. One of the main features of the weather on the 28th and 29th was low clouds, with a ceiling as low as 300 feet. Such conditions certainly restricted the ability of the Germans to get an accurate overview of what was happening. On the 30th it was clearer in the afternoon, and the skies finally cleared by noon of the 31st. From then through June 4, it remained clear. The sea was described as rough on the 28th, but as calm on the 30th, and as having "high surf" on the afternoon of the 31st. When they had good weather, "for the first time" in the war, the Luftwaffe were "successfully challenged" by Britain's Royal Air Force. The RAF were outnumbered, but shot down far more planes of the Luftwaffe than they lost. The evacuation continued, each day making the defense weaker, yet each day they held out. May 30: 53,000; the 31st, 68,000; June 1: 64,000. The Germans were able to press their bombing after the weather cleared, but surprisingly, at this time the Luftwaffe did not fly at night. After June 1, the British stopped evacuating by day, but continued to do so on the nights of June 2nd and 3rd, rescuing 64,000 more. On the morning of June 4, the remaining force of 40,000 French soldiers surrendered. But 278,000 British and 60,000 French, more than a third of a million men, had escaped.[42]

That day Churchill said to the House of Commons:

Even though large tracts of Europe and many old and famous
States have fallen or may fall into the grip of the Gestapo and all
the odious apparatus of Nazi rule, we shall not flag or fail. We shall
go on to the end, we shall fight in France, we shall fight in the seas
and oceans, we shall fight with growing confidence and growing
strength in the air, we shall defend our island, whatever the cost
may be; we shall fight on the beaches, we shall fight on the landing grounds, we shall fight in the fields and in the streets, we shall
fight in the hills; we shall never surrender, and even if, which I do
not for a moment believe, this island or a large part of it were sub-
jugated and starving, then our Empire beyond the seas, armed and
guarded by the British Fleet, would carry on the struggle, until, in
God's good time, the New World, with all its power and might,
steps forth to the rescue and liberation of the Old.[43]

In time, the New World, America, did step forth "to the rescue and liberation of the Old."

The Miracle at Midway

THEME: A Major Turning Point in World War II in the Pacific; The Unlikely Circumstances

Walter Lord wrote a book on the battle of Midway, entitled *Incredible Victory*. Indeed, so many unlikely elements went into the victory of the United States over the Japanese in this battle that it does indeed appear incredible.

On December 7, 1941, without having issued a declaration of war, the Japanese attacked the part of the U.S. naval fleet stationed at Pearl Harbor, at the island of Oahu, Hawaii. Eight battleships were moored there, and all eight were damaged, including three that were sunk. Several other vessels were also damaged. However, *none of the U.S. aircraft carriers that were stationed in the Pacific were in Pearl Harbor the day of the attack.*

On April 18, 1942, 16 U.S. planes made a raid on Tokyo (the "Doolittle Raid"). They accomplished little, except to shock the Japanese and convince them to expand their area of control. They decided to capture Midway.[44]

In the battle of the Coral Sea, May 7 to 8, the U.S. lost an aircraft carrier, and a second carrier, the *Yorktown*, was badly damaged. The Coral Sea lies between Australia and New Guinea. The Japanese thought the *Yorktown* was either sunk, or so badly damaged that it would be impossible for the ship to aid the Americans in defending Midway.[45] One Japanese carrier was damaged, and another lost most of its planes.

U.S. intelligence had deciphered enough of the Japanese codes, to believe that the Japanese were going to strike Midway. Japanese radio traffic carried references to a place code named AF. To determine the identity of AF for certain, the Americans at Midway sent a fake radio message about a water shortage. The Japanese were not aware that the message was prearranged by means of an undersea cable between Hawaii and Midway. Soon afterward, U.S. intelligence intercepted a coded Japanese message about a water shortage at AF.[46]

Now sure that the Japanese would attack Midway, the U.S. began sending additional planes, equipment, and forces to Midway, to defend these two small islands.

On May 15th, a Japanese patrol plane saw an American task force with two carriers, *Hornet* and *Enterprise*, east of the Solomon Islands.[47] The Solomons are east of New Guinea, in the South Pacific. The Japanese believed that the Americans were unaware of the plan to invade Midway. Hence, as that plan was developed and carried out, the planners thought that the *Yorktown* was out of commission, and the other two carriers were thousands of miles away. They expected no carriers to oppose their invasion. Once the invasion was underway, they expected the American fleet to come from Hawaii and fall into a trap.[48] The U.S. ships, even if the two carriers showed up, would be greatly outnumbered. The original plan called for six carriers in the Japanese attack force. Because of the battle in the Coral Sea, two of those carriers remained behind. Two more would be in the force sent to attack the Aleutians, another with a group of warships (including seven battleships) somewhat behind the attack force, waiting to ambush the Americans when they came out to defend Midway, and another with the invasion and occupation force coming from the south. Hence, in all, the Japanese forces included eight carriers, but with their forces divided, only four would be in the force that would first hit Midway. They would strike on June 4. After the planes from the carriers had bombed Midway, the invasion force would arrive to land troops.

The Japanese plan also called for cordons of submarines between Hawaii and Midway, to alert their other forces when the U.S. warships came from Pearl Harbor to Midway. These cordons were to be in place by June 1.[49] In addition, under "Operation K," Japanese seaplanes would fly to French Frigate Shoals. There, submarines would meet and refuel them and the seaplanes would fly on to Pearl Harbor to see what the Americans were doing, and what ships were there.[50]

With their plans all set, the various Japanese task forces set sail, some for the Aleutians, some for Midway. They were convinced that the Americans knew nothing of their plans. In order to keep this secrecy, they maintained radio silence.

Meanwhile, the U.S. carriers steamed to Pearl Harbor as quickly as possible. On May 28, Task Force 16, including the carriers *Hornet* and *Enterprise* left for an area northeast of Midway, to lie in wait for the Japanese. The *Yorktown*, which was to go out in Task Force 17, was so badly damaged that it could have taken weeks to repair. Admiral Nimitz told the repair experts, "We must have this ship back in three days." Incredibly, they did it. Many of those working to ready the ship, whether those in the repair crews or those loading her with bombs, worked close to 48 hours straight. To allow the Navy the massive electricity needed for the repair equipment, the Hawaiian Electric Company staged power "failures" in first one area, then another, shifting power to the shipyard in Pearl Harbor. There the race with time to repair the *Yorktown* went on, even when she left dry dock for the harbor on May 29. The next day she left for the open sea and her last battle.[51]

The Japanese reconnaissance did not go well. A practice run of "Operation K" worked flawlessly, but not the real thing. This time, when Japanese tanker-submarines arrived at French Frigate Shoals for "Operation K" they found American ships there. They waited, but the U.S. ships didn't leave. Wanting secrecy, the Japanese officer in charge postponed the operation from May 30 to May 31, then canceled it.[52] The submarine cordons ran late and would not be in place until June 3. The Japanese did not know it, but by then, of course, they would be too late to see the U.S. fleet moving west from Hawaii. Japan's strike force moving toward Midway did not hear about the failure of "Operation K" nor that the cordons would be late.[53] Radio silence!

On the morning of June 4, 1942, as they had done each day since May 30th, American search planes took to the sky about 4:15 a.m.[54] Half an hour later as dawn approached, the Japanese carriers launched half of their planes for an attack on Midway. The rest they held in reserve for a possible attack on the U.S. fleet, if it showed up. The Japanese also launched seven search planes of their own, to look for that fleet. Most of these left about 4:30, except for plane No. 4 of the cruiser *Tone*. Because of catapult problems, *that plane left a half hour late.*[55]

About 5:34, one of the U.S. search planes reported seeing two Japanese carriers, and a few minutes later another reported seeing many enemy planes heading toward Midway. These messages went to Midway, and were also heard by the waiting elements of the U.S. fleet.[56]

An hour later the Japanese planes struck Midway. They found almost no U.S. planes on the ground; those had flown off half an hour before, some to fight the incoming enemy planes, some to go after the enemy carriers.[57] It became clear to the Japanese that their first strike on Midway would not suffice. They would need to hit it again. Around 7 a.m., their planes began to break off their attack on Midway, and fly back toward their carriers.

Meanwhile, at 7:02 the *Enterprise* and *Hornet* began launching their planes to attack the Japanese carriers. About the same time, some of the planes that took off from Midway began their attacks on the Japanese carriers. The *Yorktown* launched its planes beginning about 8:38. The Japanese fighters ("Zeros") flying cover for their carriers were very effective in shooting down many of the American planes, except for the high flying bombers, such as the B-17s. For more than three hours, the Japanese carriers largely escaped any damage from attacks by eight different groups of U.S. planes, some from Midway, and some from the American carriers.

The first attacks on the Japanese carriers by planes from Midway convinced the Japanese commander to send a second strike on Midway. The matter of whether to hit Midway or U.S. ships held great significance. If the planes were to go after ships, they should carry torpedoes or armor piercing bombs. If they wanted to go after Midway, they should all carry bombs that would explode on contact. Deciding to go for Midway again, meant that the reserve planes held back from the first strike needed to rearm, to change their loads.

While this rearming was underway, about 7:28 the *Tone*'s No. 4 plane, the one that flew out a half hour late, radioed back that the crew had found a U.S. fleet of ten surface ships. This changed the plans again. But at 8:09 the pilot of No. 4 finally identified what kind of ships: five cruisers and five destroyers. No carriers? Then hitting the ships could wait. They would go back to sending a second wave against Midway. At 8:20 the pilot reported again. This time he had seen a U.S. carrier. This brought another change of plan, and back to torpedoes and armor piercing bombs. At the same time, planes were returning from the first strike on Midway, and getting low on fuel. The Zeros that had been flying cover would also need to be refueled. Admiral Nagumo wanted some of those Zeros to go with the strike force to hit that U.S. carrier. He decided to bring down the returning planes and rearm them, refuel the fighters, complete rearming the planes that had been held for the second wave, and go after the carrier at 10:30.[58]

The eight apparently fruitless American attacks on the Japanese fleet had effects. It kept the Japanese occupied, dodging bombs and torpedoes, disrupted their fleet's formation, requiring more Zeros to fly cover, hence adding to the refueling problems, and delayed their launch of a strike against the carrier sighted, namely the *Yorktown*. Finally, they were almost ready. Yet temporarily, they were in a vulnerable position. Fewer fighters were flying cover. Those flying cover were trying to deal with the last attack of torpedo planes and so none were high up. The flight decks of the carriers were covered with planes, and in some cases, the bombs removed in the rearming.[59]

At that moment, from 10:22 to 10:28 a.m., three groups of dive bombers, two from the *Enterprise* and one from the *Yorktown*, descended on three of the Japanese carriers. Within those few minutes, the bombers tore up the flight decks and rendered all three carriers into flaming infernos. The fires set off explosions of planes, bombs, ammunition, torpedoes, gas tanks, and the conflagration could not be extinguished. Before long the crews had to abandon all three carriers.[60]

The *Hiryu*, the lone remaining Japanese carrier capable of functioning, began launching planes about a half hour later for an attack on the *Yorktown*. An hour after that, about noon, those planes closed in on the *Yorktown*. They managed to get three bombs to hit the carrier, and left the *Yorktown* burning.[61]

The pilot of a Japanese scout plane sent out that morning found the other two American carriers about 11:30 a.m., *but his radio didn't work*. He was only able to report this finding when he returned about 12:50 p.m. The Japanese now knew that there were three U.S. carriers, and when they sent out another attack force from the Hiryu at 1:31, this time of torpedo planes, they wanted to hit the *Enterprise* and *Hornet*. They found the *Yorktown*. Her crew had succeeded in putting out the fires caused by the bombs of the earlier attack. Hence, the Japanese pilots thought this must be a different carrier from the one hit a couple of hours before. They hit the *Yorktown* with two torpedoes, and those who escaped the fire of the American ships and fighters returned to the *Hiryu*. The Japanese now thought they had an even air battle, one carrier to one.[62]

On the *Hiryu*, Admiral Yamaguchi wanted to send another strike at 4:30, but the few pilots he had left were exhausted. Some had been flying since dawn, and had not eaten since before that. He postponed it until 6:00 p.m., to let them eat and get some rest.

At 5:03 American dive bombers from the *Enterprise*, and some "orphans" from the *Yorktown*, struck the *Hiryu*. Hit by at least four bombs, the last Japanese carrier in the strike force joined the other three as another inferno.[63] While the Japanese command would consider other maneuvers, and the Americans would also sink a Japanese cruiser, the battle was decided. Over the next few days all four Japanese carriers and the *Yorktown* sank into the depths of the Pacific Ocean. After the bombing of the *Hiryu*, at 6:30 p.m., news collected from a scout plane disrupted the Japanese consideration of strategies to still win the battle. The pilot saw the *Enterprise* and *Hornet*, and made two reports regarding the carriers and the cruisers and destroyers that accompanied them; the second report was a correction of the first. Someone added the two reports together, and the Japanese thought the Americans still had four carriers in the area.[64] Their officers, so shocked at the loss of their own four carriers, were willing to believe anything.

The Internment of American Citizens of Japanese Ancestry

THEME: Principles of the Constitution

In February of 1942, President Franklin Roosevelt issued Executive Order No. 9066. Under authority of that order, Lt. General John L. DeWitt issued orders that after May 9, 1942, all persons of Japanese ancestry were excluded from the West Coast of the United States, and were removed to "relocation centers." The pretext was the fear that these people would commit espionage or sabotage if left in their homes. To General DeWitt, the fact that no sabotage had occurred clearly indicated that sabotage would occur. [?!] On the other hand, F.B.I. Director J. Edgar Hoover clearly did not believe the relocation and internment was necessary. He said, "The necessity for mass evacuation is based primarily upon public and political pressure rather than on factual data."[65]

Over 110,000 people[66] were removed from their homes and interned in camps in various obscure locations. They were kept there for years. Many lost homes, businesses, and other property and possessions. Over 70,000 of these people were American citizens. The rest were resident aliens. This government action has been called an "evacuation," but that is a mere euphemism.

The constitutional validity of these orders came before the Supreme Court in 1944 in the case of Korematsu v. United States.[67] The orders contained three parts: exclusion from a specific area; a requirement to report to an "assembly center"; and removal to a "relocation center," there to be kept for an indefinite period. The majority opinion in Korematsu, written by Justice Hugo Black, chose to deal only with the validity of the first of the three parts. The court found the order constitutional. In his opinion, Black referred to questions of loyalty: "Approximately five thousand American citizens of Japanese ancestry refused to swear unqualified allegiance to the United States and to renounce allegiance to the Japanese Emperor, and several thousand of the evacuees requested repatriation to Japan." He does not say how many of those requesting repatriation were U.S. citizens. He also does not say whether the five thousand he referred to who refused "to swear unqualified allegiance" were all part of the "evacuees," or were drawn from a larger number across the entire country.

These people were forced from their homes and livelihoods, and imprisoned for an indefinite period, that extended into years. They were not accused of doing anything wrong. This action was solely because of their ethnicity. Considering these factors, it may not be surprising that a small percentage would consider returning to the home of their ancestors, or would refuse to swear allegiance to the country that imprisoned them. The military, with the aid and acquiescence of Franklin Roosevelt, imprisoned citizens without charges, without warrants, without indictment by a grand jury, without trial by a jury. In violation of the Fourth, Fifth, and Sixth Amendments, they were "deprived of . . . liberty [and] property, without due process of law." In essence, the orders were a bill of attainder enacted not by the legislature (a violation of Article I Section 9 Clause 3), but by the executive and the military.

The court's decision was by 6-3, with Justices Roberts, Murphy and Jackson dissenting.

The sole justice still on the court not appointed by Roosevelt, Justice Roberts, wrote a scathing dissent. He protested against ruling solely on the first of the three parts of the orders–the exclusion–without considering the other two. This, he said,

> is to shut our eyes to reality. . . . it is the case of convicting a citizen as a punishment for not submitting to imprisonment in a concentration camp, based on his ancestry, and solely because of his ancestry, without evidence or inquiry concerning his loyalty and good disposition towards the United States. . . . Constitutional rights have been violated.

Justice Black objected to the term "concentration camp." He has a point. Certainly these camps were not like the concentration camps of the German Nazis or the Russian Communists. They might, perhaps, more appropriately be compared to prisoner of war camps.

The military sought to justify these camps due to fear of Japanese invasion of the West Coast. According to the order, people of Japanese ancestry could not reside in the designated area after May 9, 1942. After the battle of Midway, on June 4, 1942, in reality, that threat of invasion was gone. Twenty six days. Yet the internment lasted for years.

The Freedom and Neutrality of Switzerland During World War II

THEME: Peace and Freedom Require Strength in Opposing Tyranny; Benefits of An Armed Citizenry

Switzerland is a small and landlocked country. She maintained a neutral status during both World War I and World War II. The presence of the Alps may have helped. Yet there was another key factor.

What this author has read he has also verified in conversation with a friend, Louis Ringger, who grew up in Switzerland, lived there until after World War II, and during that war served in the Swiss military. Much like the militia were defined in America at her founding, every able bodied man below the age of sixty is part of the Swiss military. They move to a different category when they turn forty and again at fifty. They are expected to be armed and trained. During World War II the Swiss military was constantly training, preparing and guarding their homeland.

Hitler expected to invade Switzerland. The Swiss felt particularly threatened at certain distinct times. For instance, when Germany was not engaged on either its eastern or western front, as after the fall of Poland and before Germany invaded France; or again, after the fall of France and before Germany invaded Russia. After the fall of France, Switzerland was completely surrounded by the Axis. (Germany, with what was formerly Austria, Italy, and conquered France, on the North, East, South, and West respectively.) At times, Germany had a substantial number of divisions near the Swiss border. What kept Germany from invading Switzerland? It was certainly not her neutral status. Hitler cared nothing for that, as he showed with Belgium and Holland. It was the armed Swiss citizenry and Swiss preparedness. Undoubtedly, Hitler was dissuaded, or at least put off, from invading Switzerland by predicted estimates of heavy German casualties.

CHAPTER SEVEN

The Post War Era to the Present

The Cold War: Why Not Victory?

THEME: Peace and freedom require strength and opposing tyranny, and in war there is no substitute for victory

After World War II, the United States found that we had a new tyrannical enemy: Communism, a worldwide conspiracy, with Russia as its main bastion and our primary enemy.

In 1917 Russians for the first time formed a freely elected government; but in October of that year, Communists lead by Lenin overthrew the government. Lenin became the dictator over Russia, followed later by Joseph Stalin, and later by Nikita Khrushchev. Communism is one of the most brutal, repressive, intrusive, and dictatorial governmental forms ever devised. Both Lenin and Stalin murdered millions, as did Mao Tse Tung (or Zedong), the Communist dictator who took over China in 1949. In comparison to Hitler, Lenin was probably not far behind in the number of deaths he was responsible for. Stalin and Mao probably killed more than Hitler.

In the Soviet Union, or the U.S.S.R. ("Union of Soviet Socialist Republics"), the government arrested tens of millions for political or imagined offenses, and sent them to "corrective labor camps." Many died there. Aleksandr Solzhenitsyn was arrested because of letters he wrote to a friend, in which he criticized Stalin. He was sentenced to eight years in these camps, and to exile in Siberia after that. He wrote a masterful account of these camps, their history, their practices, their nature, entitled the *Gulag Archipelago*. It is grim reading–like the accounts of Nazi Germany, only worse, because it went on so much longer and hurt so many more people.[1]

From the first, world domination was the goal. Lenin taught his followers the strategy for communism to follow to take over the world. He said approximately this: "First we will take eastern Europe, then the masses of Asia, then we will encircle the United States which will be the last bastian of capitalism. We will not have to attack. It will fall like an overripe fruit into our hands."

After World War II, the first and second parts of Lenin's strategy seemed accomplished. Poland, Czechoslovakia, Hungary, Romania, Bulgaria, Yugoslavia, Albania, Latvia, Lithuania, and Estonia all were taken over by Communism. In essence, the West lost to Communism what they had fought Hitler for. Churchill spoke of Eastern Europe having disappeared behind an "Iron Curtain." Then China fell. Khrushchev threatened, "We will bury you."

A never ending stream of people seeking freedom escaped from Communist countries to the West, and many more tried to escape. Many died in the attempt. So many escaped from East Berlin to West Berlin, that the Communists built a wall of concrete and barbed wire to divide the city, and to prevent any further escapes. Border guards shot people who tried to escape over the wall. All of this did not stop the attempts. There is a famous photograph of an East German border guard escaping over the barbed wire.[2] Two families secretly made a hot air balloon and flew over the border from East to West Germany to freedom (remembered in the movie *Night Crossing*). Sometimes people from Iron Curtain countries that were allowed to travel outside (comparatively few received such a privilege) simply refused to go back. They "defected," and sought political asylum in free countries. Eighty one passengers from Poland defected at once, leaving their ship at a free port to seek asylum. In 1976 a Russian fighter pilot flew his MIG jet to Japan, and asked for asylum in the United States.[3]

The war between Communism and the free countries of the West sometimes meant shooting and combat, as in Korea and Vietnam. At other times more subtle forms of warfare were used, and so it was called the "Cold War."

In 1943, Colonel Carter Clarke of the U.S. Army, working in Military Intelligence, ordered work begun to break the Soviet code used in cables between Soviet agents in America and Moscow. This eventually became known as the Venona Project. This secret project continued until 1980. About 3,000 Soviet cables from 1942 to 1945 were at least partly decoded and translated. The Army released the contents to the public in 1995.

After the fall of the Soviet Union in 1991, investigators from the West were allowed access to some records from the Soviet side. Any accurate history of the Cold War must acknowledge the facts brought to light or confirmed by these sources.

The Cold War is generally considered to have begun after World War II.

However, from the standpoint of the Communists, their war started earlier. Because world conquest was the goal of Russia's Communist rulers from the beginning, the Cold War against the West in general and the United States in particular, began *before* World War II. Communist infiltration of the U.S. government, and infiltration by Soviet espionage agents (spies serving Russia) began at the latest by the early 1930s. Most of these spies and infiltrators were American Communists. The Communist Party of the United States ("CPUSA") itself, at high levels, was deeply involved in facilitating espionage against the United States.[4]

In 1938, Whittaker Chambers, who had been part of a Communist network, dropped out of that network. He took his family and went into hiding for a time, to keep from being killed by the Communists. The following year, he met with an Assistant Secretary of State, and reported on those he knew to be Soviet agents. The FBI also interviewed Chambers about two years later. In August 1948 he testified before the House Committee on Un-American Activities (HCUA), a committee of the U.S. House of Representatives. At that time Richard Nixon was a member of Congress from California and served on that committee. Nixon believed Chambers, and helped keep alive the investigation sparked by Chambers' testimony.

In 1945, Elizabeth Bentley, another former member of a Communist network, went to the F.B.I. She also identified dozens of secret Soviet agents. With the information from Soviet records and from Venona to confirm much of what Chambers and Bentley said, in addition to the solid evidence that Chambers eventually provided, it is certain that they told the truth.

There is much that we now know for certain. What is here described below about Communist infiltration of the U.S. government during the administrations of Franklin Roosevelt and Harry Truman is not speculation; it is not partisanship; it is not so-called "McCarthyism"; it is fact.

All of the following agencies of government were infiltrated by Communists, and specifically, those acting as Soviet espionage agents (spies):

- the White House;[5]
- the State Department;[6]
- the Treasury Department;[7]
- the Manhattan Project and Los Alamos (atomic bomb development);[8]

- the War Department;[9]
- the Army's Signal Intelligence Service, predecessor to the National Security Agency;[10]
- the Office of Strategic Services (similar to, and predecessor to the Central Intelligence Agency, or CIA);[11]
- the Federal Bureau of Investigation (FBI);[12]
- the Justice Department - Foreign Agent Registration;[13]
- the Justice Department - anti-trust section;[14]
- the National Bureau of Standards;[15]
- the wartime mail censorship office;[16]
- the Lend-Lease Administration;[17]
- the U.S. Army and Navy;[18]
- the Strategic Directorate of the Allied Joint Staff;[19]
- the staff of the Senate Subcommittee on War Mobilization;[20]
- the Office of the Coordinator of Inter-American Affairs;[21]
- the War Production Board;[22]
- the Board of Economic Warfare;[23]
- the Office of War Information;[24]
- the Bureau of Shipping;[25]
- the Interior Department;[26]
- the National Labor Relations Board;[27]
- the Railroad Retirement Board;[28]
- the Army's Aberdeen Proving Ground.[29]

In addition to the espionage agents, there were also underground Communists working for the government in many departments. These people worked for the Communist cause, as a "fifth column" within the U.S., and in particular within the U.S. government.[30]

Of course the number of Soviet agents varied from one government agency to another. In some, only a few have been identified. On the other hand, there were at least nine in the Treasury Department, twenty three in the State Department and other diplomatic agencies, and in the OSS at least fifty Communists of whom at least fifteen were Soviet agents. (Considering the ratio of Communists to known espionage agents in the OSS, if there were a similar ratio in the State Department, the twenty three identified espionage agents there would imply that there could easily have been 57 Communists in that department as charged by McCarthy.)[31] In Haynes and Klehr's book *Venona: Decoding Soviet Espionage in America*, the authors list 349 Americans and U.S. residents as covert Soviet agents, found in the Soviet cables decoded by the Venona Project. Of these, 171 have been identified. The other 178 are known only by code names.[32] They also list another 139 Americans or U.S. residents as Soviet agents (5 under cover names) where the source of the identification was not Venona.[33] Some of those may be among the 178 cover names from Venona.

We must keep in mind that the Venona Project only decoded a fraction of the cables available. Several thousand were never broken. The cables were only from a four year period, 1942 to 1945. Much of the records from the Soviet Union have never become public. Hence it is not only possible, but likely, that these sources have only revealed a fraction of the Communist infiltration of the period from the 1930s through the 1950s.

A number of these agents held high positions: Alger Hiss, Assistant to the Secretary of State; Harry Dexter White, Assistant Secretary of the Treasury; Lauchlin Currie, administrative assistant to President Franklin Roosevelt; Laurence Duggan, head of the State Department's Division of American Republics (dealing with Latin America); Duncan Lee, aide to the head of the OSS.[34] There were also several people who were prominent in the Soviets' espionage into the development of the atomic bomb. The information gleaned certainly allowed the Soviet Union to develop their own bomb years sooner than they otherwise would have done. Among those involved were Klaus Fuchs, Harry Gold, David and Ruth Greenglass, and Julius and Ethel Rosenberg.[35]

For decades some on the political left in the U.S. have attempted to deny the guilt of Hiss, White, Currie, Duggan, and the Rosenbergs. The Venona cables leave no room for doubt. Venona was kept secret, and hence was not used as evidence in the trials of Hiss or the Rosenbergs. Hiss was convicted of perjury, and the Rosenbergs of espionage without evidence from Venona, because other evidence was strong enough without it.

In 1948 when Whittaker Chambers testified before the House Committee on Un-American Activities, he showed by his knowledge a close acquaintance with Alger Hiss. He knew many details about Hiss' private life.[36] Hiss at first denied knowing Chambers. He repeatedly changed his story. Investigation soon showed that he had lied to the Committee on a number of points, including the clandestine transfer of an automobile.[37] Eventually, Chambers also produced documents that he received from both Hiss and Harry Dexter White (and others) about 1938, and had since kept hidden. These included documents in the handwriting of Hiss and White, and documents typed on Hiss' typewriter. Those from Hiss were copied confidential State Department documents. These documents were evidence of espionage, but the statute of limitations had run out, and Hiss was convicted only of perjury.[38]

On September 2, 1939, Whittaker Chambers met with Adolf Berle, an Assistant Secretary of State for security. Isaac Levine, who had arranged the meeting, was also present. Chambers told Berle about infiltration of the government and some other organizations, and gave him a couple of dozen names, including Alger Hiss.[39] Thirteen of those named by Chambers have been confirmed through Venona or other sources to have carried out espionage for the Soviets.[40] Levine later told Chambers that Berle had gone to President Roosevelt with this information. The President laughed, and then dismissed Berle in a rude and vulgar manner. According to Chambers account in *Witness*, the warning went to the President at least twice more, once through Walter Winchell, and again through Ambassador William Bullitt. Nothing happened.[41]

Yet when Roosevelt met with Churchill and Stalin at Yalta, in February 1945, Alger Hiss was there as an advisor to Roosevelt. It has been said that Hiss had little to do with the outcome. Yet it is also true that he wrote part of the Yalta agreement.[42] Critics have attacked the agreement for what many view as allowing Stalin to take control of Poland. Roosevelt died two months later. When Chambers' charges against Hiss became public in 1948, President Truman called it "a red herring."[43] The Justice Department considered trying to indict Chambers.[44] Even after Hiss was convicted on solid, overwhelming evidence, Truman's Secretary of State, Dean Acheson, said, "I do not intend to turn my back on Alger Hiss." (Later, he tried to explain away the comment.)[45]

From Venona we learn that Harry Dexter White advised the Soviets regarding their takeover of Poland. He also advised them that they could seize Latvia, Lithuania, and Estonia, without U.S. opposition, even though U.S. officials were publicly saying otherwise. Lauchlin Currie, administrative assistant to President Roosevelt, also advised the Soviets on taking control of Poland. He assured them that they could ignore Roosevelt's public stand on Poland.[46]

Both Alger Hiss and Harry Dexter White were part of the U.S. delegation to the conference in San Francisco that formed the United Nations. White, at least, influenced the outcome, especially in giving the Soviet Union a veto in the Security Council.[47] White, for certain, and Hiss probably, sought to influence U.S. policy toward China, seeking to undermine Chiang Kai-shek's Nationalist Chinese, thereby to aid the Chinese Communists.[48]

Some books make a point about Republicans making Communist infiltration of the U.S. government a partisan issue. It's hard to see how Republicans could have failed to make it an issue, given the following facts:

- Roosevelt's reaction to the warning brought him by Adolf Berle;
- his choice to have Hiss with him at Yalta, after being informed that he was a Communist;
- the indications from Elizabeth Bentley and other sources of widespread infiltration;
- Truman's reaction to the Hiss case;
- Truman's appointment of Harry Dexter White to the International Monetary Fund, according to some sources after he was warned by the FBI that White was a Communist.

Truman did put in place a loyalty policy for government employees, but not until 1947, after the Republican victories in the 1946 election had put the Republicans in the majority in both houses of Congress.

Why did Democrats react in the partisan way that they did? First, not all of them did. For instance, once the documentary evidence came forth, it was a Democrat in the Justice Department that prosecuted Alger Hiss. However, many, including two Presidents, prominent members of the press and Congress, and many others, reacted by denying reality, defending the Communists, and attacking the informants and the investigators, often viciously. Roosevelt ignored the problem. Truman called it a red herring. Some spread vicious lies about Chambers–that he had been in a mental institution, that he was a drunkard, etc. Prominent journalist James Reston asked Chambers in a note whether he had published a book of poetry under the name G. Crosley in 1905. (Hiss had claimed he knew Chambers as George Crosley.) Chambers wrote back to Reston that in 1905 he was four years old. Reston later said that Chambers refused to answer his question.[49] Why? No doubt part of it was partisanship, not wanting to admit that while in power, they had placed the security of the United States at risk. Part of it may have been friendship. Hiss, White, and others in high position, had many friends among those with whom they had worked for years. Even Chambers, who knew what Hiss was, and who brought forth the charges and the evidence against him, was reluctant to cause harm to those who were previously his friends. He sought to shield them for a time, but in the end he had to bring forth the evidence, in documents and microfilm, in order to fight Communism.

Chambers offered this explanation (in 1952):

> The simple fact is that when I took up my little sling and aimed at Communism, I also hit something else. What I hit was the forces of that great socialist revolution, which, in the name of liberalism, spasmodically, incompletely, somewhat formlessly, but always in the same direction, has been inching its ice cap over the nation for two decades. . . . It was the forces of this revolution that had smothered the Hiss Case (and much else) for a decade, and fought to smother it in 1948. These were the forces that made the phenomenon of Alger Hiss possible; had made it possible for him to rise steadily in Government and to reach the highest post *after* he was already under suspicion as a Communist in many quarters, including Congress, and under the scrutiny of the F.B.I. Alger Hiss is only one name that stands for the whole Communist penetration of Government. He could not be exposed without raising the question of the real political temper and purposes of those who had protected and advanced him, and with whom he was so closely identified that they could not tell his breed from their own.[50]

In 1962, a book written by Barry Goldwater, a Republican Senator from Arizona, made the best seller list. It's title was *Why Not Victory?* Goldwater had called for victory in the Cold War. For this, he had been ridiculed by those on the political left in America, such as Senator Fulbright of Arkansas. Senator Fulbright said we should just live with the Soviet Union, and deal with our problems the best we can. He did not believe in victory in such a war. He asked what it would mean, and would we have to occupy Russia? Senator Goldwater wrote *Why Not Victory?* "to make a case for victory," something no one had ever had to do before in any war America had ever fought. Yet this was a war whose outcome would determine America's survival as a free nation.

Senator Goldwater said that an American President had many means to put pressure on the Soviet Union; that winning the Cold War did not mean nor require a shooting war; and that we would not have to occupy Russia, because most Russians were not Communists.

While Goldwater lost the presidential election in 1964 by a wide margin, there can be little doubt that he and his philosophy had an influence on one of his most ardent supporters, Ronald Reagan. Sixteen years later, Reagan was elected President. As President, he raised the stakes in the arms race to a point that the Russians could not follow. He kept pressure on the Soviet Union, which he called the "Evil Empire." He put economic pressure on Russia through a trade embargo and other means. He invaded Grenada, and freed the people there from the Communists that took over during the Carter administration. He lent support to various anti-Communist forces in various countries around the world. One of these was the union called "Solidarity" in Poland, which received financial aid from the West through a variety of means. Reagan sought to defend America from potential attack by Russian nuclear missiles by proposing an anti-missile defense system called the Strategic Defense Initiative (SDI). The Soviet leader, Mikhail Gorbachev, knew that success of SDI would make the Russian missiles obsolete. He sought in negotiations to get Reagan to abandon SDI. Reagan refused. In a speech in Berlin in 1987, he spoke of the Berlin wall and urged the Soviet leader, "Mr. Gorbachev, tear down this wall!" In 1989, the wall came down. (It was not torn down by the Soviets, however.) Reagan's greatest legacy as President was Victory in the Cold War, as the Iron Curtain came down, the Soviet Union disintegrated, and Communism in Russia and Eastern Europe fell, shortly after he left office.

We did not have a shooting war with Russia, nor did we occupy it after the fall of Communism.

The Vietnam War

One part of the war with Communism was the Vietnam War. This war in Southeast Asia caused great division among the American public.

After the French were defeated in the battle of Dien Bien Phu in 1954, Vietnam was divided between North Vietnam, controlled by the Communists with their capital in Hanoi, and South Vietnam, with their capital in Saigon. The Communists sought to take over South Vietnam as well, through the Viet Cong and the North Vietnamese Army. The United States was a member of SEATO, the Southeast Asia Treaty Organization, whose purpose was to oppose Communist aggression in the region. The United States gave aid to South Vietnam with the same purpose.

Some books make no distinction between the Viet Cong, or VC, Communist guerillas in South Vietnam trying to overthrow the government, and the North Vietnamese Army, or the NVA, an invading army from Communist North Vietnam. This was not primarily a "civil war," between South Vietnam and the VC. It was a war of aggression by the North.

The Tet Offensive in 1968 was a military disaster for the Communists. In most of South Vietnam, the Viet Cong were never again an effective force. Thereafter our troops primarily fought the NVA.

However, the Tet Offensive had considerable propaganda value in the United States. Many people here no longer believed that we were making progress in the war. With so much opposition to the war here at home, as a nation we lacked the will to win. Ironically, we had the capability, and we were winning.

The NVA had supply and infiltration routes through Laos and Cambodia. They maintained base camps in Cambodia. They could cross into South Vietnam, carry out attacks, and cross back into Cambodia.

After Richard Nixon became President, the U.S. took new military steps, not tried in the several years we had been in the war. For instance, for the first time we mined Haiphong harbor, where most of the war supplies used by the NVA entered North Vietnam. These supplies came mainly from Russia and its Communist satellites in Eastern Europe. To some of us, it seemed a bit like shutting the barn door after the horse was out; but better late than never.

In May 1970, President Nixon sent troops into Cambodia. U.S. troops in Cambodia found many caches of weapons, ammunition, and equipment, which they took away from the NVA. At the end of June the U.S. pulled out of Cambodia.

This writer saw people in Vietnam leave their homes, taking what little they could carry, perhaps a pig or a few chickens, and leave to escape the oppression of the NVA. U.S. troops helped them onto helicopters, and they were flown off to start over somewhere safer.

When the U.S. signed a "peace treaty" in Paris in 1973, the U.S. concluded the withdrawal of forces from Vietnam that Nixon began in 1970. The peace treaty meant nothing to the Communists, and the war continued without any interruption.

At the fall of South Vietnam in 1975, refugees fled by any means they could, to avoid death at the hands of the Communists. In neighboring Cambodia, the government also fell to Communism, to the Khmer Rouge. Millions died, either murdered directly by the Khmer Rouge, or driven from the cities into the country, where many more died in slavery, from forced hard labor, disease, and starvation rations. Cambodia during this period has since been called "The Killing Fields."

Myths and Facts from the Carter, Reagan, Bush, Clinton, and Bush Eras

THEMES: Understanding Economics and the Free Market; Following Truth Wherever It Leads

Throughout the Carter years, inflation worsened. In 1980 the annual inflation rate reached about 15 to18 percent for two quarters.[51] The prime interest rate (the rate banks charge their best customers) reached 21.5 percent. A recession was bound to come, and did, continuing into the first of the Reagan years. Many economists insist that the only institution capable of producing long term inflation, is government. But in July 1979, President Carter tried to blame the country's economic problems on the American people, by saying that America was suffering from a "crisis of the American spirit." He went on to say, "There is growing disrespect for government and for churches and for schools, the news media and other institutions. This is not a message of happiness or reassurance, but it is the truth and it is a warning."

What Carter and his pollster, Pat Caddell, respectively, called a "crisis of confidence" or a "malaise" was viewed differently by others. On the basis of surveys, Richard Harwood described it this way: "It was rather an expression of a widespread loss of faith in the competence of the great institutions in our society, most notably in the competence of the institution of government and the men who directed it." People were "disillusioned and even cynical about the performance of [the nation's] political leaders."[52]

On November 4, 1979, militant Iranians seized the U.S. Embassy and took fifty three American citizens hostage. For over a year, nothing Carter did could free them, neither negotiations nor military action. He made an attempt to rescue the hostages by use of the military, but this effort failed miserably. Eight soldiers died in the desert in Iran, due to helicopter failure, and the mission was aborted. To many, this seemed to symbolize that national defense, including providing our troops with proper equipment and the means to properly maintain it, was not a high priority for Jimmy Carter.

The hostages were released on the day of President Reagan's inauguration. Some people consider that a coincidence, merely the culmination of what President Carter had been working toward for months. Others believe it was not a coincidence. National defense was a high priority for Ronald Reagan, and everyone knew it.

Some history texts mention that in the 1980 election, Reagan received 51 percent of the popular vote, and 489 electoral votes (out of 538). They do not mention Carter's percentage, nor the independent candidacy of John Anderson. One could draw the conclusion that this was a close race in the popular vote, and that the vote in the electoral college was greatly askew from the popular vote. Both conclusions would be false. The vote was not close. The results were:

	Popular Vote	%	Electoral Vote
Reagan	43,267,462	51	489
Carter	34,968,548	41	49
Anderson	5,588,014	7	0[53]

While this "landslide" victory for the Republican candidate brought with it Republican gains in Congress, the Democrats still held a majority in the House of Representatives.

At this period, the nation suffered from the worst economic conditions since the great depression. The inflation and high interest rates pushed the economy into a severe recession. From January 1977 to January 1981, the Consumer Price Index rose by 49 percent. Strong growth in new jobs in 1977 declined to virtually nothing by 1980. The civilian unemployment rate, which had been reduced from 7.5 percent in January 1977 to 5.6 percent in May 1979, began to grow again, reaching 7.5 percent in January 1981. As the recession took hold, unemployment grew to 10.8 percent by December 1982.

Early in Reagan's first term, Congress passed and the President signed a bill enacting a major tax cut—a 25 percent across the board reduction phased in over three years. That is, the income tax rates for all brackets were reduced by one fourth; 5 percent the first year, 10 percent the second, and 10 percent the third. He also sought to reduce government regulation. There followed one of the longest peace time periods of economic growth in America's history. Some books refuse to mention this.

Unemployment declined to 5.4 percent by January 1989. From January 1983 to January 1989, civilian employment levels grew by 17,547,000 (new jobs). Gross Domestic Product (GDP), adjusted for inflation, which had risen only 5.9 percent from January 1977 to January 1981, grew by 26.3 percent from then until January 1989. In the period from January 1981 to January 1983, the GDP declined by 1.5 percent. Then it grew by 28.2 percent over the next six years.[54]

Some pervasive myths continue about the Reagan administration. First, that Reagan cut spending on "social programs." Actually such spending continued to increase each year. What Reagan did was to reduce the rate of increase. Second, that defense spending grew to become some extraordinarily large fraction (somewhat vague, but at least half) of the federal budget. Actually, defense spending was about one quarter of the federal budget, or a little more. There were some in the media who contributed to perpetuating this myth. For example, on one occasion the Denver Post printed a purported breakdown of one of Reagan's budgets on its front page. They showed two pie charts, one of where the federal government's money came from (income tax, social security tax, excise tax, etc.), and one of where it went, the programs or departments where the money was spent. The spending chart showed national defense as well over half of the spending, but it was false. The chart left out all the spending on so called "entitlements"–social security, medicare, welfare, public housing, food stamps, etc. had all been left off the chart.

The third myth blames the large federal deficits of the Reagan years solely on the tax cut. Although tax rates had been reduced, because of the economic growth, Federal revenue increased significantly. The deficit remained large anyway, because Federal spending increased faster.

From 1980 to 1988, Federal revenue grew by 75.8 percent, from $517.1 billion to $909.3 billion. Federal expenditures, however, grew by 80.1 percent, from $590.9 billion to $1,064.5 billion. In other words, revenue grew by $392.2 billion, but spending grew by $473.6 billion. (Or, if one wishes to raise the question about which Presidency has responsibility for the budget in the year of transition, we can compare 1981 to 1989. In that case, revenue grew by $391.9 billion, but spending grew by $465.6 billion.)[55]

At one point during his presidency, Reagan made an agreement with congressional leaders to reduce the deficit. Reagan would not veto a tax increase (not as large as the previous tax cut), and in exchange these Congressmen agreed to cut federal spending by an equal amount. However, those in Congress did not keep their part of the bargain, and instead of spending reductions, there were spending increases larger than the tax increase, hence making the deficit larger. If Reagan can be criticized in this, it should be for not using the veto more often, especially against spending bills.

The deficit brings us to the fourth myth. One book falsely claims that the deficit during Reagan's administration caused interest rates to rise. Interest rates peaked in late 1980 while Carter was in office, and declined during Reagan's presidency. (The peak occurred in December 1980, with the prime rate at 21.5 percent. By January 1983, it had fallen to 11.0 percent, and continued to decline until it reached 7.5 percent in September 1986. From there it rose to 10.5 percent in January 1989, before continuing its decline to 6.0 percent in January 1993.)[56]

Various economic myths have grown out of the period between 1992 and the present.

During the 1992 presidential campaign, President George H. W. Bush's candidacy suffered from the economic recession that the country went through at that time. Al Gore, running for Vice President on the ticket with Bill Clinton, asserted that Bush's presidency was the "worst economic record since Herbert Hoover." Mr. Gore conveniently chose to forget the record of Jimmy Carter. Oddly enough, when Bush claimed that the country was on the verge of recovery, it was true. The recession ended and the recovery began while Bush was still in office, but not early enough to help him in the election.

For eight years Clinton took credit for economic expansion, and a balanced budget in the latter part of his time in office. However, after the 1994 election, the Republicans held a majority in both houses of Congress, and Clinton could not get his programs into law. This and the defeat of Clinton's plan to nationalize the health care industry played a major part in both the economic expansion and the balanced budget.

An important event occurred in 1996 when Congress passed a welfare reform bill. This change in the law placed a limit on how long people could be on welfare at a time, and required them to work in order to receive welfare. Previously, the system had tended to create dependency. Some families had been on welfare continuously for three or four generations. Such an unhealthy state destroys self respect and self reliance; it encourages people to think that others owe them a living. That may be called the "entitlement" philosophy. That is not compassion.

Questions

Question 1: What did Reagan do to end the Carter recession and bring prolonged strong economic growth?

Question 2: In 1960 the highest tax bracket was over 90 percent. What is the difference between such high taxes and slavery?

September 11, 2001, and the War on Terror

THEME: Peace and freedom require strength and opposing tyranny, and in war there is no substitute for victory; connections between al Qaeda and Iraq under Saddam Hussein?

On the morning of September 11, 2001, arab terrorists–Islamic extremists–hijacked four planes, commercial airliners. They flew one of these into the Pentagon, in Arlington, Virginia. Two others they flew into the twin towers of the World Trade Center in New York City. They chose these particular flights because they were scheduled to fly from the east coast to the west coast, and therefore were filled with jet fuel. Upon impact the fuel burst into flame; the high temperatures of these fires caused the steel frameworks to weaken, and both buildings in New York collapsed with great loss of life. We may never know precisely how many were killed, but estimates run about 3,000.

On the fourth hijacked plane, some of the passengers heard by cell phone from their families about the other planes flying into buildings. Thus knowing the intent of the hijackers, they tried to take back control of the aircraft. It crashed in a field in Pennsylvania and all aboard were killed; but the passengers prevented the hijackers from attacking their target, probably a building in Washington, D.C.

Within a short time after these attacks, officials in the U.S. government determined who the hijackers were, their countries of origin, and the organization behind them. These attacks on America were planned and carried out by al Qaeda, an Islamic terrorist organization led by Osama bin Laden. He and his group were primarily based in Afghanistan, where they were harbored by that country's ruling clique, the Taliban.

The September 11 attacks were not the first time al Qaeda had struck at the United States. Years earlier, during the Clinton administration, they had bombed the World Trade Center, and a ship of our navy, the U.S.S. Cole. The U.S. made no effective response. However, this time President George W. Bush received Congressional approval for U.S. forces to respond, in concert with dozens of other countries. America sought to destroy al Qaeda's ability to strike the United States or anyone else, to bring al Qaeda's leaders to justice, and because they harbored terrorists, to bring down the Taliban. Coalition forces took down the Taliban, killed or captured many of al Qaeda's leaders, sending others into hiding, and destroyed al Qaeda training camps. The United States helped to organize a new government in Afghanistan.

By February 2003, President Bush was urging action against Saddam Hussein in Iraq. Again with Congressional approval and joined by a coalition of dozens of other nations, United States armed forces entered Iraq and overthrew the regime of Saddam Hussein.

Where did this regime come from? What were its offenses? Why did President Bush want to remove Saddam Hussein from power?

Bernard Lewis, Cleveland E. Dodge Professor Emeritus of Near Eastern Studies, Princeton University, in a lecture on July 16, 2006, outlined the origin of the Baath Party, the organization behind Saddam Hussein. He begins with the fall of France to Nazi Germany early in World War II.

> In the year 1940, the government of France surrendered to the Axis and formed a collaborationist government in a place called Vichy. The French colonial empire was, for the most part, beyond the reach of the Nazis, which meant that the governors of the French colonies had a free choice: To stay with Vichy or to join Charles de Gaulle, who had set up a Free French Committee in London. The overwhelming majority chose Vichy, which meant that Syria-Lebanon—a French mandated territory in the heart of the Arab East—was now open to the Nazis. The governor and his high officials in the administration in Syria-Lebanon took their orders from Vichy, which in turn took orders from Berlin. The Nazis moved in, made a tremendous propaganda effort, and were even able to move from Syria eastwards into Iraq and for a while set up a pro-Nazi, fascist regime. It was in this period that political parties were formed that were the nucleus of what later became the Baath Party. The Western Allies eventually drove the Nazis out of the Middle East and suppressed these organizations. But the war ended in

1945, and the Allies left. A few years later the Soviets moved in, established an immensely powerful presence in Egypt, Syria, Iraq and various other countries, and introduced Soviet-style political practice. The adaptation from the Nazi model to the Communist model was very simple and easy, requiring only a few minor adjustments, and it proceeded pretty well. That is the origin of the Baath Party and of the kind of governments that we have been confronting in the Middle East in recent years.[57]

Hence, when some commentators refer to the terrorists and their extremist middle eastern organizations and allies as "Islamo-fascist," that's fairly accurate as applied to Saddam Hussein and his Baath Party.

During the 1980s, the Iraqi government killed 180,000 ethnic Kurds and destroyed hundreds of mountain villages. In 1988 they used nerve gas and mustard gas against the Kurds in Halabjah, and killed 5,000 in one day. In 1990 Iraq invaded Kuwait, where they treated the citizens brutally. In 1991, in the first "Gulf War," the United States, with the help of Britain, defeated Iraq's armies and drove them out of Kuwait. However, Saddam Hussein and his regime were allowed to stay in power. In order to end the war, Iraq had to agree to certain conditions. These conditions included the requirement to destroy all "weapons of mass destruction" (such as nerve gas, mustard gas, and the means of delivery), "to cease all development of such weapons, and to stop all support for terrorist groups."[58] Iraq was also forbidden to fly over what was called the "no fly zone"; the United States and Britain would continue to fly over this area to ensure compliance. Primarily, this was to protect the Kurds in northern Iraq. Inspection teams from the U.N. sought to ensure compliance with the agreement to destroy chemical and biological weapons, and the abandoning of development of chemical, biological, or nuclear weapons.

Saddam Hussein allowed the inspectors into Iraq for a time, but expelled them in 1998. Hence, the U.S. had to rely on intelligence operations to try to determine whether or not the government of Iraq was complying with the agreement with respect to the development of such weapons. By 2002 the best intelligence available indicated that Iraq continued to work on development of such weapons, including a program to develop nuclear weapons. Inspectors were again allowed into the country for a time, but were withdrawn when the U.S. pushed for military action against Iraq.

After Saddam Hussein's removal from power, searches were conducted for these weapons and programs. Little was found. However, given the delay of months between United States warnings and the actual invasion of Iraq, there are at least four possible explanations. The intelligence could have been wrong; or, weapons stores and programs could have been dismantled and hidden; or, they could have been shipped out of the country, such as to neighboring Syria; or, as some have suggested, Saddam could have been seeking to continue such development, but been deceived by his own scientists.

Other parts of the 1991 agreement were clearly not followed. President Bush reported that in the year prior to his October 7, 2002 speech, "the Iraqi military has fired upon American and British pilots more than 750 times."[59] That alone, could constitute justification for war.

President Bush mentioned that "Over the years, Iraq has provided safe haven to terrorists such as Abu Nidal, whose terror organization carried out more than 90 terrorist attacks in 20 countries that killed or injured nearly 900 people, including 12 Americans. Iraq has also provided safe haven to Abu Abbas, who was responsible for seizing the Achille Lauro [a ship that was hijacked] and killing an American passenger."[60]

The evidence of ties between Saddam Hussein's regime and terrorist organizations is clear, abundant, and indisputable. Some politicians have sought to make the point that there was no connection between Saddam Hussein and the September 11, 2001 attacks on the United States. No one, including President Bush, ever claimed that there was such a connection. However, while some have sought to deny it, there was a connection with al Qaeda, and other terrorists.

Federal Judge Gilbert S. Merritt spent time in Iraq where he served to help in rebuilding Iraq's judiciary. While he was there, an Iraqi lawyer showed him a document. This document showed that Abid Al-Karim Muhamed Aswod was an Iraqi intelligence officer in Pakistan, and was "responsible for the coordination of activities with the Osama bin Laden group." The document was signed by Uday Saddam Hussein.[61] (Uday was Saddam's son.)

Journalist Stephen F. Hayes, was staying at the al Rashid Hotel in Baghdad, when on October 26, 2003, there was a rocket attack on the hotel. Afterward, there was an investigation. He reports,

> Everywhere investigators looked, they turned up evidence that pointed to a collaborative effort between Saddam loyalists and Islamic fundamentalists affiliated with al Qaeda. . . . [Saddam's] government harbored several of the world's most notorious terrorists–Abu Abbas and Abu Nidal among them. Within days of the 1993 attack on the World Trade Center, his government facilitated the escape from U.S. authorities of the Iraqi who mixed the chemicals for that bombing. Less than two months later, his intelligence service botched an attempt to assassinate George H. W. Bush on a visit to Kuwait. By the late 1990s, he was supplying chemical weapons expertise to terrorist-friendly Islamic fundamentalists in Sudan. He wired $150,000 to his intelligence chief in Prague to blow up the U.S. government's headquarters of Radio Free Europe.[62]

The Iraqi mentioned above in connection with the 1993 attack on the World Trade Center was Abdul Rahman Yasin.

> According to the bipartisan Senate Intelligence Committee report, Yasin promptly "fled to Iraq with Iraqi assistance." His travel was arranged by the second secretary of the Iraqi embassy in Amman, Jordan. In 1994, a reporter for ABC News went to the home of Yasin's father in Baghdad and spoke with neighbors who reported that Yasin . . . was "working for the government." So an Iraqi participant in an al Qaeda attack on the U.S. mainland fled to Iraq–with Iraqi government assistance–after those attacks.

On October 2, 2002, an al Qaeda affiliated group in the Philippines called Abu Sayyaf, carried out a terrorist bombing that wounded an American soldier and killed another, Sergeant First Class Mark Wayne Jackson. A week later the same group tried to set off another bomb at an elementary school, but failed. "Authorities recovered the cell phone that was to have set it off and analyzed incoming and outgoing calls." In addition to "several calls to and from Abu Sayyaf leaders," they found "a call to a top official in the Iraqi embassy in Manila." Further investigation showed frequent contact between the Iraqi official and Abu Sayyaf, "both before and after the attack that killed SFC Jackson." In addition, "Twice in two years, Abu Sayyaf leaders boasted about receiving funding from Iraq."[63]

Since the overthrow of Saddam Hussein, the U.S. has captured millions of documents, tapes, computer hard drives, etc. Some of what we have learned from these sources include the following:

> In 1995, a senior Iraqi intelligence official met with Osama bin Laden. After the meeting, Saddam Hussein agreed to broadcast al Qaeda propaganda on Iraqi government-run television and to let the relationship develop through discussion and agreement.
>
> In 1998, a confidante of bin Laden visited Baghdad as a guest of the Iraqi regime, staying in the Iraqi capital for two weeks at government expense. The document corroborated telephone intercepts the U.S. government had not previously been able to understand . . .
>
> A fax from the Iraqi Embassy in the Philippines to the Iraqi Foreign Ministry in Baghdad, dated June 6, 2001, confirms that the Iraqi regime had been providing arms and weapons to Abu Sayyaf—the al Qaeda affiliate in the Philippines responsible for the death of Mark Wayne Jackson.
>
> Iraqi financial records confirm that the government supported, harbored and financed Abdul Rahman Yasin, the 1993 World Trade Center bomber, throughout the 1990s.[64]

The regime of Saddam Hussein routinely used rape and torture as weapons against Iraq's own people.[65] Since the overthrow of his regime in May 2003, mass graves have been found confirming its use of mass murder. According to the U.S. Agency for International Development, as of January 2004, 270 mass graves had been reported, of which 53 sites had been confirmed. "'We've already discovered just so far the remains of 400,000 people in mass graves,' said British Prime Minister Tony Blair on November 20 in London."[66] Reports from a few individuals who survived mass government killings report that at one site, in addition to mass shootings, many others were thrown into a large fire and burned to death.[67]

Some politicians declared the war in Iraq a failure, and stated that the U.S. was losing, at the very time that "the surge" ordered by General Petraius was showing remarkable success. The end result in Iraq and the Middle East, will depend upon the decisions of Americans at the polls and through their leaders, and upon the courage and determination of the Iraqis themselves.

Kelo v. City of New London, 545 U.S. 469 (2005)

THEME: Principles of the Constitution - restriction on Eminent Domain?

The battle for freedom in America did not end with the Declaration of Independence, nor with the Constitution and the Bill of Rights, nor with the freeing of the slaves, nor with victory in World War II or the Cold War. It continues today. Eternal vigilance is the price of freedom.

The Fifth Amendment states that "No person shall . . . be deprived of life, liberty or property without due process of law; nor shall private property be taken for public use without just compensation." The power of government to take private property for public use is called "eminent domain." For example, taking a strip of land to build a road, or to widen one, or to make a public park. The Fifth Amendment requires that such taking be for public use, and that just compensation be given.

Since ratification of the Fourteenth Amendment, the Supreme Court has held most of the Bill of Rights, including most of the Fifth Amendment, applicable to the states, as well as the national government. However, over the course of time, the Supreme Court has, in effect, changed the wording of the Fifth Amendment. That body has no authority to do that—such a change should only happen through the amendment process outlined in Article V—but for a long time now they have used their own wording, namely, substituting "public purpose" for "public use."

With this change, some cities have gone so far from public use as to condemn and seize private property to give to other private entities. They force people from their homes and destroy established businesses and people's livelihoods, because they think a Costco or a Walmart will bring in more sales tax revenue. This they claim is a "public purpose."

The city of New London, Connecticut, condemned all properties in a sizable area. Pfizer Corporation was one of the beneficiaries of their plan. For some of the seized property, the city did not even have a plan for what to do with it. Some of those whose homes would be taken went to court to try to save their homes. The case went to the U.S. Supreme Court, where in 2005 the court ruled 5-4 in favor of the city.

In the Kelo case, the majority opinion relied heavily on Berman v. Parker, 348 U.S. 26 (1954). Justice William O. Douglas, writing the opinion for the Court in that case, said (at page 33), "The concept of the public welfare is broad and inclusive. . . . The values it represents are spiritual as well as physical, aesthetic as well as monetary. It is within the power of the legislature to determine that the community should be beautiful as well as healthy, spacious as well as clean, well-balanced as well as carefully patrolled. . . . If those who govern the District of Columbia decide that the Nations Capital should be beautiful as well as sanitary, there is nothing in the Fifth Amendment that stands in the way."

Justice Douglas seemed to think that any reason was sufficient to seize someone's property, even though government was not going to use the property, but was going to give it to another private owner. Apparently, even someone's opinion that the new use of the property would be prettier than the old one would be sufficient reason. But the wording of the fifth amendment is not "public welfare," nor "public purpose," but "public use."

Justice Clarence Thomas in his dissent in Kelo said,

> The most natural reading of the Clause is that it allows the government to take property only if the government owns, or the public has a legal right to use, the property, as opposed to taking it for any public purpose or necessity whatsoever . . . [After explaining that the word "use" implies to employ or make use of,] When the government takes property and gives it to a private individual, and the public has no right to use the property, it strains language to say that the public is employing the property, regardless of the incidental benefits that might accrue to the public from the private use. The term public use, then, means that either the government or its citizens as a whole must actually employ the taken property.

The consequence of the Berman case, the case of Hawaii Housing Authority v. Midkiff, 467 U.S. 229 (1984), and Kelo, has been the loss of any protection from the Supreme Court under the terms of the eminent domain clause of the Fifth Amendment. It is true that Justice Stevens in his majority opinion in Kelo asserted, ". . . it has long been accepted that the sovereign may not take the property of A for the sole purpose of transferring it to another private party B, even though A is paid just compensation. . . . Nor would the City be allowed to take property under the mere pretext of a public purpose, when its actual purpose was to bestow a private benefit." However, such assurances have no meaning when the majority's view of acceptable reasons is so broad that they always rule in government's favor. Such assurances have no practical meaning when a mere increase in tax revenue is sufficient purpose. Nor is there any practical way for the Court to know in most cases whether the stated purpose is a mere pretext, unless the justices are to become mind readers. *The "purpose" is not even relevant.* According to the Constitution the relevant question is "public use." The Court has taken it upon itself to virtually eliminate part of our Bill of Rights.

In his dissent, Justice Thomas said,

> The Court has elsewhere recognized "the overriding respect for the sanctity of the home that has been embedded in our traditions since the origins of the Republic," . . . when the issue is only whether the government may search a home. [The Fourth Amendment's requirement of a warrant, etc.] Yet today the Court tells us that we are not to "second-guess the City's considered judgments," . . . when the issue is, instead, whether the government may take the infinitely more intrusive step of tearing down petitioners' homes. Something has gone seriously awry with this Court's interpretation of the Constitution. Though citizens are safe from the government in their homes, the homes themselves are not.

The consequence of these decisions is that in instances by the thousands and perhaps the tens of thousands across the country, cities are seizing private property from A to give it to private party B. Indeed, the Institute for Justice has identified 10,000 such attempts. In Detroit, Michigan, the city seized an entire neighborhood (Poletown) of 465 acres for transfer to General Motors.

East Saint Louis, Illinois, seized property belonging to a mosque for transfer to a private developer. Bristol, Connecticut, seized homes and a farm for transfer to a private "industrial park." Home owners are particularly vulnerable to such seizure, because they do not generate sales tax. Even more vulnerable are non-profit groups such as churches or charitable or service organizations, because they generate neither sales nor property taxes. The City of North Hempstead, New York, condemned St. Luke's Pentecostal Church. The Becket Fund for Religious Liberty in their Amicus Brief for the Kelo case documented many such attempts: South Bend, Indiana, condemning the City Chapel; Belleville, Missouri, seeking to condemn a Moose Lodge for the benefit of Home Depot; Cleveland, Ohio, seeking to condemn property of the American Legion for private office and retail development; Cypress Redevelopment Agency sought to condemn the Cottonwood Christian Center to transfer to a Costco.

Well did Justice Sandra Day O'Connor say in her dissent in the Kelo case:

> It holds that the sovereign may take private property currently put to ordinary private use, and give it over for new, ordinary private use, so long as the new use is predicted to generate some second-ary benefit for the public–such as increased tax revenue, more jobs, maybe even aesthetic pleasure. . . . The specter of condemnation hangs over all property. Nothing is to prevent the State from re-placing any Motel 6 with a Ritz-Carlton, any home with a shop-ping mall, or any farm with a factory.

No doubt such actions save expense for the private parties gaining posses-sion of the condemned property. In a free market they must either raise their offer to purchase the property to a high enough price to change an unwilling seller into a willing one–if such a price exists–or they must look elsewhere. We call that the right of the owner to his or her property, and to control of that property. It is an essential part of what we call freedom.

District of Columbia v. Heller, 554 U.S. ___ (2008)

THEME: Principles of the Constitution - Self Defense and the Right to Keep and Bear Arms

The right to use force in self defense is a basic, inherent right. Indeed, it is the origin of the force of government. The District of Columbia tried to outlaw that right.

In 1975 the District of Columbia passed ordinances to ban handguns, and to ban the possession of an operable firearm in the home. Ownership of some rifles and shotguns were considered permissible, but they had to be kept disassembled, or otherwise rendered unusable, such as by a trigger lock. There was no exception in the ordinance for the immediate need of an operable firearm for self defense, for instance, in the event of a break in.

Such drastic measures have not kept D.C. from having one of the highest murder rates in the country. The District has a serious crime problem. The ordinances likely did not help. Disarming honest citizens removes one of the deterrents to crime. Defenseless victims are a magnet for criminals. So they should be learning in the United Kingdom (Britain), where disarming the public and essentially outlawing self defense has led to a great surge in crime. The District should have learned the same thing. "D.C.'s murder rate—which had been declining before the handgun ban took effect—tripled in the first 15 years after the ban, and has consistently been the highest of any major U.S. city."[68]

The other side of the same coin, is that armed citizens do deter crime. In state after state—Florida, for instance—when laws have been adopted expanding allowance for citizen "concealed carry" of firearms, crime has decreased.

Legal challenge to the D.C. ordinances went to the Supreme Court and was decided in the case of D.C. v. Heller in 2008. The Supreme Court ruled both ordinances unconstitutional, and violations of the Second Amendment:

. . . the inherent right of self-defense has been central to the Second Amendment right. The handgun ban amounts to a prohibition of an entire class of "arms" that is overwhelmingly chosen by American society for that lawful purpose. The prohibition extends, moreover, to the home, where the need for defense of self, family and property is most acute. . . . In sum, we hold that the District's ban on handgun possession in the home violates the Second Amendment, as does its prohibition against rendering any lawful firearm in the home operable for the purpose of immediate self-defense.

The court rejected the idea that the right only applies to service in the militia. Justice Scalia in the majority opinion said that "the Second Amendment right is exercised individually and belongs to all Americans." He also pointed out, "It has always been widely understood that the Second Amendment, like the First and Fourth Amendments, codified a *pre-existing* right. The very text of the Second Amendment implicitly recognizes the pre-existence of the right and declares only that it 'shall not be infringed.'"

D.C. v. Heller thus affirmed that the Second Amendment is binding on the national government and entities whose authority derives from it, such as the District of Columbia. In the case of Barron v. Baltimore, 32 U.S. (7 Pet.) 243 (1833), the Supreme Court judged the Bill of Rights not binding on the states. However, since the Fourteenth Amendment in 1868, the Court has held that the Fourteenth Amendment makes numerous parts of the Bill of Rights binding on the states. The case of D.C. v. Heller did not specifically raise the issue of whether the Second Amendment is applicable to the states through the Fourteenth. Justice Scalia did refer to one of the purposes of the Fourteenth–namely, to prevent southern state governments from interfering with the right of blacks to own firearms. Hence, the Court's opinion did *imply* that the Second Amendment applies to the states.

D.C. v. Heller was decided by a 5-4 vote. It should have been unanimous. It seems incredible that four justices would conclude, as stated in one of the dissenting opinions, that D.C.'s ordinances were "reasonable." How can it be "reasonable" to outlaw self defense? Justice Stevens dissenting opinion resorted to the intellectually dishonest method of dismissing evidence that was inconvenient for his line of argument. If historical use of the terms "keep" or "bear arms" related to a military situation, he used it. If such use related to other situations, such as hunting or self defense, he sought to disqualify it. This indicates a prejudiced mind.

There was a recent article published about the police chief of Washington, D.C. As of July 2009, she has held the office for about two and a half years. According to the article, the murder rate in the city has gone down by 14 percent from July 2008 to July 2009. It's something to consider that such a decline may not all be due to the work of this police chief and her staff. Part of that decline may be due to the outcome of this court case, for the decision in D.C. v. Heller was announced on June 26, 2008.

A friend of the author in Colorado related the following story. She was returning home to her apartment one night, when a man asked her the time. She stopped to look at her watch, and on looking up to reply, found that the man had approached to within a few feet of her. He seized her, and dragged her into his van. She struggled, and managed to escape his grasp long enough to make it to the front seats, where she tried to open the passenger door. The handle was gone. He tried to drag her into the back, but she held onto the passenger seat with a tight grip. He tried to drive away with her, but she grabbed the gear shift and threw it into reverse. Fortunately, a man from the apartment complex, who knew her, appeared at the door of the van with a gun. His arrival, ARMED, enabled her to exit the van and escape from her assailant.

Millions of times every year, firearms are lawfully used to defend self, family, or friends—in most cases, without being fired. Without private possession of firearms, my friend's story would have had a much different ending, and not a happy one. The police cannot intervene while every crime is being committed; much less can they prevent every crime. Most of their work is in striving to solve crimes after they happen, and to imprison the criminals. If my friend had been forced to wait for the intervention of police, probably, she would not have been spared.

This author is opposed to what some euphemistically call "gun control." Instead, he favors "crime control." To prevent crime, we should be concerned with results. When we see that states and cities with the most restrictive gun laws have far more crime than states with less restrictive laws, we should draw conclusions about what works, and what doesn't. Furthermore, when laws prevent gun ownership for the honest, then after the police and the army, only the criminals, who care nothing about such laws, have guns. Then indeed are we closer to that anarchy described by Madison, "where the weaker individual is not secured against the violence of the stronger."[69] But let a four foot eight, eighty year old widow, have a handgun and know how to use it, and she can be the equal, or more than the equal, of a man, no matter how large and strong, who tries to break into her home.

Now to the advocates of "gun control," we should ask this question: Whose side are you on—the law abiding citizens, or the criminals? The author's friend and her rescuer, or her attacker?

Looking Ahead

America has a great destiny. It was not founded to fail. As Americans we must be moral and vigilant. We need to keep the principles of the Declaration of Independence and the Constitution in our hearts, and seek to live by them. Then America will remain powerful, prosperous, and free.

Appendix A. The Olive Branch Petition

Adopted by the Second Continental Congress, and Signed July 8, 1775.

To the King's most excellent Majesty

Most gracious Sovereign,

[OBP-1]   We your Majesty's faithful subjects of the colonies of New Hampshire, Massachusetts bay, Rhode Island and Providence plantations, Connecticut, New York, New Jersey, Pennsylvania, the counties of New Castle Kent and Sussex on Delaware, Maryland, Virginia, North Carolina and South Carolina, in behalf of ourselves and the inhabitants of these colonies, who have deputed us to represent them in general Congress, entreat your Majesty's gracious attention to this our humble petition.

[OBP-2]   The union between our Mother Country and these colonies, and the energy of mild and just government, produced benefits so remarkably important, and afforded such an assurance of their permanency and increase, that the wonder and envy of other nations were excited, while they beheld Great Britain rising to a power the most extraordinary the world had ever known.

[OBP-3]   Her rivals observing, that there was no probability of this happy connection being broken by civil dissensions, and apprehending its future effects, if left any longer undisturbed, resolved to prevent her receiving such continual and formidable accessions of wealth and strength, by checking the growth of those settlements from which they were to be derived.

[OBP-4]   In the prosecution of this attempt events so unfavorable to the design took place, that every friend to the interests of Great Britain and these colonies entertained pleasing and reasonable expectations of seeing an additional force and extension immediately given to the operations of the union hitherto experienced, by an enlargement of the dominions of the Crown, and the removal of ancient and warlike enemies to a greater distance.

[OBP-5]   At the conclusion therefore of the late war, the most glorious and advantageous that ever had been carried on by British arms, your loyal colonists having contributed to its success, by such repeated and strenuous exertions, as frequently procured them the distinguished approbation of your Majesty, of the late king, and of Parliament, doubted not but that they should be permitted with the rest of the empire, to share in the blessings of peace and the emoluments of victory and conquest. While these recent and honorable acknowledgments of their merits remained on record in the journals and acts of that august legislature the Parliament, undefaced by the imputation or even the suspicion of any offence, they were alarmed by a new system of statutes and regulations adopted for the administration of the colonies, that filled their minds with the most painful fears and jealousies; and to their inexpressible astonishment perceived the dangers of a foreign quarrel quickly succeeded by domestic dangers, in their judgement of a more dreadful kind.

[OBP-6]   Nor were their anxieties alleviated by any tendency in this system to promote the welfare of the Mother Country. For though its effects were more immediately felt by them, yet its influence appeared to be injurious to the commerce and prosperity of Great Britain.

[OBP-7]   We shall decline the ungrateful task of describing the irksome variety of artifices practiced by many of your Majesty's ministers, the delusive pretenses, fruitless terrors, and unavailing severities, that have from time to time been dealt out by them, in their attempts to execute this impolitic plan, or of tracing through a series of years past the progress of the unhappy differences between Great Britain and these colonies which have flowed from this fatal source.

[OBP-8]   Your Majesty's ministers persevering in their measures and proceeding to open hostilities for enforcing them, have compelled us to arm in our own defense, and have engaged us in a controversy so peculiarly abhorrent to the affections of your still faithful colonists, that when we consider whom we must oppose in this contest, and if it continues, what may be the consequences, our own particular misfortunes are accounted by us, only as parts of our distress.

[OBP-9]   Knowing to what violent resentments and incurable animosities, civil discords are apt to exasperate and inflame the contending parties, we think ourselves required by indispensable obligations to Almighty God, to your Majesty, to our fellow subjects, and to ourselves, immediately to use all the means in our power not incompatible with our safety, for stopping the further effusion of blood, and for averting the impending calamities that threaten the British Empire.

[OBP-10]   Thus called upon to address your Majesty on affairs of such moment to America, and probably to all your dominions, we are earnestly desirous of performing this office with the utmost deference for your Majesty; and we therefore pray, that your royal magnanimity and benevolence may make the most favorable construction of our expressions on so uncommon an occasion. Could we represent in their full force the sentiments that agitate the minds of us your dutiful subjects, we are persuaded your Majesty would ascribe any seeming deviation from reverence, in our language, and even in our conduct, not to any reprehensible intention but to the impossibility of reconciling the usual appearances of respect with a just attention to our own preservation against those artful and cruel enemies, who abuse your royal confidence and authority for the purpose of effecting our destruction.

[OBP-11]   Attached to your Majesty's person, family and government with all the devotion that principle and affection can inspire, connected with Great Britain by the strongest ties that can unite societies, and deploring every event that tends in any degree to weaken them, we solemnly assure your Majesty, that we not only most ardently desire the former harmony between her and these colonies may be restored but that a concord may be established between them upon so firm a basis, as to perpetuate its blessings uninterrupted by any future dissensions to succeeding generations in both countries, and to transmit your Majesty's name to posterity adorned with that signal and lasting glory, that has attended the memory of those illustrious personages, whose virtues and abilities have extricated states from dangerous convulsions, and by securing happiness to others, have erected the most noble and durable monuments to their own fame.

[OBP-12]   We beg leave further to assure your Majesty that notwithstanding the sufferings of your loyal colonists during the course of the present controversy, our breasts retain too tender a regard for the kingdom from which we derive our origin to request such a reconciliation as might in any manner be inconsistent with her dignity or her welfare. These, related as we are to her, honor and duty, as well as inclination induce us to support and advance; and the apprehensions that now oppress our hearts with unspeakable grief, being once removed, your Majesty will find your faithful subjects on this continent ready and willing at all times, as they ever have been with their lives and fortunes to assert and maintain the rights and interests of your Majesty and of our Mother Country.

[OBP-13]   We therefore beseech your Majesty, that your royal authority and influence may be graciously interposed to procure us relief from our afflicting fears and jealousies occasioned by the system before mentioned, and to settle peace through every part of your dominions, with all humility submitting to your Majesty's wise consideration, whether it may not be expedient for facilitating those important purposes, that your Majesty be pleased to direct some mode by which the united applications of your faithful colonists to the throne in pursuance of their common councils, may be improved into a happy and permanent reconciliation; and that in the meantime measures be taken for preventing the further destruction of the lives of your Majesty's subjects; and that such statutes as more immediately distress any of your Majesty's colonies be repealed: For by such arrangements as your Majesty's wisdom can form for collecting the united sense of your American people, we are convinced, your Majesty would receive such satisfactory proofs of the disposition of the colonists towards their sovereign and the parent state, that the wished for opportunity would soon be restored to them, of evincing the sincerity of their professions by every testimony of devotion becoming the most dutiful subjects and the most affectionate colonists.

[OBP-14]   That your Majesty may enjoy a long and prosperous reign, and that your descendants may govern your dominions with honor to themselves and happiness to their subjects is our sincere and fervent prayer.

Appendix B:
The Declaration of Independence

In Congress, July 4, 1776,

The Unanimous Declaration of the Thirteen United States of America.

[DI-1]   When in the Course of human events, it becomes necessary for one people to dissolve the political bands which have connected them with another, and to assume among the Powers of the earth, the separate and equal station to which the Laws of Nature and of Nature's God entitle them, a decent respect to the opinions of mankind requires that they should declare the causes which impel them to the separation.

[DI-2]   We hold these truths to be self-evident, that all men are created equal, that they are endowed by their Creator with certain inalienable Rights, that among these are Life, Liberty and the pursuit of Happiness. That to secure these rights, Governments are instituted among Men, deriving their just powers from the consent of the governed, That whenever any Form of Government becomes destructive of these ends, it is the Right of the People to alter or to abolish it, and to institute new Government, laying its foundation on such principles and organizing its powers in such form, as to them shall seem most likely to effect their Safety and Happiness. Prudence, indeed, will dictate that Governments long established should not be changed for light and transient causes; and accordingly all experience hath shown, that mankind are more disposed to suffer, while evils are sufferable, than to right themselves by abolishing the forms to which they are accustomed. But when a long train of abuses and usurpations, pursuing invariably the same Object evinces a design to reduce them under absolute Despotism, it is their right, it is their duty, to throw off such Government, and to provide new Guards for their future security. Such has been the patient sufferance of these Colonies; and such is now the necessity which constrains them to alter their former Systems of Government. The history of the present King of Great Britain is a history of repeated injuries and usurpations, all having in direct object the establishment of an absolute Tyranny over these States. To prove this, let Facts be submitted to a candid world.

[DI-3]   He has refused his Assent to Laws, the most wholesome and necessary for the public good.

[DI-4]   He has forbidden his Governors to pass Laws of immediate and pressing importance unless suspended in their operation till his Assent should be obtained; and when so suspended, he has utterly neglected to attend to them.

[DI-5]   He has refused to pass other Laws for the accommodation of large districts of people, unless those people would relinquish the right of Representation in the Legislature, a right inestimable to them and formidable to tyrants only.

[DI-6]   He has called together legislative bodies at places unusual, uncomfortable, and distant from the depository of their Public Records, for the sole purpose of fatiguing them into compliance with his measures.

[DI-7]   He has dissolved representative Houses repeatedly, for opposing with manly firmness his invasions on the rights of the people.

[DI-8]   He has refused for a long time, after such dissolutions, to cause others to be elected; whereby the Legislative Powers, incapable of Annihilation, have returned to the People at large for their exercise; the State remaining in the mean time exposed to all the dangers of invasion from without, and convulsions within.

[DI-9]   He has endeavored to prevent the population of these States; for that purpose obstructing the Laws of Naturalization of Foreigners; refusing to pass others to encourage their migration hither, and raising the conditions of new appropriations of Lands.

[DI-10]   He has obstructed the Administration of Justice, by refusing his Assent to Laws for establishing Judiciary Powers.

[DI-11]   He has made Judges dependent on his will alone, for the tenure of their offices, and the amount and payment of their salaries.

[DI-12]   He has erected a multitude of New Offices, and sent hither swarms of Officers to harass our people, and eat out their substance.

[DI-13]   He has kept among us, in times of peace, Standing Armies without the Consent of our legislatures.

[DI-14]   He has affected to render the Military independent of and superior to the Civil Power.

[DI-15]   He has combined with others to subject us to a jurisdiction foreign to our constitution, and unacknowledged by our laws; giving his Assent to their acts of pretended legislation:

[DI-16]   For quartering large bodies of armed troops among us:

[DI-17]   For protecting them by a mock Trial, from Punishment for any Murders which they should commit on the Inhabitants of these States:

[DI-18]   For cutting off our Trade with all parts of the world:

[DI-19]   For imposing taxes on us without our Consent:

[DI-20]   For depriving us in many cases, of the benefits of Trial by Jury:

[DI-21]   For transporting us beyond Seas to be tried for pretended offences:

[DI-22]   For abolishing the free system of English Laws in a neighboring Province, establishing therein an Arbitrary government, and enlarging its Boundaries so as to render it at once an example and fit instrument for introducing the same absolute rule into these Colonies:

[DI-23]   For taking away our Charters, abolishing our most valuable Laws, and altering fundamentally the Forms of our Governments:

[DI-24]   For suspending our own Legislatures, and declaring themselves invested with Power to legislate for us in all cases whatsoever.

[DI-25]   He has abdicated Government here, by declaring us out of his Protection and waging War against us.

[DI-26]   He has plundered our Seas, ravaged our Coasts, burnt our towns, and destroyed the lives of our people.

[DI-27]   He is at this time transporting large armies of foreign mercenaries to complete the works of death, desolation and tyranny, already begun with circumstances of Cruelty and perfidy scarcely paralleled in the most barbarous ages, and totally unworthy the Head of a civilized nation.

[DI-28]   He has constrained our fellow Citizens taken Captive on the high Seas to bear Arms against their Country, to become the executioners of their friends and Brethren, or to fall themselves by their Hands.

[DI-29]   He has excited domestic insurrections amongst us, and has endeavored to bring on the inhabitants of our frontiers, the merciless Indian

Savages, whose known rule of warfare, is an undistinguished destruction of all ages, sexes and conditions.

[DI-30] In every stage of these Oppressions We have Petitioned for Redress in the most humble terms: Our repeated Petitions have been answered only by repeated injury. A Prince, whose character is thus marked by every act which may define a Tyrant, is unfit to be the ruler of a free people.

[DI-31] Nor have We been wanting in attentions to our British brethren. We have warned them from time to time of attempts by their legislature to extend an unwarrantable jurisdiction over us. We have reminded them of the circumstances of our emigration and settlement here. We have appealed to their native justice and magnanimity, and we have conjured them by the ties of our common kindred to disavow these usurpations, which, would inevitably interrupt our connections and correspondence. They too have been deaf to the voice of justice and of consanguinity. We must, therefore, acquiesce in the necessity, which denounces our Separation, and hold them, as we hold the rest of mankind, Enemies in War, in Peace Friends.

[DI-32] We, therefore, the Representatives of the United States of America, in General Congress, Assembled, appealing to the Supreme Judge of the world for the rectitude of our intentions, do, in the Name, and by Authority of the good People of these Colonies, solemnly publish and declare, that these United Colonies are, and of Right ought to be Free and Independent States; that they are Absolved from all Allegiance to the British Crown, and that all political connection between them and the State of Great Britain, is and ought to be totally dissolved; and that as Free and Independent States, they have full Power to levy War, conclude Peace, contract Alliances, establish Commerce, and to do all other Acts and Things which Independent States may of right do. And for the support of this Declaration, with a firm reliance on the protection of Divine Providence, we mutually pledge to each other our Lives, our Fortunes and our sacred Honor.

JOHN HANCOCK.

New Hampshire
Josiah Bartlett
Wm. Whipple
Matthew Thornton

Massachusetts Bay
Saml. Adams
John Adams
Robt. Treat Paine
Elbridge Gerry

Rhode Island
Step. Hopkins
William Ellery

Connecticut
Roger Sherman
Sam'el Huntington
Wm. Williams
Oliver Wolcott

New York
Wm. Floyd
Phil. Livingston
Frans. Lewis
Lewis Morris

New Jersey
Richd. Stockton
Jno. Witherspoon
Fras. Hopkinson
John Hart
Abra. Clark

Pennsylvania
Robt. Morris
Benjamin Rush
Benja. Franklin
John Morton
Geo. Clymer
Jas. Smith
Geo. Taylor
James Wilson
Geo. Ross

Delaware
Caesar Rodney
Geo. Read
Tho. M:Kean

Maryland
Samuel Chase
Wm. Paca
Thos. Stone
Charles Carroll of
   Carrollton

Virginia
George Wythe
Richard Henry Lee
Th. Jefferson
Benja. Harrison
Thos. Nelson, Jr.
Francis Lightfoot Lee
Carter Braxton

North Carolina
Wm. Hooper
Joseph Hewes
John Penn

South Carolina
Edward Rutledge
Thos. Heyward Junr.
Thomas Lynch Junr.
Arthur Middleton

Georgia
Button Gwinnett
Lyman Hall
Geo. Walton

Appendix C:
The Constitution of the United States

WE THE PEOPLE, of the United States in order to form a more perfect Union, establish justice, insure domestic tranquility, provide for the common defense, promote the general welfare and secure the blessings of liberty to ourselves and our posterity, do ordain and establish this Constitution for the United States of America.

ARTICLE I

Section 1. All legislative Powers herein granted shall be vested in a Congress of the United States, which shall consist of a Senate and House of Representatives.

Section 2. The House of Representatives shall be composed of Members chosen every second Year by the People of the several States, and the Electors in each State shall have the Qualifications requisite for Electors of the most numerous Branch of the State Legislature.

No Person shall be a Representative who shall not have attained to the Age of twenty five Years, and been seven Years a Citizen of the United States, and who shall not, when elected, be an Inhabitant of that State in which he shall be chosen.

Representatives and direct Taxes shall be apportioned among the several States which may be included within this Union, according to their respective Numbers, which shall be determined by adding to the whole Number of free persons, including those bound to Service for a Term of Years, and excluding Indians not taxed, three fifths of all other Persons. The actual Enumeration shall be made within three Years after the first Meeting of the Congress of the United States, and within every subsequent Term of ten Years, in such Manner as they shall by Law direct. The Number of Representatives shall not exceed one for every thirty Thousand, but each State shall have at least one Representative; and until such enumeration shall be made, the State of New Hampshire shall be entitled to choose three, Massachusetts eight, Rhode Island and Providence Plantations one, Connecticut five, New York six, New Jersey four, Pennsylvania eight, Delaware one, Maryland six, Virginia ten, North Carolina five, South Carolina five, and Georgia three.

When vacancies happen in the Representation from any State, the Executive Authority thereof shall issue Writs of Election to fill such Vacancies.

The House of Representatives shall choose their Speaker and other Officers; and shall have the sole Power of Impeachment.

Section 3. The Senate of the United States shall be composed of two Senators from each State, chosen by the Legislature thereof, for six Years; and each Senator shall have one Vote.

Immediately after they shall be assembled in Consequence of the first Election, they shall be divided as equally as may be into three classes. The Seats of the Senators of the first Class shall be vacated at the Expiration of the second Year, of the second Class at the Expiration of the fourth Year, and of the third Class at the Expiration of the sixth Year, so that one third may be chosen every second Year; and if Vacancies happen by Resignation, or otherwise, during the Recess of the Legislature of any State, the Executive thereof may make temporary Appointments until the next Meeting of the Legislature, which shall then fill such Vacancies.

No person shall be a Senator who shall not have attained to the Age of thirty Years, and been nine Years a Citizen of the United States, and who shall not, when elected, be an Inhabitant of that State for which he shall be chosen.

The Vice President of the United States shall be President of the Senate, but shall have no Vote, unless they be equally divided.

The Senate shall choose their other Officers, and also a President pro tempore, in the Absence of the Vice President, or when he shall exercise the Office of President of the United States.

The Senate shall have the sole Power to try all Impeachments. When sitting for that Purpose, they shall be on Oath or Affirmation. When the President of the United States is tried, the Chief Justice shall preside: And no Person shall be convicted without the Concurrence of two thirds of the Members present.

Judgment in Cases of Impeachment shall not extend further than to removal from Office, and disqualification to hold and enjoy any Office of honor, Trust or Profit under the United States: but the Party convicted shall nevertheless be liable and subject to Indictment, Trial, Judgment and Punishment, according to Law.

Section 4. The Times, Places and Manner of holding Elections for Senators and Representatives, shall be prescribed in each State by the Legislature thereof; but the Congress may at any time by Law make or alter such Regulations, except as to the Places of choosing Senators.

The Congress shall assemble at least once in every Year, and such Meeting shall be on the first Monday in December, unless they shall by Law appoint a different Day.

Section 5. Each House shall be the Judge of the Elections, Returns and Qualifications of its own Members, and a Majority of each shall constitute a Quorum to do Business; but a smaller Number may adjourn from day to day, and may be authorized to compel the Attendance of absent Members, in such Manner, and under such Penalties as each House may provide.

Each House may determine the Rules of its Proceedings, punish its Members for disorderly Behavior, and, with the Concurrence of two thirds, expel a Member. Each House shall keep a Journal of its Proceedings, and from time to time publish the same, excepting such Parts as may in their Judgment require

Secrecy; and the Yeas and Nays of the Members of either House on any question shall, at the Desire of one fifth of those Present, be entered on the Journal.

Neither House, during the Session of Congress, shall, without the Consent of the other, adjourn for more than three days, nor to any other Place than that in which the two Houses shall be sitting.

Section 6. The Senators and Representatives shall receive a Compensation for their Services, to be ascertained by Law, and paid out of the Treasury of the United States. They shall in all Cases, except Treason, Felony and Breach of the Peace, be privileged from Arrest during their Attendance at the Session of their respective Houses, and in going to and returning from the same; and for any Speech or Debate in either House, they shall not be questioned in any other Place.

No Senator or Representative shall, during the Time for which he was elected, be appointed to any civil Office under the Authority of the United States which shall have been created, or the Emoluments whereof shall have been increased during such time; and no Person holding any Office under the United States, shall be a Member of either House during his Continuance in Office.

Section 7. All Bills for raising Revenue shall originate in the House of Representatives; but the Senate may propose or concur with Amendments as on other Bills.

Every Bill which shall have passed the House of Representatives and the Senate, shall, before it become a Law, be presented to the President of the United States; If he approve he shall sign it, but if not he shall return it, with his Objections to that House in which it shall have originated, who shall enter the Objections at large on their Journal, and proceed to reconsider it. If after such Reconsideration two thirds of that House shall agree to pass the Bill, it shall be sent, together with the Objections, to the other House, by which it shall likewise be reconsidered, and if approved by two thirds of that House, it shall become a Law. But in all such Cases the Votes of both Houses shall be determined by yeas and Nays, and the Names of the Persons voting for and against the Bill shall be entered on the Journal of each House respectively. If any Bill shall not be returned by the President within ten Days (Sundays excepted) after it shall have been presented to him, the Same shall be a Law, in like Manner as if he had signed it, unless the Congress by their Adjournment prevent its Return, in which Case it shall not be a law.

Every Order, Resolution, or Vote to which the Concurrence of the Senate and House of Representatives may be necessary (except on a question of Adjournment) shall be presented to the President of the United States; and before the Same shall take Effect, shall be approved by him, or being disapproved by him, shall be repassed by two thirds of the Senate and House of Representatives, according to the Rules and Limitations prescribed in the Case of a Bill.

Section 8. The Congress shall have Power To lay and collect Taxes, Duties, Imposts and Excises, to pay the Debts and provide for the common Defense and general Welfare of the United States; but all Duties, Imposts and Excises shall be uniform throughout the United States;

To borrow Money on the credit of the United States;

To regulate Commerce with foreign Nations, and among the several States, and with the Indian Tribes;

To establish an uniform Rule of Naturalization, and uniform Laws on the subject of Bankruptcies throughout the United States;

To coin Money, regulate the Value thereof, and of foreign Coin, and fix the Standard of Weights and Measures;

To provide for the Punishment of counterfeiting the Securities and current Coin of the United States;

To establish Post Offices and post Roads;

To promote the Progress of Science and useful Arts, by securing for limited Times to Authors and Inventors the exclusive Right to their respective Writings and Discoveries;

To constitute Tribunals inferior to the Supreme Court;

To define and punish Piracies and Felonies committed on the high Seas, and Offences against the Law of Nations;

To declare War, grant Letters of Marque and Reprisal, and make Rules concerning Captures on Land and Water;

To raise and support Armies, but no Appropriation of Money to that Use shall be for a longer Term than two Years;

To provide and maintain a Navy;

To make Rules for the Government and Regulation of the land and naval Forces;

To provide for calling forth the Militia to execute the Laws of the Union, suppress Insurrections and repel Invasions;

To provide for organizing, arming, and disciplining, the Militia, and for governing such Part of them as may be employed in the Service of the United States, reserving to the States respectively, the Appointment of the Officers, and the Authority of training the Militia according to the discipline prescribed by Congress;

To exercise exclusive Legislation in all Cases whatsoever, over such District (not exceeding ten Miles square) as may, by Cession of particular States, and the Acceptance of Congress, become the Seat of the Government of the United

States, and to exercise like Authority over all Places purchased by the Consent of the Legislature of the State in which the Same shall be, for the Erection of Forts, Magazines, Arsenals, dock-Yards, and other needful Buildings;–And

To make all Laws which shall be necessary and proper for carrying into Execution the foregoing Powers, and all other Powers vested by this Constitution in the Government of the United States, or in any Department or Officer thereof.

Section 9. The Migration or Importation of such Persons as any of the States now existing shall think proper to admit, shall not be prohibited by the Congress prior to the Year one thousand eight hundred and eight, but a Tax or duty may be imposed on such Importation, not exceeding ten dollars for each Person.

The Privilege of the Writ of Habeas Corpus shall not be suspended, unless when in Cases of Rebellion or Invasion the public Safety may require it.

No bill of Attainder or ex post facto Law shall be passed.

No Capitation, or other direct, Tax shall be laid, unless in Proportion to the Census or Enumeration herein before directed to be taken.

No Tax or Duty shall be laid on Articles exported from any State.

No Preference shall be given by any Regulation of Commerce or Revenue to the Ports of one State over those of another: nor shall Vessels bound to, or from, one State, be obliged to enter, clear, or pay Duties in another.

No Money shall be drawn from the Treasury, but in Consequence of Appropriations made by Law; and a regular Statement and Account of the Receipts and Expenditures of all public Money shall be published from time to time.

No Title of Nobility shall be granted by the United States: and no Person holding any Office of Profit or Trust under them, shall, without the Consent of the

Congress, accept of any present, Emolument, Office, or Title, of any kind whatever, from any King, Prince or foreign State.

Section 10. No State shall enter into any Treaty, Alliance, or Confederation; grant Letters of Marque and Reprisal; coin Money; emit Bills of Credit; make any Thing but gold and silver Coin a Tender in Payment of Debt.; pass any Bill of Attainder, ex post facto Law, or Law impairing the Obligation of Contracts, or grant any Title of Nobility.

No State shall, without the Consent of the Congress, lay any Imposts or Duties on Imports or Exports, except what may be absolutely necessary for executing its inspection Law: and the net Produce of all Duties and Imposts, laid by any State on Imports or Exports, shall be for the Use of the Treasury of the United States; and all such Laws shall be subject to the Revision and Control of the Congress.

No State shall, without the Consent of Congress, lay any Duty of Tonnage, keep Troops, or Ships of War in time of Peace, enter into any Agreement or Compact with another State, or with a foreign Power, or engage in War, unless actually invaded, or in such imminent Danger as will not admit of delay.

ARTICLE II

Section 1. The executive Power shall be vested in a President of the United States of America. He shall hold his Office during the Term of four Years, and, together with the Vice President, chosen for the same Term, be elected as follows:

Each State shall appoint, in such Manner as the Legislature thereof may direct, a Number of Electors, equal to the whole Number of Senators and Representatives to which the State may be entitled in the Congress: but no Senator or Representative, or Person holding an Office of Trust or Profit under the United States, shall be appointed an Elector.

The Electors shall meet in their respective States, and vote by Ballot for two persons, of whom one at least shall not be an Inhabitant of the same State with themselves. And they shall make a List of all the Persons voted for, and of the Number of Votes for each; which List they shall sign and certify, and transmit sealed to the Seat of the Government of the United States, directed to the President of the Senate. The President of the Senate shall, in the Presence of the Senate and House of Representatives, open all the Certificates, and the Votes shall then be counted. The Person having the greatest Number of Votes shall be the President, if such Number be a Majority of the whole Number of Electors appointed; and if there be more than one who have such Majority, and have an equal Number of Votes, then the House of Representatives shall immediately choose by Ballot one of them for President; and if no person have a Majority, then from the five highest on the List the said House shall in like Manner choose the President. But in choosing the President, the Votes shall be taken by States, the Representation from each State having one Vote; A quorum for this Purpose shall consist of a Member or Members from two thirds of the States, and a Majority of all the States shall be necessary to a Choice. In every Case, after the Choice of the President, the Person having the greatest Number of Votes of the Electors shall be the Vice President. But if there should remain two or more who have equal Votes, the Senate shall choose from them by Ballot the Vice President.

The Congress may determine the Time of choosing the Electors, and the Day on which they shall give their Votes; which Day shall be the same throughout the United States.

No Person except a natural born Citizen, or a Citizen of the United States, at the time of the Adoption of this Constitution, shall be eligible to the Office of President; neither shall any Person be eligible to that Office who shall not have attained to the Age of thirty five Years, and been fourteen Years a Resident within the United States.

In Case of the Removal of the President from Office, or of his Death, Resignation, or inability to discharge the Powers and Duties of the said Office, the

Same shall devolve on the Vice President, and the Congress may by Law provide for the Case of Removal, Death, Resignation or Inability, both of the President and Vice President, declaring what Officer shall then act as President, and such Officer shall act accordingly, until the Disability be removed, or a President shall be elected.

The President shall, at stated Times, receive for his Services a compensation, which shall neither be increased nor diminished during the Period for which he shall have been elected, and he shall not receive within that Period any other Emolument from the United States, or any of them.

Before he enter on the Execution of his Office, he shall take the following Oath or Affirmation: "I do solemnly swear (or affirm) that I will faithfully execute the Office of President of the United States, and will to the best of my Ability, preserve, protect and defend the Constitution of the United States."

Section 2. The President shall be Commander in Chief of the Army and Navy of the United States, and of the Militia of the several States, when called into the actual Service of the United States; he may require the Opinion, in writing, of the principal Officer in each of the executive Departments, upon any Subject relating to the Duties of their respective Offices, and he shall have Power to grant Reprieves and Pardons for Offenses against the United States, except in Cases of Impeachment.

He shall have Power, by and with the Advice and Consent of the Senate, to make Treaties, provided two thirds of the Senators present concur; and he shall nominate, and by and with the Advice and Consent of the Senate, shall appoint Ambassadors, other public Ministers and Consuls, Judges of the supreme Court, and all other Officers of the United States, whose Appointments are not herein otherwise provided for, and which shall be established by Law: but the Congress may by Law vest the Appointment of such inferior Officers, as they think proper, in the President alone, in the Courts of Law, or in the Heads of Departments.

The President shall have Power to fill up all Vacancies that may happen during the Recess of the Senate, by granting Commissions which shall expire at the End of their next Session.

Section 3. He shall from time to time give to the Congress Information of the State of the Union, and recommend to their Consideration such Measures as he shall judge necessary and expedient; he may, on extraordinary Occasions, convene both Houses, or either of them, and in Case of Disagreement between them, with Respect to the Time of Adjournment, he may adjourn them to such Time as he shall think proper; he shall receive Ambassadors and other public Ministers; he shall take Care that the Laws be faithfully executed, and shall Commission all the Officers of the United States.

Section 4. The President, Vice President and all civil Officers of the United States, shall be removed from Office on Impeachment for, and Conviction of, Treason, Bribery, or other high Crimes and misdemeanors.

ARTICLE III

Section 1. The judicial Power of the United States, shall be vested in one Supreme Court, and in such inferior Courts as the Congress may from time to time ordain and establish. The Judges, both of the supreme and inferior Courts, shall hold their Offices during good Behavior, and shall, at stated Times, receive for their Services, a Compensation, which shall not be diminished during their Continuance in Office.

Section 2. The judicial Power shall extend to all Cases, in Law and Equity, arising under this Constitution, the Laws of the United States, and Treaties made or which shall be made, under their Authority;–to all Cases affecting Ambassadors, other public Ministers and Consuls;-to all Cases of admiralty and maritime Jurisdiction;–to Controversies to which the United States shall be a Party;–to Controversies between two or more States;–between a State and Citizens of another State;–between Citizens of different States,–between Citizens of the same State claiming Lands under Grants of different States, and between a State, or the Citizens thereof, and foreign States, Citizens or Subjects.

In all Cases affecting Ambassadors, other Public Ministers and Consuls, and those in which a State shall be Party, the supreme Court shall have original Jurisdiction. In all the other Cases before mentioned, the supreme Court shall have appellate Jurisdiction, both as to Law and Fact, with such Exceptions, and under such Regulations as the Congress shall make.

The Trial of all Crimes, except in Cases of Impeachment, shall be by Jury; and such Trials shall be held in the State where the said Crimes shall have been committed; but when not committed within any State, the Trial shall be at such Place or Places as the Congress may by Law have directed.

Section 3. Treason against the United States, shall consist only in levying War against them, or in adhering to their Enemies, giving them Aid and Comfort. No person shall be convicted of Treason unless on the Testimony of two Witnesses to the same overt Act, or on Confession in open Court.

The Congress shall have Power to declare the Punishment of Treason, but no Attainder of Treason shall work Corruption of Blood, or Forfeiture except during the Life of the Person attainted.

ARTICLE IV

Section 1. Full Faith and Credit shall be given in each State to the Public Acts, Records, and judicial Proceedings of every other State. And the Congress may by general Laws prescribe the Manner in which such Acts, Records and Proceedings shall be proved, and the Effect thereof.

Section 2. The citizens of each State shall be entitled to all Privileges and Immunities of Citizens in the several States.

A Person charged in any State with Treason, Felony, or other Crime, who shall flee from Justice, and be found in another State, shall on Demand of the executive Authority of the State from which he fled, be delivered up, to be removed to the State having Jurisdiction of the Crime.

No Person held to Service or Labor in one State, under the Laws thereof, escaping into another, shall in Consequence of any Law or Regulation therein, be discharged from such Service or Labor, but shall be delivered up on Claim of the Party to whom such Service or Labor may be due.

Section 3. New States may be admitted by the Congress into this Union; but no new States shall be formed or erected within the Jurisdiction of any other State; nor any State be formed by the Junction of two or more States, or Parts of States, without the Consent of the Legislatures of the States concerned as well as of the Congress.

The Congress shall have Power to dispose of and make all needful Rules and Regulations respecting the Territory or other Property belonging to the United States; and nothing in this Constitution shall be so construed as to Prejudice any Claims of the United States, or of any particular State.

Section 4. The United States shall guarantee to every State in this Union a Republican Form of Government, and shall protect each of them against Invasion; and on Application of the Legislature, or of the Executive (when the Legislature cannot be convened) against domestic Violence.

ARTICLE V

The Congress, whenever two thirds of both Houses shall deem it necessary, shall propose Amendments to this Constitution, or, on the Application of the Legislatures of two thirds of the several States, shall call a Convention for proposing Amendments, which, in either Case, shall be valid to all Intents and Purposes, as Part of this Constitution, when ratified by the Legislatures of three fourths of the several States, or by Conventions in three fourths thereof, as the one or the other Mode of Ratification may be proposed by the Congress; Provided that no Amendment which may be made prior to the Year One thousand eight hundred and eight shall in any Manner affect the first and fourth Clauses in the Ninth Section of the first Article; and that no State, without its Consent, shall be deprived of its equal Suffrage in the Senate.

ARTICLE VI

All Debts contracted and Engagements entered into, before the Adoption of this Constitution, shall be as valid against the United States under this Constitution, as under the Confederation.

This Constitution, and the Laws of the United States which shall be made in Pursuance thereof; and all Treaties made, or which shall be made, under the Authority of the United States, shall be the supreme Law of the Land; and the Judges in every State shall be bound thereby, any Thing in the Constitution or Laws of any State to the Contrary notwithstanding.

The Senators and Representatives before mentioned, and the Members of the several State Legislatures and all executive and judicial Officers, both of the United States and of the several States, shall be bound by Oath or Affirmation, to support this Constitution; but no religious Test shall ever be required as a Qualification to any Office or Public Trust under the United States.

ARTICLE VII

The Ratification of the Conventions of nine States, shall be sufficient for the Establishment of this Constitution between the States so ratifying the Same.

Done in Convention by the Unanimous Consent of the States present the Seventeenth Day of September in the Year of our Lord one thousand seven hundred and Eighty seven and of the Independence of the United States of America the Twelfth. In witness whereof We have hereunto subscribed our Names,

Go. WASHINGTON   Presidt and deputy from Virginia

New Hampshire	*New Jersey*	*Delaware*	*North Carolina*
John Langdon	Wil: Livingston	Geo: Read	Wm. Blount
Nicholas Gilman	David Brearley	Gunning	Richd Dobbs
	Wm. Paterson	Bedford jun	Spaight
Massachusetts	Jona: Dayton	John Dickinson	Hu Williamson
Nathaniel		Richard Bassett	
Gorham	*Pennsylvania*	Jaco: Broom	*South Carolina*
Rufus King	B. Franklin		J. Rutledge
	Thomas Mifflin	*Maryland*	Charles
Connecticut	Robt Morris	James McHenry	Cotesworth
Wm. Saml.	Geo. Clymer	Dan of St Thos.	Pinckney
Johnson	Thos. FitzSimons	Jenifer	Charles Pinckney
Roger Sherman	Jared Ingersoll	Danl Carroll	Pierce Butler
	James Wilson		
New York	Gouv Morris	*Virginia*	*Georgia*
Alexander		John Blair	William Few
Hamilton		James Madison Jr.	Abr Baldwin

Articles in addition to, and Amendment of, the Constitution of the United States of America, proposed by Congress, and ratified by the Legislatures of the several States, pursuant to the fifth Article of the original Constitution.

(The first ten amendments compose the Bill of Rights, and went into effect December 15, 1791.)

AMENDMENT 1

Congress shall make no law respecting an establishment of religion, or prohibiting the free exercise thereof; or abridging the freedom of speech, or of the press; or the right of the people peaceably to assemble, and to petition the government for a redress of grievances.

AMENDMENT 2

A well regulated Militia, being necessary to the security of a free State, the right of the people to keep and bear Arms, shall not be infringed.

AMENDMENT 3

No Soldier shall, in time of peace be quartered in any house, without the consent of the Owner, nor in time of war, but in a manner to be prescribed by law.

AMENDMENT 4

The right of the people to be secure in their persons, houses, papers, and effects, against unreasonable searches and seizures, shall not be violated, and no Warrants shall issue, but upon probable cause, supported by Oath or affirmation, and particularly describing the place to be searched, and the persons or things to be seized.

AMENDMENT 5

No person shall be held to answer for a capital, or otherwise infamous crime, unless on a presentment or indictment of a Grand Jury, except in cases arising in the land or naval forces, or in the Militia, when in actual service in time of War or public danger; nor shall any person be subject for the same offence to be twice put in jeopardy of life or limb; nor shall be compelled in any criminal case to be a witness against himself, nor be deprived of life, liberty, or property, without due process of law; nor, shall private property be taken for public use, without just compensation.

AMENDMENT 6

In all criminal prosecutions, the accused shall enjoy the right to a speedy and public trial, by an impartial jury of the State and district wherein the crime shall have been committed, which district shall have been previously ascertained by law, and to be informed of the nature and cause of the accusation; to be confronted with the witnesses against him; to have compulsory process for obtaining witnesses in his favor, and to have the Assistance of Counsel for his defense.

AMENDMENT 7

In Suits at common law, where the value in controversy shall exceed twenty dollars, the right of trial by jury shall be preserved, and no fact tried by a jury, shall be otherwise re-examined in any Court of the United States, than according to the rules of the common law.

AMENDMENT 8

Excessive bail shall not be required, nor excessive fines imposed, nor cruel and unusual punishments inflicted.

AMENDMENT 9

The enumeration in the Constitution, of certain rights, shall not be construed to deny or disparage others retained by the people.

AMENDMENT 10

The powers not delegated to the United States by the Constitution, nor prohibited by it to the States, are reserved to the States respectively, or to the people.

AMENDMENT 11 (January 8, 1798)

The Judicial power of the United States shall not be construed to extend to any suit in law or equity, commenced or prosecuted against one of the United States, by Citizens of another State, or by Citizens or Subjects of any Foreign State.

AMENDMENT 12 (September 25, 1804)

The Electors shall meet in their respective states, and vote by ballot for President and Vice-President, one of whom, at least, shall not be an inhabitant of the same state with themselves; they shall name in their ballots the person voted for as President, and in distinct ballots the person voted for as Vice-President, and they shall make distinct lists of all persons voted for as President and of all persons voted for as Vice-President, and of the number of votes for each, which lists they shall sign and certify, and transmit sealed to the seat of the government of the United States, directed to the President of the Senate;–The President of the Senate shall, in the presence of the Senate and House of Representatives, open all the certificates and the votes shall then be counted;–

The person having the greatest number of votes for President, shall be the President, if such number be a majority of the whole number of Electors appointed; and if no person have such majority, then from the persons having the highest numbers not exceeding three on the list of those voted for as President, the House of Representatives shall choose immediately, by ballot, the President. But in choosing the President, the votes shall be taken by states, the representation from each state having one vote; a quorum for this purpose shall consist of a member or members from two-thirds of the states, and a majority of all the states shall be necessary to a choice. And if the House of Representatives shall not choose a President whenever the right of choice shall devolve upon them, before the fourth day of March next following, then the Vice-President shall act as President, as in the case of the death or other constitutional disability of the President.–The person having the greatest number of votes as Vice-President, shall be the Vice-President, if such number be a majority of the whole number of Electors appointed, and if no person have a majority, then from the two highest numbers on the list, the Senate shall choose the Vice-President; a quorum for the purpose shall consist of two-thirds of the whole number of Senators, and a majority of the whole number shall be necessary to a choice. But no person constitutionally ineligible to the office of President shall be eligible to that of Vice-President of the United States.

AMENDMENT 13 (December 18, 1865)
Section 1. Neither slavery nor involuntary servitude, except as a punishment for crime whereof the party shall have been duly convicted, shall exist within the United States, or any place subject to their jurisdiction.

Section 2. Congress shall have power to enforce this article by appropriate legislation.

AMENDMENT 14 (July 20, 1868)
Section 1. All persons born or naturalized in the United States, and subject to the jurisdiction thereof, are citizens of the United States and of the State wherein they reside. No State shall make or enforce any law which shall abridge the privileges or immunities of citizens of the United States; nor shall any State

deprive any person of life, liberty, or property, without due process of law; nor deny to any person within its jurisdiction the equal protection of the laws.

Section 2. Representatives shall be apportioned among the several States according to their respective numbers, counting the whole number of persons in each State, excluding Indians not taxed. But when the right to vote at any election for the choice of electors for President and Vice President of the United States, Representatives in Congress, the Executive and Judicial officers of a State, or the members of the Legislature thereof, is denied to any of the male inhabitants of such State, being twenty-one years of age, and citizens of the United States, or in any way abridged, except for participation in rebellion, or other crime, the basis of representation therein shall be reduced in the proportion which the number of such male citizens shall bear to the whole number of male citizens twenty-one years of age in such State.

Section 3. No person shall be a Senator or Representative in Congress, or elector of President and Vice President, or hold any office, civil or military, under the United States, or under any State, who, having previously taken an oath, as a member of Congress, or as an officer of the United States, or as a member of any State legislature, or as an executive or judicial officer of any State, to support the Constitution of the United States, shall have engaged in insurrection or rebellion against the same, or given aid or comfort to the enemies thereof. But Congress may by a vote of two-thirds of each House, remove such disability.

Section 4. The validity of the public debt of the United States, authorized by law, including debt incurred for payment of pensions and bounties for services in suppressing insurrection or rebellion, shall not be questioned. But Neither the United States nor any State shall assume or pay any debt or obligation incurred in aid of insurrection or rebellion against the United States, or any claim for the loss or emancipation of any slave; but all such debts, obligations and claims shall be held illegal and void.

Section 5. The Congress shall have power to enforce, by appropriate legislation, the provisions of this article.

AMENDMENT 15 (March 30, 1870)

Section 1. The right of citizens of the United States to vote shall not be denied or abridged by the United States or by any State on account of race, color, or previous condition of servitude.

Section 2. The Congress shall have power to enforce this article by appropriate legislation.

AMENDMENT 16 (February 25, 1913)

The Congress shall have power to lay and collect taxes on incomes, from whatever source derived, without apportionment among the several States, and without regard to any census or enumeration.

AMENDMENT 17 (May 31,1913)

The Senate of the United States shall be composed of two senators from each State, elected by the people thereof, for six years; and each Senator shall have one vote. The electors in each State shall have the qualifications requisite for electors of the most numerous branch of the State legislature.

When vacancies happen in the representation of any State in the Senate, the executive authority of such State shall issue writs of election to fill such vacancies: *Provided,* That the legislature of any State may empower the executive thereof to make temporary appointments until the people fill the vacancies by election as the legislature may direct.

This amendment shall not be so construed as to affect the election or term of any Senator chosen before it becomes valid as part of the Constitution.

AMENDMENT 18 (January 29, 1919)

Section 1. After one year from the ratification of this article, the manufacture, sale, or transportation of intoxicating liquors within, the importation thereof into, or the exportation thereof from the United States and all territory subject to the jurisdiction thereof for beverage purposes is hereby prohibited.

Section 2. The Congress and the several States shall have concurrent power to enforce this article by appropriate legislation.

Section 3. This article shall be inoperative unless it shall have been ratified as an amendment to the Constitution by the legislatures of the several States, as provided in the Constitution, within seven years from the date of the submission hereof to the States by the Congress.

AMENDMENT 19 (August 26, 1920)
The right of citizens of the United States to vote shall not be denied or abridged by the United States or by any State on account of sex.

The Congress shall have power to enforce this article by appropriate legislation.

AMENDMENT 20 (February 6, 1933)
Section 1. The terms of the President and Vice-President shall end at noon on the twentieth day of January, and the terms of Senators and Representatives at noon on the third day of January, of the years in which such terms would have ended if this article had not been ratified; and the terms of their successors shall then begin.

Section 2. The Congress shall assemble at least once in every year, and such meeting shall begin at noon on the third day of January, unless they shall by law appoint a different day.

Section 3. If, at the time fixed for the beginning of the term of the President, the President-elect shall have died, the Vice President-elect shall become President. If a President shall not have been chosen before the time fixed for the beginning of his term or if the President-elect shall have failed to qualify, then the Vice President-elect shall act as President until a President shall have qualified; and the Congress may by law provide for the case wherein neither a President-elect nor a Vice President-elect shall have qualified, declaring who shall then act as President, or the manner in which one who is to act shall be selected, and such person shall act accordingly until a President or Vice President shall have qualified.

Section 4. The Congress may by law provide for the case of the death of any of the persons from whom the House of Representatives may choose a President whenever the right of choice shall have devolved upon them, and for the case of the death of any of the persons from whom the Senate may choose a Vice President whenever the right of choice shall have devolved upon them.

Section 5. Sections 1 and 2 shall take effect on the 15th day of October following the ratification of this article.

Section 6. This article shall be inoperative unless it shall have been ratified as an amendment to the Constitution by the legislatures of three-fourths of the several States within seven years from the date of its submission.

AMENDMENT 21 (December 5, 1933)
Section 1. The eighteenth article of amendment to the Constitution of the United States is hereby repealed.

Section 2. The transportation or importation into any State, Territory or possession of the United States for delivery or use therein of intoxicating liquors, in violation of the laws thereof, is hereby prohibited.

Section 3. This article shall be inoperative unless it shall have been ratified as an amendment to the Constitution by conventions in the several States, as provided in the Constitution, within seven years from the date of the submission thereof to the States by the Congress.

AMENDMENT 22 (March 1, 1951)
Section 1. No person shall be elected to the office of the President more than twice, and no person who has held the office of President, or acted as President, for more than two years of a term to which some other person was elected President shall be elected to the office of the President more than once. But this Article shall not apply to any person holding the office of President when this Article was proposed by the Congress, and shall not prevent any person who may be holding the office of President, or acting as President, during the term

within which this Article becomes operative from holding the office of President or acting as President during the remainder of such term.

Section 2. This Article shall be inoperative unless it shall have been ratified as an amendment to the Constitution by the legislatures of three-fourths of the several States within seven years from the date of its submission to the States by the Congress.

AMENDMENT 23 (April 3, 1961)
Section 1. The District constituting the seat of Government of the United States shall appoint in such manner as the Congress may direct:

A number of electors of President and Vice President equal to the whole number of Senators and Representatives in Congress to which the District would be entitled if it were a State, but in no event more than the least populous State; they shall be in addition to those appointed by the States, but they shall be considered, for the purposes of the election of President and Vice President, to be electors appointed by a State; and they shall meet in the District and perform such duties as provided by the twelfth article of amendment.

Section 2. The Congress shall have power to enforce this article by appropriate legislation.

AMENDMENT 24 (February 4, 1964)
Section 1. The right of citizens of the United States to vote in any primary or other election for President or Vice President, for electors for President or Vice President, or for Senator or Representative in Congress, shall not be denied or abridged by the United States or any State by reason of failure to pay any poll tax or other tax.

Section 2. The Congress shall have power to enforce this article by appropriate legislation.

AMENDMENT 25 (February 10, 1967)

Section 1. In case of the removal of the President from office or of his death or resignation, the Vice President shall become President.

Section 2. Whenever there is a vacancy in the office of the Vice President, the President shall nominate a Vice President who shall take office upon confirmation by a majority vote of both houses of Congress.

Section 3. Whenever the President transmits to the President pro tempore of the Senate and Speaker of the House of Representatives his written declaration that he is unable to discharge the powers and duties of his office, and until he transmits to them a written declaration to the contrary, such powers and duties shall be discharged by the Vice President as Acting President.

Section 4. Whenever the Vice President and a majority of either the principal officers of the executive departments or of such other body as Congress may by law provide, transmit to the President pro tempore of the Senate and the Speaker of the House of Representatives their written declaration that the President is unable to discharge the powers and duties of his office, the Vice President shall immediately assume the powers and duties of the office as Acting President.

Thereafter, when the President transmits to the President pro tempore of the Senate and the Speaker of the House of Representatives his written declaration that no inability exists, he shall resume the powers and duties of his office unless the Vice President and a majority of either the principal officers of the executive department or of such other body as Congress may by law provide, transmit within four days to the President pro tempore of the Senate and the Speaker of the House of Representatives their written declaration that the President is unable to discharge the powers and duties of his office. Thereupon Congress shall decide the issue, assembling within forty-eight hours for that purpose if not in session. If the Congress, within twenty-one days after receipt of the latter declaration, or, if Congress is not in session, within twenty-one days after Congress is required to assemble, determines by two-thirds vote of both

Houses that the President is unable to discharge the powers and duties of his office, the Vice President shall continue to discharge the same as Acting President; otherwise, the President shall resume the powers and duties of his office.

AMENDMENT 26 (July 1, 1971)

Section 1. The right of citizens of the United States, who are eighteen years of age or older, to vote shall not be denied or abridged by the United States or by any State on account of age.

Section 2. The Congress shall have power to enforce this article by appropriate legislation.

AMENDMENT 27 (May 7, 1992)

No law, varying the compensation for the services of the Senators and Representatives, shall take effect, until an election of Representatives shall have intervened.

Appendix D:
Cross References Between the Declaration of Independence and the Constitution

Explanation of Cross Reference with Example

The Reference Key for the Declaration of Independence gives a short designation, such as DI-2, for parts of the Declaration, showing the words with which that part begins. In the case of DI-2, "We hold these Truths to be self-evident." Since DI-3 begins with, "He has refused his Assent to Laws," etc., looking at the Declaration, we find that DI-2 must end with, "To prove this, let Facts be submitted to a candid World."

The Cross Reference then relates the principles in each part of the Declaration to sections of the Constitution. For example, in the Reference Key for the Declaration, we see the following:

DI-11   "He has made Judges dependent on his Will alone, . . ."

Looking up the entire passage, it reads as follows:

He has made Judges dependent on his Will alone, for the Tenure
of their Offices, and the Amount and Payment of their Salaries.

Because the king could control how much each judge could be paid, and could
remove them at will, this would have a strong tendency to pressure each judge
to decide cases the way the king wanted them decided, whether according to
law or not.

Next to DI-11 in the Cross Reference we find "Art III Sect 1" referring to
Article three, Section one of the Constitution. Within that section we find this
sentence:

The Judges, both of the supreme and inferior Courts, shall hold
their Offices during good Behavior, and shall, at stated Times, receive for their Services, a Compensation, which shall not be diminished during their Continuance in Office.

Hence, judges cannot have their salaries reduced or be fired because they decided a case differently than Congress or the President may have preferred.

Abbreviated Paragraph or Clause Reference Key for the Declaration of Independence

DI-1   "When in the Course of human Events . . ."

DI-2   "We hold these Truths to be self-evident, . . ."

DI-3   "He has refused his Assent to Laws, the most wholesome and necessary . . ."

DI-4   "He has forbidden his Governors to pass Laws . . . unless suspended . . ."

DI-5   "He has refused to pass other Laws . . . unless . . . relinquish the Right of Representation in the Legislature . . ."

DI-6   "He has called together Legislative Bodies at Places unusual, . . ."

DI-7   "He has dissolved Representative Houses repeatedly, for opposing . . ."

DI-8   "He has refused for a long Time, after such Dissolutions, to cause others to be elected. . ."

DI-9   "He has endeavored to prevent the Population of these States . . ."

DI-10 "He has obstructed the Administration of Justice, by refusing . . . Judiciary Powers."

DI-11 "He has made Judges dependent on his Will alone, . . ."

DI-12 "He has erected a Multitude of new Offices, and sent hither Swarms of Officers . . ."

DI-13 "He has kept among us, in Times of Peace, Standing Armies . . ."

DI-14 "He has affected to render the Military independent of and superior to the Civil Power."

DI-15 "He has combined with others to subject us to a Jurisdiction foreign to . . ."

DI-16 "For quartering large Bodies of Armed Troops among us;"

DI-17 "For protecting them, by a mock Trial, from Punishment . . ."

DI-18 "For cutting off our Trade with all Parts of the World;"

DI-19 "For imposing Taxes on us without our Consent;"

DI-20 "For depriving us, in many Cases, of the Benefits of Trial by Jury;"

DI-21 "For transporting us beyond Seas to be tried for pretended Offences;"

DI-22 "For abolishing the free System of English Laws in a neighboring Province . . ."

DI-23   "For taking away our Charters, abolishing our most valuable Laws, and altering . . ."

DI-24   "For suspending our own Legislatures, and declaring themselves . . ."

DI-25   "He has abdicated Government here, by declaring us out of his Protection . . ."

DI-26   "He has plundered our Seas, ravaged our Coasts, burnt our Towns, and destroyed . . ."

DI-27   "He is, at this Time, transporting large Armies of foreign Mercenaries . . ."

DI-28   "He has constrained our fellow Citizens . . ."

DI-29   "He has excited domestic Insurrections amongst us, and has endeavoured . . ."

DI-30   "In every stage of these Oppressions . . . repeated Petitions . . . repeated Injury. . . ."

DI-31   "Nor have we been wanting in Attentions to our British Brethren. . . ."

DI-32   "We, therefore, the Representatives of the United States of America, . . ."

Reference Key for the Constitution

  Art: Article

 Sect: Section

   Cl: Clause

  Am: Amendment

For example, Art I Sect 9 Cl 2 represents Article one, Section nine, Clause two.

Cross References Between the Declaration of Independence and the Constitution

Declaration References	Constitution References
DI-1	Separate and equal station among the powers of the earth - Sovereignty Preamble; Art I Sect 1; Art II Sect 1; Art III Sect 1; Art VI Cl 2, 3
DI-2	Fundamental Statement of Rights Preamble; Art I Sect 2 Cl 1; Art I Sect 9 Cl 2, 3, 4, 5, 6, 8; Art I Sect 10 Cl 1; Am 1-10 Right to Alter Art V Laying its Foundation on such Principles, and organizing its Powers in such Form . . . Art I Sect 2 Cl 1, 2, Sect 3 Cl 1-3; Art I Sect 7 Cl 2, 3; Art II Sect 1 Cl 1, 5; Art III Sect 1, Sect 3; Art IV Sect 1, Sect 2 Cl 1, Sect 4; Art V; Art VI Cl 2, 3 general structure under Art I-III; separation of powers; checks; limited government of enumerated powers, for instance, Art I Sect 8
DI-3	Art I Sect 7 Cl 2, 3
DI-4	Art I Sect 7 Cl 2, 3
DI-5	Art I Sect 1, 2, 3
DI-6	Art I Sect 8 Cl 17; Art I Sect 5 Cl 4
DI-7	Art II Sect 3
DI-8	Preamble; Art I Sect 4 Cl 2; Am 20 Sect 2
DI-9	Art I Sect 8 Cl 4
DI-10	Art III Sect 1, 2; Art I Sect 8 Cl 9; Am 11
DI-11	Art III Sect 1
DI-12	Art I Sect 6 Cl 2; general structure under Art I-III; separation of powers, checks, limited government of enumerated powers (e.g., Art I Sect 8)
DI-13	Art I Sect 8 Cl 12, 14, 15, 16; especially Cl 12.

DI-14	Art II Sect 2 Cl 1
DI-15	Art I-III, and general structure; Art VI Cl 2, 3; Art II Sect 1 Cl 5, Sect 2 Cl 2; especially Art I Sect 1
DI-16	Am 3
DI-17	Art III Sect 2 Cl 3; Am 6
DI-18	Art I Sect 10 Cl 2, 3; Art I Sect 8 Cl 1, 3; Art I Sect 9 Cl 5, 6
DI-19	Art I Sect 7 Cl 1; Art I Sect 8 Cl 1
DI-20	Art III Sect 2 Cl 3; Am 6, 7
DI-21	Art III Sect 2 Cl 3; Am 6
DI-22, 23, 24	Art V; Art I Sect 1
DI-25-29	Preamble; Art I Sect 8 Cl 10-16; Art II Sect 2 Cl 1
DI-30	Am 1; Art II
DI-31	
DI-32	Preamble

Actions of the King and Royal Governors and Acts of Parliament
Related to the Declaration of Independence

Reference	Action
DI-2	Violations of American rights not specifically mentioned in the Declaration, would include the Hat Act (1732), with severe restrictions on who was allowed to make hats; the Iron Act (1750) forbidding iron mills in America; the use of "writs of assistance" (e.g., with the Townshend duties of 1767), a sort of uncontrolled search warrant; by a 1772 act, certain trade could only use ships built in Great Britain; closing the port of Boston, June 1, 1774.
DI-3	For example, colonial attempts to stop the transporting of slaves to America, either "by prohibitions, [or] by imposing duties which might amount to a prohibition," were "defeated by his Majesty's negative."
DI-4	". . . his Majesty [has] permitted our laws to lie neglected, in England, for years, neither confirming them by his assent, nor annulling them by his negative . . . And . . . by his instructions, has laid his Governors under such restrictions that they can pass no law, of any moment, unless it have such suspending clause [i.e., suspending the law until the king's agreement is obtained]."
DI-5	King George III instructed Virginia's Governor, to forbid "the division of a county, unless the new county will consent to have no representative" in the Virginia Assembly.
DI-7	Virginia's Royal Governors dissolved the Assembly in springs of 1769, 1773, and 1774.
DI-8	"After dissolving one House of Representatives, they have refused to call another . . ."
DI-9	". . . his Majesty has lately taken on him to advance the terms of purchase and holding, to the double of what they were . . ."
DI-11	Act for regulating the government of Massachusetts Bay (1774). See detail under DI-23.

DI-13   The British kept armies in America from the end of the French and Indian War in 1763 until Independence, stationed in various places, including New York, then Boston.

DI-15   The king supported the acts of Parliament, as described below.

DI-16   Quartering Acts (ten acts from 1765 to 1776).

DI-17   Act for the suppression of riots and tumults in Massachusetts Bay (1774). By this act, at the choice of the governor, anyone accused of murder in Massachusetts could be tried in Great Britain.

DI-18   Navigation Acts; Sugar Act (1764); trade act of 1768; New England Restraining Act (1775); Restraining Act on Pennsylvania, New Jersey, Maryland, Virginia, and South Carolina (1775). Various acts imposed various restrictions on where the colonies could trade. The two acts from 1775 restricted the colonies' trade to only Great Britain, Ireland, and the West Indies. An act in 1776 prohibited all American trade.

DI-19   Stamp Act (1765); Sugar Act (1764) duties on sugar, molasses, syrup, indigo, coffee, pimento, wine, silk, calico, linen cloth; a trade act in 1766 with more of the same; Townshend Act (1767) duties on glass, lead, paint colors, tea, paper; Tea Act (1773).

DI-20   Sugar Act (1764); trade act of 1768. Both called for violations to be tried in an admiralty or vice-admiralty court, which did not use juries.

DI-21   Act for the suppression of riots and tumults in Massachusetts Bay (1774). See DI-17.

DI-22   Quebec Act (1774). This act extended the boundary of Quebec south to the Ohio River, and provided an appointed rather than elected government.

DI-23   The Act for regulating the government of Massachusetts Bay (1774), changed the charter and structure of Massachusetts government. The council was to be appointed by the king, judges and sheriffs appointed or removed by the governor, and assembly denied except with the permission of the governor. In 1687 the Parliament tried to repeal the Connecticut charter. The colony refused to give it up. A few years later William and Mary recognized this charter, after coming to the throne in the "Glorious Revolution" of 1688.

DI-24   Act suspending the New York legislature (1767); Declaratory Act (1766), which claimed that Parliament "had, hath, and of right ought to have, full power and authority to make laws . . . of sufficient force and validity to bind the colonies . . . in all cases whatsoever."

DI-25   King George III declared the colonies in rebellion and out of his protection, August 23, 1775 (without waiting to see the Olive Branch Petition, presented September 1, 1775).

DI-26   The British attacked Lexington and Concord, and Breed's Hill and Bunker Hill. Charlestown, Massachusetts, was destroyed by fire due to British cannon. "Lord Dunmore [Royal Governor of Virginia] has commenced hostilities in Virginia. That people bore with everything, till he attempted to burn the town of Hampton." (Jefferson, *Letter to John Randolph, Esq.*, November 29, 1775)

DI-27   King George III hired German mercenaries. (Hessians)

DI-28   Impressment of sailors, the same practice that helped to bring on the War of 1812.

DI-29   The British successfully solicited the Mohawk tribe to fight Americans. For the truthfulness of Jefferson's description of the Amerindian methods of warfare, consult Francis Parkman's *The Conspiracy of Pontiac* (1851, 1870, history of events in 1763-64).

DI-30   America's numerous petitions, including those passed by colonial legislatures, from 1764 about the proposed Stamp Act, to much later, and by the First and Second Continental Congresses, to the Olive Branch Petition of 1775, were all treated the same. Bodies of the British government, whether the king, the Privy Council, or the Parliament, would not receive or respond to any of these petitions, except through scorn heaped on agents of the colonies, new infringements on America's liberty, and open warfare.

DI-31   The writings of Richard Bland, John Dickinson, Thomas Jefferson, etc., could potentially have affected the views of the British public. Benjamin Franklin tried for ten years to reconcile England and America and found it could not be done. In spite of their efforts, the Parliamentary elections of 1768 and 1774 still resulted in majorities willing to follow the unjust and coercive policies described in the Declaration of Independence.

The quotes in the descriptions above relative to DI-3, 4, 5, 8 and 9 are taken from Thomas Jefferson's *A Summary View of the Rights of British America* (1774). This description of the acts of the king, the governors who were chosen by the king and acted as his agents, and of Parliament, does not mention specifics for DI-6, 10, 12, and 14. However, with justifications cited for part or all of the other 25 points, I am willing to trust Jefferson's honesty on those four.

Some books say that the king was not a tyrant, nor guilty of the offenses Jefferson listed in the Declaration. This list of actions shows that he was—either directly, or through the royal governors, over whom he held the power of appointment and removal, or by consenting to the actions of Parliament. This list should not be thought complete, but it may be sufficient.

Exposition on the Cross Reference,
with Principles from the Declaration of Independence
and the Constitution

DI-1   A few years ago, a prominent political figure took the position that America's foreign policy needed to pass some kind of "global test." The first paragraph of the Declaration tells us that when the United States found it "necessary . . . to dissolve the Political Bands [that] connected them with" Great Britain, "a decent Respect to the Opinions of Mankind requires that they should declare the causes which impel them to the Separation." Hence the Founders wrote and adopted the Declaration to explain what they were doing and why. However, they did not need the permission of the rest of mankind to do it. To require that, would destroy "the separate and equal Station to which the Laws of Nature and of Nature's God entitle them," and make them slaves to the rest of mankind. Those "Laws of Nature" entitled them to take the action they did, as said in DI-32, "in the Name, and by Authority of the good People of these Colonies." That "separate and equal station" "among the powers of the earth" is called Sovereignty.

That sovereignty is assured in the Constitution by the identification of Congress as the sole legislative body; the President as the executive; defining the courts and their jurisdiction; and by defining the Constitution as the supreme law of the land.

DI-2   Fundamental Statement of Rights: "We hold these Truths to be self-evident, that all Men are created equal, that they are endowed by their Creator with certain inalienable Rights, that among these are Life, Liberty, and the Pursuit of Happiness—That to secure these Rights, Governments are instituted among Men, deriving their just Powers from the Consent of the Governed . . ."

The Constitution states its purposes in the Preamble, including justice and liberty. Article I Section 2 Clause 1 invokes the consent of the governed. Article I Sections 9 and 10, and Amendments 1 through 10, place specific limits on government to secure those rights spoken of by Jefferson in DI-2. Among the rights specifically mentioned are these: the writ of habeas corpus, which prevents government from arresting and holding a citizen without charge (Art I Sect 9 Cl 2); protection against bills of attainder, which inflict a punishment without trial; protection against ex post facto laws, which make an action a crime after it happened (Art I Sect 9 Cl 3, Sect 10 Cl 1); freedom of religion; freedom of speech; freedom of the press; freedom of assembly; the right to petition (Am 1); the right to keep and bear arms (Am 2); freedom from having troops quartered in your house (Am 3); freedom from unreasonable search and seizure (Am 4); when accused, the right to trial by jury, to counsel for your defense, to bring in witnesses in your favor, and to a local trial (Am 6); freedom from being forced to testify against yourself, and from being tried twice for the same offense (Am 5); freedom from excessive bail and from cruel and unusual punishment (Am 8).

The Right to Alter: ". . . that whenever any Form of Government becomes destructive of these Ends, it is the Right of the People to alter or to abolish it, and to institute new Government . . ."

Article V provides the means to amend the Constitution. Typically amendments are proposed by the vote of two thirds of both Houses of Congress, followed by ratification by the Legislatures of three fourths of the States, or by Conventions in three fourths of the States.

". . . to institute new Government, laying its Foundation on such Principles, and organizing its Powers in such Form, as to them shall seem most likely to effect their Safety and Happiness."

This is what the Founders did by writing and adopting the Constitution. The general structure of the government under the Constitution embodied several principles: federalism, representation and election, separation of powers, checks between departments, limited government of enumerated powers, trial by jury, a bill of rights, etc. Each branch was elected or appointed by a different method. The Founders so designed it as to give the people a strong voice in their government, while making it difficult for any one faction to gain control of all branches. By separating the legislative, executive and judicial powers, giving each department checks upon the others, and listing only certain powers that the people authorized their government to exercise, they hoped to preserve those inalienable rights spoken of in DI-2.

DI-3   "He has refused his Assent to Laws, the most wholesome and necessary for the public Good."

Article I Section 7 Clauses 2 and 3 of the Constitution describe how a bill or resolution becomes law. After passing both houses of Congress, the next step is for the bill to receive the approval of the President. The President can disapprove (veto) the bill and return it to Congress; that is part of the system of checks. However, if disapproved, the Congress can still pass the bill into law if each house passes it by a two thirds vote.

DI-4   "He has forbidden his Governors to pass Laws. . . unless suspended" until approved by the king, "and when so suspended, he has utterly neglected to attend to them."

In Article I Section 7 Clause 2 we find that if the President neglects a bill passed by Congress, it becomes law without his signature, if not returned "within ten Days (Sundays excepted) after it shall have been presented to him."

DI-5 This clause of the Declaration refers to the king's instruction to Virginia's governor not to allow the division of a county unless the new county would have no representation in the legislature.

Article I Sections 1, 2, and 3, assure the representation of the people in Congress, directly in the House of Representatives through election, and indirectly in the Senate through election of Senators by state legislatures, who are elected by the people. (The people now elect Senators directly as a result of Amendment 17.)

DI-6 "He has called together Legislative Bodies at Places unusual, uncomfortable, and distant from the Depository of their public Records, for the sole Purpose of fatiguing them into Compliance with his Measures."

In the Constitution, Article I Section 8 Clause 17 calls for the creation of "such District. . . as may . . . become the Seat of the Government of the United States," and gives Congress authority "To exercise exclusive Legislation" over such District. The District of Columbia, or Washington, D.C., has become this seat of government. It is where Congress always meets, and where its public records reside. Article I Section 5 Clause 4 specifies that "Neither House, during the Session of Congress, shall, without the Consent of the other, adjourn for more than three days, nor to any other Place than that in which the two Houses shall be sitting." No other person, department, or entity, is given any authority to determine where Congress shall meet.

DI-7   This is the complaint against the king for dissolving colonial legislatures.

The President may not dissolve Congress. Under Article II Section 3, he may call Congress into special session if there is a need ("he may, on extraordinary Occasions, convene both Houses, or either of them"), and "he may adjourn them to such Time as he shall think proper," but only "in Case of Disagreement between them, with Respect to the Time of Adjournment." Hence, if the two houses cannot agree on a time of adjournment, he can decide.

DI-8   In this part of the Declaration, Jefferson complains that after dissolving colonial legislatures, the king "has refused for a long Time, after such Dissolutions, to cause others to be elected."

In Article I Section 4 Clause 2, the Constitution requires that "The Congress shall assemble at least once in every Year." That clause named the first Monday in December as a date for that meeting, but allowed the Congress to "appoint a different day." Amendment 20 Section 2 named a different day, January third, but still allowed Congress to "appoint a different day" if they choose.

Another aspect of DI-8 is that Jefferson describes the consequences of a dissolved legislature is these terms: "the State remaining in the mean time exposed to all the Dangers of Invasion from without, and Convulsions within." This pair of concerns finds an exact match in the purposes of government stated in the Preamble, to "insure domestic Tranquility, [and] provide for the common defense."

DI-9   In this complaint, the Declaration says that the king has "obstruct[ed] the Laws for Naturalization of Foreigners."

Article I Section 8 Clause 4 gives Congress the power to "establish an uniform Rule of Naturalization," the process by which immigrants can become citizens.

DI-10   The king has "obstructed the Administration of Justice, by refusing his Assent to Laws for establishing Judiciary Powers."

Article III Section 1 does the establishing of the same, with these words: "The judicial Power of the United States, shall be vested in one supreme Court, and in such inferior Courts as the Congress may from time to time ordain and establish." Section 2 then specifies the extent of that judicial power; this was modified by Amendment 11. Article I Section 8 Clause 9 gave Congress power "To constitute Tribunals inferior to the supreme Court."

DI-11   "He has made Judges dependent on his Will alone, for the Tenure of their Offices, and the Amount and Payment of their Salaries." Because the king could control how much each judge could be paid, and could remove them at will, this would have a strong tendency to pressure each judge to decide cases the way the king wanted them decided, whether according to law or not. Article III Section 1 states, "The Judges, both of the supreme and inferior Courts, shall hold their Offices during good Behavior, and shall, at stated Times, receive for their Services, a Compensation, which shall not be diminished during their Continuance in Office." Hence, judges cannot have their salaries reduced or be fired because they decided a case differently than Congress or the President may have preferred.

DI-12   "He has erected a Multitude of new Offices, and sent hither Swarms of Officers to harass our People, and eat out their Substance."

The structure described earlier, with its separation of powers, its checks, and the limits on what government is allowed to do under the Constitution, should provide an answer to this complaint. A government kept within the bounds of the Constitution would be free of such a multitude of harassing officers. Its cost would also remain reasonable.

DI-13   "He has kept among us, in Times of Peace, Standing Armies, without the consent of our Legislatures." Standing armies have historically been a threat to freedom. Certainly a standing army from another jurisdiction, not of your own people, would especially threaten freedom.

Under Article I Section 8 Clauses 12, 14, 15 and 16, Congress was given power to raise armies, to organize, arm, and call forth the militia, and to make rules for governing such forces. Especially important is Clause 12, which states, "To raise and support Armies, but no Appropriation of Money to that Use shall be for a longer Term than two years." Every two years one third of the Senate and the entire House of Representatives are up for election. Hence this clause requires that every new Congress must appropriate funds for the maintenance of the army, the reserves, and the national guard, or those bodies would cease to exist. (The national guard is not the militia, and was created by act of Congress under clause 12 for raising and supporting armies, not under clause 15 or 16 that deal with the militia.) By the rules which they enact and the amounts they appropriate, Congress can effectively determine the size of the army, and whether it exists at all. It exists then, only with the consent of our national legislature.

DI-14   "He has affected to render the Military independent of and superior to the Civil Power." As with DI-13, this complains of a matter that seriously threatened the people's freedom.

Article II Section 2 Clause 1 begins, "The President shall be Commander in Chief of the Army and Navy of the United States, and of the Militia of the several States, when called into the actual Service of the United States." The Constitution thus makes the military subject to an elected, civil, officer.

DI-15 "He has combined with others [namely, Parliament] to subject us to a Jurisdiction foreign to our Constitution, and unacknowledged by our Laws; giving his Assent to their Acts of pretended Legislation." Jefferson here makes clear the colonies' position that Parliament had no legal nor moral right to legislate for the colonies.

Article I Section 1, "All legislative Powers herein granted shall be vested in a Congress of the United States, which shall consist of a Senate and House of Representatives." This specifies who shall make law for the United States. Article VI Cl 2 makes the Constitution the supreme law of the land, along with laws made in pursuance thereof, and treaties. Cl 3 requires that all government officers at all levels take an oath (or affirmation) to support the Constitution. With regard to treaties, the President may make them with the consent of the Senate (Art II Sect 2 Cl 2), but only a natural born citizen who has lived within the United States for at least fourteen years, and thirty five years of age, may serve as President (Art II Sect 1 Cl 5).

DI-16 (DI-16 through DI-24 list some of the "Acts of pretended Legislation" mentioned in DI-15 as attempts to subject the colonies to a foreign jurisdiction.) "For quartering large Bodies of Armed Troops among us."

Amendment 3, from the Bill of Rights: "No Soldier shall, in time of peace be quartered in any house, without the consent of the

Owner, nor in time of war, but in a manner to be prescribed by law."

DI-17 "For protecting them, by a mock Trial, from Punishment for any Murders which they should commit on the Inhabitants of these States." By the "Act for the suppression of riots and tumults in Massachusetts Bay," any murder committed in Boston could be tried in Britain. Considering the time and difficulty of travel between the two at the time, it seems doubtful that American witnesses would actually make the trip. British witnesses would be going home. Justice would not likely be served.

Under Article III Section 2 Clause 3, "The Trial of all Crimes, . . . shall be held in the State where the said Crimes shall have been committed." Amendment 6 also required that such trials be held in "the State and district wherein the crime shall have been committed; which district shall have been previously ascertained by law."

DI-18 "For cutting off our Trade with all Parts of the World." Many acts of Parliament sought to restrict the trade of the American colonies, and they grew more restrictive toward the end. These acts sought to benefit Britain at America's expense. In many cases, ships intending to bring goods to America were required to go first to Britain and there be taxed. Just before Independence, the Restraining acts of 1775 sought to prevent all trade for several colonies. After Independence, some of the states sought to follow the British example, by making laws giving preferences that led to trade wars between the states.

Hence the Constitution sought to rectify matters by clearing away all trade barriers between the states, making external trade laws uniform, and forbidding the taxing of exports. Article I

Section 10 Clause 2: "No State shall, without the Consent of the Congress, lay any Imposts or Duties on Imports or Exports, except what may be absolutely necessary for executing its inspection Laws." Hence no state can tax external trade, except as described, and cannot derive any net revenue from such. Any net goes to the national government, not the state. Clause 3 forbids states from "lay[ing] any Duty of Tonnage." Article I Section 8 Clause 1 gives Congress the power to impose taxes on imports, "but all Duties, Imposts and Excises shall be uniform throughout the United States." In the same section, Clause 3 gives Congress the power "To regulate Commerce with foreign Nations, and among the several States." This power is restricted by Article I Section 9 Clauses 5 and 6: "No Tax or Duty shall be laid on Articles exported from any State. No Preference shall be given by any Regulation of Commerce or Revenue to the Ports of one State over those of another: nor shall Vessels bound to, or from, one State, be obliged to enter, clear, or pay Duties in another."

DI-19   "For imposing Taxes on us without our Consent."

Article I Section 7 Clause 1 requires that "All Bills for raising Revenue shall originate in the House of Representatives." Thus bills on taxes must begin in the House closest to the people, and directly elected by them. Article I Section 8 Clause 1 gave Congress the power to "lay and collect Taxes, Duties, Imposts and Excises, to pay the Debts and provide for the common Defense and general Welfare of the United States." The national government needed this power to tax in order to survive. However, it was never intended to be an unlimited grant of power. Rather, it was only to pay the nation's debts, to provide for the common defense, and to carry out the other things authorized in Article I Section 8, which is all one sentence, of which Clause 1 is a part. Unfortunately, the clause has been used to justify raising taxes for any purpose whatsoever; and the words "general welfare" have been used to justify spending for the welfare of *specific* people; or even, for any purpose whatsoever. The list of the powers of Congress in Article I Section 8, was meant to limit the power of Congress to specific objects. This interpretation of Clause 1 has rendered the power of Congress virtually unlimited, and destroyed the purpose of the rest of the section. Madison spoke about this in the Federalist No. 41. (The quotation from Madison will be followed by an explanation in, I hope, simpler language.) Said he:

> But what color can [such an interpretation] have, when a specification of the objects alluded to by these general terms immediately follows and is not even separated by a longer pause than a semicolon? If the different parts of the same instrument ought to be so expounded as to give meaning to every part which will bear it, shall one part of the same sentence be excluded altogether from a share in the meaning; and shall the more doubtful and indefinite terms be retained in their full extent, and the clear and precise expressions be denied any signification whatsoever? For what purpose could the enumeration of particular powers be inserted, if these and all others were meant to be included in the preceding general power? Nothing is more natural nor common than first to use a general phrase, and then to explain and qualify it by a recital of particulars. But the idea of an enumeration of particulars which neither explain nor qualify the general meaning, and can have no other effect than to confound and mislead, is an absurdity.

In other words: The list of powers of Congress in Article I Section 8 is all one sentence. Hence those powers listed in Clauses 2 through 18 are only separated from Clause 1 by a semicolon.

Madison affirms that Clauses 2 to 18 give the specifics that explain the general terms in Clause 1. All parts of the sentence should have meaning. Clauses 2 through 18 should then clarify and explain. However, if Clause 1 is not limited by the rest of the section, but includes the powers there listed and the power to do anything and everything else for which money can be spent, then the rest of the section has no meaning. The Founders intended Section 8 to limit the powers of Congress to those listed. If the section does not do that, then the list serves no purpose. The idea that the Convention would have written such a section with no meaning, and which explains nothing, is absurd.

DI-20   "For depriving us, in many Cases, of the Benefits of Trial by Jury." A number of the acts of Parliament infringed on the right to trial by jury; for instance, by assigning cases to the court of admiralty, that did not use juries.

Article III Section 2 Clause 3 requires that "The Trial of all Crimes, except in Cases of Impeachment, shall be by Jury." When the Bill of Rights was added, Amendment 6 stated the same thing, but rephrased: "In all criminal prosecutions, the accused shall enjoy the right to a speedy and public trial, by an impartial jury of the State and district wherein the crime shall have been committed," and added the following rights in addition. Namely, "to be informed of the nature and cause of the accusation; to be confronted with the witnesses against him; to have compulsory process for obtaining witnesses in his favor, and to have the assistance of counsel for his defense."

Thomas Jefferson (in a letter to Thomas Paine, July 11, 1789) said of trial by jury, "I consider that as the only anchor ever yet imagined by man, by which a government can be held to the principles of its constitution." In order for the jury to serve such a function, it must possess both the right and the power to judge both law and fact–resolve both, as Hamilton said, "complicatedly," by a general verdict of guilty or not guilty. This means the jury have the right, by a verdict of not guilty, **to free a defendant accused of breaking an unconstitutional law.** They could also find the defendant not guilty if they concluded that the law was wrongly applied to the case, and to do so would cause an injustice. Such diverse men among our Founding Fathers as Alexander Hamilton, John Adams, John Jay, Theophilus Parsons and Thomas Jefferson, all believed the jury had the right to decide both law and fact. John Jay specifically endorsed this power of the jury speaking from the bench as Chief Justice of the Supreme Court. However, in the Sparf case in 1895 the Supreme Court ruled that the jury had to take the law from the judge.

Amendment 7 also assured trial by jury in suits at common law.

DI-21   "For transporting us beyond Seas to be tried for pretended Offences." The same act mentioned in discussing DI-17 applies here also. For a crime committed in Boston, the accused could be tried in England, and if the accused were American, DI-21 would apply. The same parts of the Constitution and Bill of Rights cited there, apply here also.

DI-22   "For abolishing the free System of English Laws in a neighboring Province, establishing therein an arbitrary Government, and enlarging its Boundaries." This refers to the Quebec Act. It may be that part of the intent in changing the method of government in Quebec was to give the French inhabitants forms that they were more accustomed to. However, that change, when combined with the boundary change, which extended Quebec all the way south to the Ohio River, alarmed the Americans. We will discuss Article V below.

DI-23   "For taking away our Charters, abolishing our most valuable Laws, and altering fundamentally the Forms of our Governments." Although many of the charters were written in a contractual form, apparently binding upon the British government, Parliament felt free to change the terms unilaterally at any time. Several times during the colonial period, charters were changed. In 1774 Parliament passed a bill to change the Massachusetts charter, and the structure and functions of its government.

Article V of our Constitution outlines the ways that amendments can be proposed and adopted. Since the Constitution's adoption, the United States have amended it twenty seven times to date. Congress has proposed amendments by a two thirds vote of each house, and those adopted have been approval by three fourths of the states, either through the state legislatures, or in one instance, by conventions held in each state.

DI-24   "For suspending our own Legislatures, and declaring themselves invested with Power to legislate for us in all Cases whatsoever." In 1767 Parliament passed a bill to suspend the New York legislature. The year before, they also passed the Declaratory Act, declaring that they could legislate for the colonies "in all cases whatsoever."

The Constitution's answers can again be found in Article V, and in Article I Section 1, which states that we have only given power to legislate for the United States to our Congress.

DI-25 to DI-29

When the king declared the colonies in America out of his protection in August 1775, **by law, the colonies no longer owed the king any allegiance.** DI-25 also tells us that the king was "waging war against us," and DI-26 to DI-29 describe the methods and means by which he did so, including with army, navy, and inciting insurrection.

The Preamble speaks of government's purposes, "to . . . insure domestic tranquility, [and] provide for the common defense." The means for doing so are outlined in Article I Section 8 Clauses 10 to 16, giving Congress power to punish piracy, to declare war, to create army and navy, and to use the militia. Article II Section 2 Clause 1 makes the President the commander in chief of all the armed forces.

DI-30

"In every stage of these Oppressions we have Petitioned for Redress in the most humble Terms: Our repeated Petitions have been answered only by repeated Injury. A Prince, whose Character is thus marked by every act which may define a Tyrant, is unfit to be the Ruler of a free People."

The first Amendment specifies that "Congress shall make no law . . . abridging the freedom of speech, or of the press, or the right of the people peaceably to assemble, and to petition the Government for a redress of grievances." Hence, Amendment 1 protects the right to petition; and since the king was judged "unfit to be the ruler of a free people," Article II creates the position of President, and makes that office an elected one.

DI-32

In 1766, Parliament in its arrogance, passed the Declaratory Act. That act declared that Parliament "*had, hath, and of right ought to have,* full power and authority to make laws and statutes of sufficient force and validity to bind the colonies . . . in all cases whatsoever." Ten years later, the Declaration of Independence answered as if in direct response to such language. The Congress chose to "solemnly Publish and Declare, That these United Colonies *are, and of Right ought to be,* Free and Independent States; that they are absolved from all Allegiance to the British

Crown, and that all political Connection between them and the State of Great-Britain, *is and ought to be* totally dissolved." Congress took this step as "the Representatives of the United States of America, in General Congress, Assembled," and "in the Name, and by Authority of the good People of these Colonies."

There are some who would suppress the study of at least part, if not all, of the Declaration from our schools, because of the repeated references to Deity contained in it. There are five such references, three of them in this final paragraph. In the first paragraph is the reference to the "Laws of Nature and of Nature's God." The second paragraph declares that all men "are endowed by their Creator with certain inalienable Rights." In the last paragraph, the representatives in Congress assembled declare the separation from Britain, "appealing to the Supreme Judge of the World for the Rectitude of our Intentions." Then in the last sentence, the document refers to the "protection of divine Providence," and makes an implied reference by use of the word "sacred." Hence they have called upon Deity to witness the uprightness of their intentions, and appealed for, or at least stated their trust in, divine protection. "And for the support of this Declaration, with a firm Reliance on the Protection of divine Providence, we mutually pledge to each other our Lives, our Fortunes, and our sacred Honor."

Abraham Lincoln, in speaking to the Young Men's Lyceum of Springfield, January 27, 1838, on "The perpetuation of our political institutions," said this:

Let every American, every lover of liberty, every well-wisher to his posterity swear by the blood of the Revolution never to violate in the least particular the laws of the country, and never to tolerate their violation by others. As the patriots of seventy-six did to the support of the Declaration of Independence, so to the support of the Constitution and laws let every American pledge his life, his property, and his sacred honor—let every man remember that to violate the law is to trample on the blood of his father, and to tear the charter of his own and his children's liberty.

Citations for Acts of Parliament

Navigation Acts
>   There were a number of these over the course of more than a century, beginning in 1651.

Sugar Act (1764)
>   4 Geo. 3 C. 15 - Statutes At Large Vol. 26, 33-52.

Stamp Act (1765)
>   5 Geo. 3 C. 12 - Statutes At Large Vol. 26, 179-204.

Declaratory Act (1766)
>   6 Geo. 3 C. 12 - Statutes At Large Vol. 27, 19-20.

trade act of 1766, duties on molasses, syrup, pimento, indigo, linen cloth
>   6 Geo. 3 C. 52 - Statutes At Large Vol. 27, 275-87

Townshend act (1766) duties on glass, lead, paint colors, tea, paper;
>   7 Geo. 3 C. 46 - Statutes At Large Vol. 27, 505-12.

trade act of 1768
>   8 Geo. 3 C. 22 - Statutes At Large Vol. 28, 70-71.

Tea Act (1773)
>   13 Geo. 3 C. 44 - Statutes At Large Vol. 30, 74-77.

Act to close the port of Boston (1774)
>   14 Geo. 3 C. 19 - Statutes At Large Vol. 30, 336-41.

Act for the suppression of riots and tumults in Massachusetts Bay. (1774)
>   14 Geo. 3 C. 39 - Statutes At Large Vol. 30, 367-71.

Act for better regulating the government of Massachusetts Bay (1774)
>   14 Geo. 3 C. 45 - Statutes At Large Vol. 30, 381-90.

Quebec Act (1774)
>   14 Geo. 3 C. 83 - Statutes At Large Vol. 30, 549-554.

New England Restraining Act (1775)
>   15 Geo 3 C. 10 - Statutes At Large Vol 31, 4-11.

Restraining Act on Pennsylvania, New Jersey, Maryland, Virginia, and South Carolina (1775).
>   15 Geo 3 C. 18 - Statutes At Large Vol 31, 37-43.

An act in 1776 prohibited all American trade
>   16 Geo 3 C. 5 - Statutes At Large Vol. 31, 135-154.

"Answers"

Common Law

1. Inherent: yours at birth, part of your nature.

Inalienable: cannot be sold or given away; because also inherent, hence part of nature.

2. Greater freedom in the Common Law approach.

3. Characteristics of Common Law: Kentucky. Characteristics of Civil Law: Colorado.

Roots of Independence

1. All but Georgia were privately financed, sometimes by individuals, sometimes by stock companies. Georgia was financed mostly by private sources, partly by appropriations from Parliament.

2. In my view, both the treaty with Virginia and the charters should have been treated as contracts that Britain was honor bound to follow. Nations will sometimes abandon or renegotiate treaties if conditions have changed and the old terms have become harmful to them. However, if one party abandons a treaty, then the other side is no longer bound by it. In that sense, when Britain failed to honor the charters, Americans were no longer obligated to associate with Britain nor submit to any governmental rule by her.

3. Yes, by the Virginia treaty and by the charters; by natural right, and the principle stated by Jefferson, that British troops must either be subject to local law or considered a hostile invasion force; and finally by the withdrawal of protection, which removed any obligation of allegiance to the king.

4. Many of the members of Parliament held offices in the government at the same time, which gave them more income. Apparently, in many cases, appointments to these offices were given by the Prime Minister in exchange for the members voting for his measures. Under Article I Section 6 Clause 2 of the U.S. Constitution, no member of Congress can hold any other government office. If appointed to such an office, to accept, the member must resign his or her seat in Congress. Furthermore, if a new office is created, or the pay for an office is increased during the term of a member of Congress, the member cannot be appointed to that office.

5. Protection, meaning for instance, that if America were attacked while under the protection of the king, that Britain would help defend her. One of the most basic purposes of government is to protect its citizens from invasion or foreign attack. By withdrawing protection, as Jefferson said in DI-25, the king had "abdicated government here."

6. Postponed for a year, to receive America's response. When the response came, Parliament refused to receive or consider it, hence abrogating the stated purpose for the delay.

7. None.

Basic Principles

1. Life and person; liberty; and the right to own and control property.

2. Enumerated powers are those specifically listed in the Constitution and thereby given to specific branches of the government. They are delegated to government by the people, who are the original holders of those powers. Their purpose is twofold; to see that appropriate powers are delegated, and to see that only those powers are granted to government that are listed. Thus, the enumeration of certain powers is intended to place limits on government, in order for the people to remain free.

3. The separation of powers seeks to prevent the accumulation of legislative, executive and judicial power in the same hands, which enables tyranny. The founders wanted the checks between departments to keep those departments from exceeding their authority. These two principles, if followed, would help keep the people free.

4. Democracies have historically been unstable, and have not respected human rights. See the quotes from Madison and Tyler.

The Structure of Government Under the U.S. Constitution

1. The members of the House of Representatives were to represent the people. Senators were to represent the states.

2. The oath of office should bind the conscience of the officer taking the oath.

3. The Constitution requires all officers in all branches (legislative, executive, judicial) at all levels (Federal, state, city, county, etc.) to take an oath to support the U.S. Constitution.

4. The President may not dissolve Congress. If the two houses cannot agree on when to adjourn, the President may adjourn Congress. He may also call them into special session if he feels the need.

5. Some of the flaws of the Weimar Republic included: allowing one house to overrule the other; having both a President and a Chancellor; allowing the President or the Reichstag to suspend much of the country's constitutional rights; allowing the legislature to delegate its authority to a single officer; allowing rule by decree.

The Declaration of Independence and the U.S. Constitution

1. See Cross References. (Appendix D)

2. That passage of the Declaration describes well what Americans did in writing the Constitution and Bill of Rights. The nine principles listed in the section on Basic Principles form the general foundation. Skousen in the *The Making of America* lists 242 principles from the Constitution through the Tenth Amendment.

The Judiciary and Judicial Review

1. Opinions differ on this. Hamilton in the Federalist no. 78, and Marshall in Marbury v. Madison give an argument for Judicial Review, and Jefferson's letter to Madison implies it. Certainly as Marshall said, "the constitution is superior to any ordinary act of the legislature." That principle should apply to **all branches** of the government, not just the judiciary.

2. The independence of the judiciary is established by the provisions that allow members thereof to hold office "during good behavior" (essentially for life or until they resign), and that their compensation cannot be "diminished during their continuance in office." Article III Section 1.

3. Some in our time would say that the courts have not kept to their own department, but have taken in many cases to legislating from the bench. The checks on the judiciary are these: impeachment and removal from office, which has almost never been effective; appointment by the President, and confirmation by the Senate; the power of the Congress to propose amendments to the Constitution; and the power of the Congress to make exceptions and regulations regarding the Supreme Court's appellate jurisdiction. Appointment and confirmation affect who becomes a judge or Justice. While important, they have no effect on a sitting court that's running amuck. They can have a preventive effect, or a corrective one if sufficient vacancies occur, perhaps after many years and a great deal of damage to the Republic.

Trial by Jury

1. There are differences of opinion on this subject. Those favoring this power of the jury, refer to it as the right or power to judge both law and fact and to resolve both by a general verdict. Those opposed to this power refer to it as "jury nullification," implying that the jury is nullifying the law. However, if the jury is upholding the Constitution, then the law in question, or as given by the judge, is at fault, and the jury is upholding the basic and fundamental law as it should be upheld. The view of the court in the Sparf case can be considered that of an entity trying to enlarge, solidify and keep its power. I believe in the principles expressed by Jay and Jefferson.

2. Some may say that defending the Constitution is not the job of the jury. On this, I'm with Jefferson. Every legitimate means to defend the Constitution should be employed. In the trial of Throckmorton in 1554, and the seven bishops in 1688, the jury settled questions of law and fact, and of what here would have been questions of Constitutional law. When men of such diverse views as Jay, Jefferson, Hamilton, and Adams all believed in the power of the jury to resolve both law and fact, there can be no doubt that juries traditionally held, and should hold, this power.

3. They clearly can only act as a check on the judiciary if they continue to have this power. This may be the only practical check on the judiciary. Impeachment as a check is clearly ineffective.

The Second Amendment

1. Logically, "the right of the people" should include essentially the same people in the First, Second, Fourth, Ninth and Tenth Amendments.

2. For myself, by context, by historical background, and by logic, the independent clause must carry more importance and meaning than the dependent clause.

3. I believe we should interpret the Constitution according to the original intent. That means, the broad meaning of the militia from that period: except for felons, every able bodied man. Clearly, the original intent would most adequately protect our freedom.

Gibbons v. Ogden

1. A few examples of interstate commerce: transporting goods by truck or by rail across state lines; people driving across state lines; transporting people by bus, van, train, or airplane, across state lines; the sale or purchase of stocks, bonds, or commodities, between people of different states, or through the use of a broker or exchange in another state; in most cases, the sale or purchase of goods over the internet; telephone calls between people in different states.

   A purchase at a store or restaurant that was part of a bus or train station, or an airport, for the convenience of persons traveling in interstate commerce, would probably be considered interstate commerce.

   A few examples of intrastate commerce: the employee-employer relationship, where the work is carried out within one state; farming, mining, or manufacturing, where the activity is carried out within one state; a purchase at a local store or restaurant, in most cases, regardless of whether the product has previously traveled across state lines. It was long considered settled law regarding goods that had traveled in interstate commerce, that once they had come to rest, and been commingled with other goods, that such goods then lost their interstate character.

   So it used to say in the section on Commerce in Corpus Juris Secundum (CJS)—and to some extent, still does. Thus in Volume 15, Section 29, page 291, we find, "The local sale of goods after they have been brought into the state from another state and have come to rest is not a transaction in interstate commerce." And on the same page, in Section 28, "Interstate commerce ceases when the product has come to rest definitely at a given point, as when the articles carried arrive at their destination and are there held for final disposal or use." But since Katzenbach v. McClung, 379 U.S. 294

(1964), there is now this in the previous sentence in Section 28: "However, with respect to the power of federal regulation, interstate commerce does not necessarily end when goods come to rest in the state of destination."[70] Hence, the Supreme Court's decisions have caused the wording in CJS to now be unclear and self contradictory.

2. For Congress to have power to regulate *all* commerce would give enormous power to the legislative branch. This power would be far greater than the power to regulate only commerce between states (interstate) and with foreign countries. As illustrated in the answer given to the previous question, the power over interstate commerce would not reach many commercial activities.

Under the Articles of Confederation, many of the states enacted tariffs and duties against other states. The resulting "trade wars" formed a major part of the reasons for creating the Constitution. In Madison's view, the founders wrote the commerce clause to end these barriers to trade between states, with Congress as the only body to whom they could give the power to correct the problem. Hence, they may not have intended it as a positive grant of power, as much as a restraining power on the abuses of the states.

Texas and Mexico

1. I will let you figure this one out.

2. Mexico did not honor either river as a boundary.

3. I can't think of any other way. Mexico could have tried to negotiate with the U.S. when President Polk sent John Slidell to Mexico City. However, perhaps because Slidell wanted to negotiate at least three different issues that they wanted kept separate, the Mexicans refused to negotiate with him. Of course, we cannot know whether a satisfactory settlement could have resulted, had they done so. In essence, Mexico chose war. If Mexican troops had not crossed the Rio Grande and battled U.S. troops, Polk may have chosen war anyway.

4. Whether the U.S. owned the ground between the two rivers could depend on whether the treaty signed by Santa Anna was valid. We could also consider the question of who exercised actual control over the area: probably Texas and the U.S. (if either party).

5. Had I served in Congress at the time, I would have voted for the Wilmot Proviso, to prohibit slavery from any territory gained in the settlement of the War with Mexico. However, when it could not get through the Senate, rather than continue the impasse or cause the Union to split, I would have consented to the Compromise of 1850.

Nullification and Secession

1. Ratification of the Constitution occurred state by state, ratified, however, by conventions, not by legislatures. During the debates on ratification, Patrick Henry objected strenuously to the wording in the Preamble, "We the People." He therefore, thought the term significant. His argument contended that if the United States was a confederation, it should be formed by the states. If formed by the people, then it must be one nation.

2. Congress cannot pass an unconstitutional law "in pursuance" of the Constitution. That seems obvious. However, states cannot nullify even such a law. They can, however, seek to overturn it. If they have "standing" to sue, they can challenge the law before the Supreme Court. Under the original terms of the Constitution (before the 17th Amendment), the state legislatures elected the Senators. Hence, as Senators' terms expired, the state legislatures could seek to replace those who voted for the unconstitutional law. Of course, the people could vote to replace the Representatives who voted for it.

3. I cannot see why any theory should take precedence over the express words of the Constitution.

4. When men from South Carolina fired on Fort Sumter, they waged war on the United States, and that constitutes treason. The South paid a terrible

price. So did the North, for that matter. It was good that Grant gave generous terms to Lee's army when they surrendered at Appomattox. One of
those terms was the assurance that they would not be tried for treason.

Lawlessness and Lincoln's Address to the Young Men's Lyceum of Springfield

1. Mob rule undermines regard for law in at least two ways. First, by bad example, which encourages imitation. Second, by convincing friends of law
and order that they are not safe, that the law will not protect them.

2. The Boston Tea Party destroyed property, but did not harm persons. We
have discussed in the section on Roots of Independence, some of the circumstances. The mobs in Jackson County, Missouri, and those discussed
by Lincoln did harm persons, and with far less cause. The mob in Jackson
County made their declaration in defiance of law. As shown earlier, the Declaration of Independence stood on solid legal grounds.

3. Personally, I agree with Lincoln, even in this era of missiles and atomic
weapons. "As a nation of freemen, we must live through all time, or die by
suicide." The greatest dangers to our freedom will arise from within.

4. No.

5. The Eleventh Amendment would almost certainly prevent any such suit.
The Fourteenth Amendment, with its passage, "No State shall make or enforce any law which shall abridge the privileges or immunities of citizens of
the United States; nor shall any State deprive any person of life, liberty, or
property, without due process of law; nor deny to any person within its jurisdiction the equal protection of the laws," could give grounds for a suit,
for Missouri certainly violated this and several other parts of the Constitution. However, one cannot say with certainty that the courts would have allowed such a suit. The Eleventh may still have provided grounds to preclude
it. Of course, this is all hypothetical.

Lincoln's Speech at Peoria in 1854

1. The quote from Bastiat describes it perfectly. Slavery and morality cannot be reconciled. The prolonged existence of a conflict between law and morality tends to dull the conscience of those who benefit from the warped law. They excuse their conduct or the unfairness of the law, and eventually conclude that it is just and right. All forms of legal plunder tend to have the same effect. Those whose conduct brings public censure may also seek legal acceptance or approval, to justify their conduct. On the other side of the slavery issue, some of the abolitionists expressed a willingness to trample the Constitution to get what they wanted. They did not seem to realize that such actions would set precedents that would endanger their own freedom. Some, such as John Brown, resorted to violence. By their actions they helped create hostility and lawlessness in their opponents. Then reason departs.

   In our day, prolonged legal plunder embedded in the laws has contributed to moral decline.

Lincoln's Reply in the Seventh Debate at Alton, 1858.

1. "You toil, and work, and earn bread, and I'll eat it." In other words, one person taking by force the product of another person's work. Hence, theft. Other aspects include controlling or dictating the course of life, and restrictions on action, for instance, preventing the slave from leaving.

Economics

1. Key economic principles include: Smith's "invisible hand"; Say's Law (demand comes from supply or production); Bastiat's principle that in evaluating any action we must consider not only what is seen, but also what is not seen.

2. Economic growth depends on: freedom, incentive, initiative, production, saving and investment.

3. Keynes seemed ignorant of Bastiat's principle of what is seen and what is not seen, and did not believe in Say's Law.

Wickard v. Filburn

1. In my opinion, Wickard v. Filburn cannot be reconciled with Gibbons v. Ogden. The later case seriously abuses the Constitution and the concept of interstate commerce. It rests upon a foundation of sand. Logically, Jackson's argument promulgates sophistry, based on hypotheticals.

2. No number is provided, because none can be provided. How many would justify the conclusion? Justice Jackson would not or could not suggest a number that would justify it. No number could justify it, because the decision is wrong.

3. Jackson's argument is deeply flawed. Logically, no one can draw any meaningful distinction between Jackson's "many others similarly situated," and any similar number of protesting taxpayers. The only real difference lies between something government wants, and something it does not want to allow.

4. I think Senator Ervin hits closer to the mark. However, I think assigning the case to a legal Smithsonian not sufficient; the Supreme Court should specifically overrule it.

Carter, Reagan, etc.

1. Cut taxes and reduce regulations.

2. Ninety percent taxes essentially amount to slavery. Because the highest rates fall on those with the highest income, the person may not be reduced to the level of poverty we associate with slavery. However, this removes any reason for the person to make the effort to continue earning. The person affected may still have some freedom of action. However, they typically cannot escape (except by leaving the country and renouncing their citizenship), as slaves sometimes escaped. Such taxes destroy incentive and damage the country's economy. Refer back to the quote from Supreme Court Justice Sutherland (see above in the section on the Constitution, subsection on Basic Principles): "To give [a man] his liberty but take from him the property which is the fruit and badge of his liberty, is to still leave him a slave."

Notes

Introduction

1. "Address to the Young Men's Lyceum of Springfield," January 27, 1838. Philip Van Doren Stern, editor, *The Life and Writings of Abraham Lincoln* (New York: The Modern Library, Random House, 1940), 232 [hereafter Stern, *Writings of Lincoln*].

2. "Letter to George Washington Lewis[?]," October 25, 1825. Adrienne Koch and William Peden, *The Life and Selected Writings of Thomas Jefferson* (New York: Random House, 1993), 661 [hereafter Koch and Peden, *Writings of Jefferson*].

3. "Letter to Colonel William Duane," August 12, 1810. Ibid., 555.

4. "Letter to Benjamin Rush," September 23, 1800. Ibid., 511.

5. *Holy Bible, John* 8:32.

FOREWORD   America - Land of Freedom and Opportunity

1. *The Federalist Papers*, No. 14 (New York: The New American Library, 1961), 104.

2. Ernest Lee Tuveson, *Redeemer Nation* (Chicago: University of Chicago Press, 1974), 25.

3. "Letter to Roger C. Weightman," June 24, 1826. Koch and Peden, *Writings of Jefferson,* 666.

4. Personal papers, 1984, published in edited form in *National Forum*, Fall, 1984, 14.

5. "Address Before the Wisconsin State Agricultural Society, Milwaukee," September 30, 1859. Stern, *Writings of Lincoln*, 561.

6. Donzella Cross Boyle, *Quest of a Hemisphere* (Appleton, Wisconsin: Western Islands, 1970), 511.

7. "Speech at Edwardsville," September 11, 1858. Stern, *Writings of Lincoln*, 483.

8. "Letter to Colonel Charles Yancey," January 6, 1816. Henry A. Washington, editor, *The Writings of Thomas Jefferson* (New York: H. W. Derby, 1861), vol. 6, 517 [hereafter, Washington, *Writings of Thomas Jefferson*].

CHAPTER ONE   For a Foundation of Freedom: Colonial and Pre-Colonial Issues

1. J. Reuben Clark, November 29, 1952. Jerreld L. Newquist, compiler, *Prophets, Principles and National Survival* (Salt Lake City: Publishers Press, 1964), 76, 78.

2. Arthur R. Hogue, *Origins of the Common Law* (Bloomington: Indiana University Press, 1966; reprinted, Indianapolis: Liberty Fund, Inc., 1985), xiii, 5 [hereafter Hogue, *Origins of Common Law*].

3. Ibid., 6. Hogue here quotes Walter Ullmann, *Principles of Government and Politics in the Middle Ages* (New York: Methuen, 1961), 166-67.

4. *Notes on Virginia*, Query XIV. Koch and Peden, *Writings of Jefferson*, 236-37.

5. "Letter to Dr. Thomas Cooper," February 10, 1814. Washington, *Writings of Thomas Jefferson*, vol. 6, 314-15. There Jefferson states, "For we know that the common law is that system of law which was introduced by the Saxons on their settlement in England, and altered from time to time by proper legislative authority from that time to the date of Magna Carta…" See also his "Letter to George Wythe," November 1, 1778. Julian P. Boyd, editor, *The Papers of Thomas Jefferson* (Princeton, New Jersey: Princeton University Press, 1950), vol. 2, 230. Jefferson there says, "The extracts from the Anglo-Saxon laws, the sources of the Common law, I wrote in their original for my own satisfaction…"

6. J. E. A. Jolliffe, *The Constitutional History of Medieval England from the English settlement to 1485*, (New York: W. W. Norton & Company, Inc., 1961), 72 [hereafter Jolliffe, *Constitutional History*].

7. "Letter to Edward Everett," October 15, 1824. Washington, *Writings of Thomas Jefferson*, vol. 7, 382. In his "Letter to Thomas Cooper," February 10, 1814, he quotes Hale to the effect that these laws were not handed down only be oral means, saying, "For all those laws have their several monuments in writing..." Washington, *Writings of Thomas Jefferson*, vol. 6, 314.

8. *Notes on Virginia*, Koch and Peden, *Writings of Jefferson*, 237.

9. Letter to Edmund Pendleton, August 13, 1776. See W. Cleon Skousen, *The Making of America – the Substance and Meaning of the Constitution* (Washington, D.C.: The National Center for Constitutional Studies, 1985), 33, 56 [hereafter Skousen, *Making of America*].

10. "A Summary View of the Rights of British America." Koch and Peden, *Writings of Jefferson*, 285.

11. Jolliffe, *Constitutional History*, 72.

12. Ibid., 74.

13. Thus Jolliffe speaks of "the feudal practice which is to be grafted upon England after the Conquest" (*Constitutional History*, 72). He also quotes Stubbs: "Feudalism in both tenure and government was, so far as it existed in England, brought full-grown from France." (*Constitutional History*, 139, quoting from Stubbs, *Constitutional History of England*, i. 273 n.) "France" refers, of course, to the Norman invasion.

14. "A Summary View of the Rights of British America." Koch and Peden, *Writings of Jefferson*, 286.

15. Ibid. In terms similar to Jefferson's account, Jolliffe speaks of "the destruction of the ancient alodial right of Englishmen and its replacement by feudal tenure," [*Constitutional History*, 139] and describes steps taken by the Normans toward that end.

16. Hogue, *Origins of Common Law*, 104.

17. "A Summary View of the Rights of British America." Koch and Peden, *Writings of Jefferson*, 286.

18. Ibid.

19. Thomas Jefferson, original draft of the Declaration of Independence. See Jefferson's *Autobiography*, Koch and Peden, *Writings of Jefferson*, 24.

20. *The Book of Popular Science* (New York: The Grolier Society, Inc., 1959), vol. 8, 217.

21. Francis Parkman's work as historian on relations with Amerindians deserves respect. He used many original sources, visited historical sites, knew fur trader Pierre Chouteau who knew Pontiac, and in the summer of 1846 Parkman lived for a time with the Sioux. In describing his experiences in *The Oregon Trail*, he admits to actions of his own that may put him in a bad light. As you may see in the next two paragraphs, he cites the facts as he knows them, regardless of which "side" they may appear to benefit.

22. Francis Parkman, *The Conspiracy of Pontiac and the Indian War After the Conquest of Canada* (New York: The Library of America, 1991), 414. [hereafter Parkman, *The Conspiracy of Pontiac*. Parkman's 1870 edition has been bound with *The Oregon Trail* in one volume under the Library of America imprint, and it is from this volume that page numbers and citations will be given.] The quote from Bancroft, *Hist. U. S.* II, 98, and from *Instructions to Endicot*, 1629, are from a footnote.

23. Ibid., 413-14. In particular, see the footnote on 414.

24. Ibid., 414-18.

25. Parkman first published *The Conspiracy of Pontiac* in 1851. He continued to research and add corrections and additional material until 1870, when he published an edition in the final form.

26. Parkman, *The Conspiracy of Pontiac*, 477.

27. Ibid., 478.

28. Ibid., 476.

29. Ibid., 593-612, especially 594-96. Regarding the drinking of the blood of the slain, see page 596, and regarding the murder of prisoners and cannibalism, see page 606.

30. Ibid., 509-10, 513-26, especially 510, 515-16, 517-19.

31. Ibid., 479.

32. Ibid., 681, 691, 683, respectively.

33. In addition to Parkman's book, some of this information is derived from a biography of Benjamin Franklin: Thomas Fleming, *The Man Who Dared the Lightning* (New York: William Morrow and Company, Inc., 1971), 114-120 [hereafter Fleming, *Man Who Dared*].

34. For example, see Wallace K. Ferguson, Geoffrey Bruun, *A Survey of European Civilization*, vol. II, *Since 1500* (Boston: Houghton Mifflin Company, 1962), 406, 408 [hereafter Ferguson and Bruun, *Survey of European Civilization*].

35. Thomas Bayly Howell, *State Trials* (London: Longman, Hurst, Rees, Orme, and Brown, 1816) vol. 1, 163-76, 219-26 [hereafter Howell, *State Trials*].

36. For example, regarding the persecution of Quakers, see the trial of William Penn and William Mead for a tumultuous assembly, in 1670, and when they were acquitted, the trial of Edward Bushell who had been on the jury. Howell, *State Trials*, vol. 6, 951-970, 999-1026.

37. Ferguson and Bruun, *Survey of European Civilization*, 520.

38. Jefferson, "An Act for establishing Religious Freedom [1779], passed in the Assembly of Virginia in the beginning of the year 1786." Koch and Peden, *Writings of Jefferson*, 290 (289-91).

CHAPTER TWO Roots of America's Declaration of Independence

1. Max Seville, *The Foundations of American Civilization–A History of Colonial America* (New York: Henry Holt and Company, 1942; Westport, Connecticut: Greenwood Press, 1970), 527 [hereafter Seville, *Foundations of American Civilization*]. R. C. Simmons, *The American Colonies from Settlement to Independence* (New York: W. W. Norton & Company, Inc., 1976), 241, 275 [hereafter Simmons, *American Colonies*]. Morton Borden, Otis Graham, Jr., et. al., *Portrait of a Nation–A History of the United States* (Lexington, Massachusetts: D. C. Heath and Company, 1973), vol. I, 16 [hereafter Borden and Graham, et. al., *Portrait of a Nation*].

2. Simmons, *American Colonies*, 12-13, 16, 23.

3. Francis Newton Thorpe, *American Charters, Constitutions, and Organic Laws 1492-1908*, 7 vols., Volume 3, 1677 [hereafter Thorpe, *American Charters, Constitutions*].

4. Lawrence H. Leder, *America 1603-1789–Prelude to a Nation* (Minneapolis: Burgess Publishing Company, 1972), 110. Seville, *Foundations of American Civilization*, 527. Simmons, *American Colonies*, 241, 275. Borden and Graham, et. al., *Portrait of a Nation*, vol. I, 16.

5. See Thomas Jefferson, *Notes On Virginia*, Koch and Peden, *Writings of Jefferson*, 217-19.

6. Thorpe, *American Charters, Constitutions*, Volume 7, 3788, 3800; Volume 3, 1880; Volume 6, 3220.

7. Ibid., Volume 1, 533.

8. Ibid., Volume 2, 773.

9. Ibid., Volume 3, 1681.

10. Ibid., Volume 1, 536; Volume 2, 777.

11. Ibid., Volume 7, 3801.

12. Ibid., Volume 3, 1840; Volume 5, 2750; Volume 6, 3220.

13. Ibid., Volume 1, 534-35.

14. Ibid., Volume 3, 1884; Volume 6, 3218; Volume 7, 3799-3800.

15. Thomas Jefferson, "A Summary View of the Rights of British America." Koch and Peden, *Writings of Jefferson*, 287.

16. *Notes on Virginia*, Query XIII. Ibid., 219-20.

17. *The Anas*. Ibid., 117.

18. "A Summary View of the Rights of British America," Ibid., 279.

19. Fleming, *Man Who Dared*, 262, 177.

20. Ibid, 275.

21. Ibid, 271-2.

22. "Letter to Dr. William Small," May 7, 1775. Koch and Peden, *Writings of Jefferson*, 334.

23. *Notes on Virginia*, Query XIII. Ibid., 221.

24. Fleming, *Man Who Dared.*, 156-57.

25. Koch and Peden, *Writings of Jefferson*, 336.

26. Fleming, *Man Who Dared*, 156.

27. *Autobiography*. Koch and Peden, *Writings of Jefferson*, 26-27.

28. "Letter to John Randolph, Esq.," November 29, 1775. Ibid., 335.

29. Skousen, *Making of America*, 24.

30. *Autobiography*. Koch and Peden, *Writings of Jefferson*, 19.

31. *Declaration of Independence*.

32. Jefferson, *Notes on Virginia*, Query XXIII. Koch and Peden, *Writings of Jefferson*, 266.

33. Fleming, *Man Who Dared*, 134.

34. Jefferson, *Notes on Virginia*, Query XXIII. Koch and Peden, *Writings of Jefferson*, 266.

35. Fleming, *Man Who Dared*, 274.

36. Ibid., 282.

37. Jefferson, *Autobiography*, Koch and Peden, *Writings of Jefferson*, 14.

38. Peter D. G. Thomas, *Tea Party to Independence–The Third Phase of the American Revolution 1773-1776* (Oxford: Clarendon Press, 1991), 261 [hereafter Thomas, *Tea Party to Independence*].

39. Jefferson, *Autobiography*. Koch and Peden, *Writings of Jefferson*, 16.

40. Ibid., 16.

41. Thomas, *Tea Party to Independence*, 262-63.

42. "Letter to John Randolph, Esq.," November 29, 1775. Koch and Peden, *Writings of Jefferson*, 335.

43. "A Summary View of the Rights of British America," Ibid., 273.

CHAPTER THREE **The Constitution of the United States**

1. Frederic Bastiat, *The Law* (France, 1850. English translation: New York: The Foundation for Economic Education, Irvington-On-Hudson, 1950), 5-6 [hereafter Bastiat, *The Law*].

2. faculties: talents and abilities, both physical and mental.

3. *The Federalist Papers,* no. 10 (e.g., (New York: "A Mentor Book," The New American Library, 1961), 78).

4. Quoted in Jerreld L. Newquist, *Prophets, Principles and National Survival* (Salt Lake City: Publishers Press, 1964), 175.

5. "Letter to Colonel Carrington," May 27, 1788. Koch and Peden, *Writings of Jefferson*, 413.

6. *The Federalist Papers*, No. 51, 322.

7. *The Federalist Papers*, No. 47, 301.

8. *Notes On Virginia*, Query XIII. Koch and Peden, *Writings of Jefferson*, 222.

9. *The Federalist Papers*, No. 10, 81.

10. Quoted in Skousen, *Making of America*, 265. On page 264, Skousen describes the experience of ancient Athens illustrating Tyler's statement.

11. *The Federalist Papers*, No. 41, 263.

12. *Autobiography*, Koch and Peden, *Writings of Jefferson*, 11-12.

13. "A Summary View of the Rights of British America." Ibid., 287.

14. Alexander Hamilton, *The Federalist Papers,* no. 78, 466-67.

15. Skousen, *Making of America*, 595.

16. "Letter to James Madison," March 15, 1789. Koch and Peden, *Writings of Jefferson*, 426.

17. Quoted in 156 U.S. 143, from 2 *John Adams' Works*, 253-55.

18. *Notes on Virgina*, Query XIV. Koch and Peden, *Writings of Jefferson*, 231.

19. Howell's *State Trials*, vol. 12, beginning at 183.

20. 3 Dall. 1. (Reports of U.S. Supreme Court cases from that period.)

21. "Letter to Thomas Paine," July 11, 1789. Koch and Peden, *Writings of Jefferson*, 442.

22. George Washington, *Farewell Address*, September 17, 1796. Newquist, *Prophets, Principles and National Survival*, 544-45.

23. *Notes On Virginia*, Query XVIII. Koch and Peden, *Writings of Jefferson*, 258.

24. From an address by Dallin H. Oaks, February 29, 1992, reported in *The Ensign*, October 1992, 60.

25. "Letter to Benjamin Rush," September 23, 1800, Koch and Peden, *Writings of Jefferson*, 511.

26. Bastiat, *The Law*, 6.

27. Ibid., 6.

28. "A Summary View of the Rights of British America." Koch and Peden, *Writings of Jefferson*, 287.

29. Ibid., 279.

30. "The Right to Keep and Bear Arms," Report of the Senate Subcommittee on the Constitution (Washington: U.S. Government Printing Office, February 1982), 1-12, quoted by Skousen, *Making of America*, 700.

31. U.S. Code, Title 10, section 31.

32. Report previously cited, quoted in Skousen, *Making of America*, 699.

33. Dave Kopel, "Gun Bans & Genocide - The Disarming Facts," *America's 1ˢᵗ Freedom*, Volume 7, Number 8 (August 2006), 33-35. Mr. Kopel cites Gregory Stanton of Genocide Watch, the U.S. State Department, Peter Verney of *Sudan Update*, and professor Eric Reeves of Smith College, among others.

34. "Letter to James Madison," December 20, 1787. Koch and Peden, *Writings of Jefferson*, 405.

35. Gibbons v. Ogden, 22 U.S. (9 Wheat.) 1, 6 L.Ed.2d 23 (1824). Such a citation indicates that the record for the case begins on page 1 of volume 22 of the U.S. Reports, which record Supreme Court decisions, with the various opinions given by the justices, including concurring and dissenting opinions.

36. *Imprimis*, Volume 35, Number 5 (May 2006), 6. Hillsdale College, Hillsdale, Michigan. Reprinted by permission from Imprimis, the national speech digest of Hillsdale College, www.hillsdale.edu.

CHAPTER FOUR Prelude and Postlude to the Civil War; Lincoln; Emancipation

1. *Encyclopedia Americana*, 1981, vol. 18, 864, 806, and various other sources.

2. Ibid., vol. 20, 536a.

3. H.W. Brands, *Lone Star Nation* (New York: Doubleday, 2004; Anchor, 2005), 387-407, especially 403-07. Page citations are from the soft cover edition (Anchor).

4. Ibid., 450-455, 466.

5. Ibid., 466.

6. Ibid., 492-93.

7. Stern, *Writings of Lincoln*, 233-34.

8. Ibid., 236. See the footnote on that page.

9. Doris Kearns Goodwin, *Team of Rivals: The Political Genius of Abraham Lincoln* (New York: Simon & Schuster, 2005), 108-09 [hereafter Goodwin, *Team of Rivals*]. She cites John Niven, *Salmon P. Chase: A Biography* (New York and Oxford: Oxford University Press, 1995), 48; Betty Fladeland, *James Gillespie Birney: Slaveholder to Abolitionist* (Ithaca, N.Y.: Cornell University Press, 1955), 136-37, 140-41; and Frederick J. Blue, *Salmon P. Chase: A Life in Politics* (Kent, Ohio: Kent State University Press, 1987), 29.

10. Stern, *Writings of Lincoln*, 235-36.

11. For the full document, see Joseph Smith, *History of the Church of Jesus Christ of Latter Day Saints* (Salt Lake City: Deseret Book Company, 1978), Volume 1, 374-76.

12. Ibid., 396. This history cites the original publication of the document quoted on pages 395-400 as the *Western Monitor*, Fayette, Missouri, August 2, 1833.

13. Ibid., 390-94.

14. Ibid., Volume 3, 165-172.

15. Ibid., 175.

16. Ibid.

17. Ibid., 182-187.

18. Ibid., 187-192.

19. Ibid., 190-91, particularly the footnote. The order of General Lucas and General Doniphan's reply are quoted from the St. Louis National Historical Company, *History of Caldwell County*, 137.

20. Goodwin, *Team of Rivals*, 193.

21. Stern, *Writings of Lincoln*, 232-33.

22. Ibid., 236-37.

23. Ibid., 237.

24. Ibid., 239.

25. Ibid., 340-42.

26. Ibid., 348.

27. Ibid., 362.

28. Ibid., 369.

29. Ibid., 374-75.

30. Ibid., 375-76.

31. Bastiat, *The Law*, 12.

32. For the quote, Goodwin, *Team of Rivals*, 110; regarding the public burning of the Constitution, James Daugherty, *Abraham Lincoln* (New York: Viking Press, 1943), 70-71.

33. Stern, *Writings of Lincoln*, 519.

34. Ibid., 529-30.

35. Ibid., 569-70.

36. Ibid., 571-72.

37. Ibid., 574.

38. Ibid., 576.

39. Ibid., 577.

40. This name applies to a mountain range and two rivers. Some sources, such as the treaties from that period, Brown's book, and the example of a town and a county in Wyoming, use two words: Big Horn. Other sources, such as the example of a town in Montana, and numerous map references, show it as one word: Bighorn. One map shows the same river named both ways. After consulting at least four map sources, this author has chosen to go with one word from a preponderance of map entries and a desire for consistency.

41. Mark H. Brown, *The Plainsmen of the Yellowstone - A History of the Yellowstone Basin* (New York: G. P. Putnam's Sons, 1961), 363, 367 [hereafter Brown, *Plainsmen of the Yellowstone*].

42. Ibid., 127.

43. Charles J. Kappler, *Indian Treaties 1778-1883* (Washington, D.C.: Government Printing Office, 1904; New York, 1973), 594 [hereafter Kappler, *Indian Treaties*].

44. Brown sometimes refers to "Kearney," but it was named after Philip Kearny (1814-1862).

45. Brown, *Plainsmen of the Yellowstone*, 153.

46. Ibid., 159-60.

47. Ibid., 161-62.

48. Ibid.,184. See Kappler, *Indian Treaties*, 1002, Article 11, points 1st through 6th.

49. Brown, *Plainsmen of the Yellowstone*, 229.

50. Ibid., 230-31.

51. Ibid., 183-87, especially 185-87.

52. Ibid., 229.

53. Ibid., 232-33, 235-37.

54. Ibid., 231-37.

55. Ibid., 232.

56. Ibid., 219, 231, 234.

57. Ibid., 198-209.

58. Ibid., 234-35, 232.

59. Ibid., 230.

60. Ibid., 219.

61. Ibid., 187, 259. For boundaries, see Kappler, *Indian Treaties*, 1008.

CHAPTER FIVE An Economics Primer

1. Adam Smith, *The Wealth of Nations* (1776; New York: Modern Library, 1965) 423. Quoted by Mark Skousen, *The Making of Modern Economics* (Armonk, New York: M. E. Sharpe, 2001), 22 [hereafter, M. Skousen, *Making of Modern Economics*].

2. For another discussion of Say's Law and its misrepresentation by John Maynard Keynes, see M. Skousen, *Making of Modern Economics*, 54-57.

3. M. Skousen, *Making of Modern Economics*, 52-54.

4. Frederic Bastiat, *Selected Essays on Political Economy* (originally written in France in 1850. Translation by Seymour Cain: Irvington-On-Hudson, New York: The Foundation for Economic Education, Inc., 1964). "What Is Seen and What Is Not Seen" takes pages 1 to 50, and the discussion of *The Broken Window* is on pages 2 to 4.

5. M. Skousen, *Making of Modern Economics*, 69-70, 75.

6. Ibid., 70-71.

7. Ibid., 86-87.

8. Ibid., 88.

9. Ibid., 84-85. Skousen refers to Julian L. Simon, *The State of Humanity* (Cambridge: Blackwell, 1995) 375, and Simon, *The Ultimate Resource 2* (Princeton, New Jersey: Princeton University Press, 1996) 92.

10. M. Skousen, *Making of Modern Economics*, 336-37.

11. Ibid., 343-45.

12. Ibid., 345.

13. Mark Skousen, *Economics On Trial — Lies, Myths, and Realities* (New York: Irwin Professional Publishing, 1991), 97-99 [hereafter, M. Skousen, *Economics On Trial*]. Skousen there gives graphs reprinted from Roger Leroy Miller, *Economics Today*, 6 edition (New York: Harper & Row, 1988) 396-97. See also M. Skousen, *Making of Modern Economics*, 373-74.

14. M. Skousen, *Making of Modern Economics*, 368-69. See also, M. Skousen, *Economics On Trial*, 63-73, where he devotes a chapter to "The Magic and Myth of the Multiplier."

15. Paul Samuelson, *Economics,* 6th edition (New York: McGraw-Hill Book Company, 1964), 223-24. He treats the "Paradox of Thrift" on pages 234-39. In M. Skousen, *Economics On Trial*, 47-62, Skousen devotes a chapter to "The Fallacy of the Paradox of Thrift."

16. M. Skousen, *Making of Modern Economics*, 368.

17. Mark Skousen, *Ideas on Liberty,* May 2002 (Irvington-On-Hudson, New York: Foundation for Economic Education).

CHAPTER SIX From the Great Depression to World War II

1. Milton and Rose Friedman, *Free to Choose* (New York: Avon Books, 1980), 71 (in the Avon Books edition; 79 in another edition) [hereafter Friedman, *Free to Choose*].

2. Robert D. Edwards and John Magee, *Technical Analysis of Stock Trends* (Boston: John Magee Inc., 1966), 403.

3. Friedman, *Free to Choose*, 75 (83 in another edition).

4. Ibid., 76 (84 in another edition).

5. M. Skousen, *Making of Modern Economics*, 371.

6. T. Harry Williams, Richard N. Currant, Frank Freidel, *A History of the United States [Since 1865]*, Second Edition, Revised (New York: Alfred A. Knopf, 1965), 529 [hereafter Williams, Current and Freidel, *History of United States*].

7. Koch and Peden, *Writings of Jefferson*, 277.

8. 317 U.S. 111.

9. Friedman, *Free to Choose*, 64.

10. Friedman, *Free to Choose*, 80.

11. For example, see the chart in Williams, Current, and Freidel, *History of United States*, 523.

12. See, for instance, Friedman, *Free to Choose*, 86.

13. Bastiat, *The Law*, 22.

14. Ibid., 23.

15. Fabian refers to the Fabian Society in England; social democrat refers to political parties at various times and in various countries, for instance in 1920s Germany.

16. Ferguson and Bruun, *A Survey of European Civilization - Since 1500*, Third Edition (Boston: Houghton Mifflin, 1962), 874.

17. William L. Shirer, *The Rise and Fall of the Third Reich* (New York: Fawcett World Library, 1960) , 324-333, especially 325 (persecution of Catholics), 329 (Hitler's contempt for Protestants), and 332 (Nazi plans to change Christianity) [hereafter Shirer, *Third Reich*]. Also, Bruce A. Van Orden, *Building Zion - The Latter Day Saints in Europe*, (Salt Lake City: Deseret Book, 1996), 145, 151, citing Blair R. Holmes and Alan F. Keele, *When Truth Was Treason: German Youth Against Hitler*, (Urbana, Illinois: University of Illinois Press, 1995), 291n. 18, quoting a Nazi official telling Otto Berndt (following the arrest of Helmuth Hubener), ". . . after we have eliminated the Jews, you Mormons are next."

18. Ferguson and Bruun, *Survey of European Civilization*, 850.

19. Shirer, *Third Reich*, 354-365.

20. Ibid., 527-29.

21. Ibid., 542, 571-77.

22. Ibid., 530.

23. Ibid., 531-35.

24. Ibid., 559-563. On the writing of Mussolini's "compromise" in Berlin, 561.

25. Ibid., 567.

26. Ibid., 571, and Jack LeVien and John Lord, *Winston Churchill: The Valiant Years* (New York: Scholastic Book Services, 1962), 8 [hereafter LeVien and Lord, *Churchill: The Valiant Years*].

27. Shirer, *Third Reich*, 568.

28. Ibid., 589-611, Hungary, 605, Poland, 612.

29. Ibid., 535.

30. LeVien and Lord, *Churchill: The Valiant Years*, 8-9.

31. Shirer, *Third Reich*, 962.

32. Ibid., 840.

33. Ibid., see footnote 839-40.

34. Ibid., 403 (3 battalions), 572 (12 divisions), 840 (23), 947 (136).

35. Ibid., 940, 941, 943.

36. Ibid., 949, 953-54, 958, 963.

37. Ibid., 959, 963-65.

38. Ibid., 968.

39. Ibid., 968.

40. LeVien and Lord, *Churchill: The Valiant Years,* 28.

41. Shirer, *Third Reich,* 968.

42. Ibid., 968-970. Some other sources give different figures as to how many of the evacuees were British, French, or as some claim, Belgian. I chose to use Shirer's figures. Regarding the weather during the evacuation, see Harold A. Winters, Gerald E. Galloway, Jr., William J. Reynolds, David W. Rhyne, *Battling the Elements - Weather and Terrain in the Conduct of War* (Baltimore: Johns Hopkins University Press, 1998), 21-23.

43. Shirer, *Third Reich,* 971; or William W. Watt, An American Rhetoric (New York: Holt, Rinehart and Winston, 1964), 255-56; or LeVien and Lord, *Churchill: The Valiant Years,* 31.

44. Walter Lord, *Incredible Victory* (New York: Harper & Row, Publishers, 1967), 5-6.

45. Ibid., 11.

46. Ibid., 17-23, 27.

47. Ibid., 15.

48. Ibid., 15.

49. Ibid., 7, 9, 44.

50. Ibid., 9, 40.

51. Ibid., *Enterprise* and *Hornet,* 35-36; *Yorktown,* 33-34, 36-39.

52. Ibid., 39-41.

53. Ibid., 44.

54. Ibid., 29, 52-53, 65, 78-79, 94.

55. Ibid., 91-92.

56. Ibid., 94-95.

57. Ibid., 97, 100-103, 110.

58. Ibid., 118-19, 124, 128, 132-35.

59. Ibid., 130-35, 159-61; bombs left lying on the deck: 132.

60. Ibid., 162-74, 179-85, 292-95.

61. Ibid., 187-88, 196-202.

62. Ibid., 214-15, 219, 223, 232.

63. Ibid., 232-36.

64. Ibid., 244.

65. Letter to Attorney General Francis Biddle, February 3, 1942.

66. One source refers to 117,000; another says 112,000; another says 120,000.

67. 323 U.S. 214.

CHAPTER SEVEN The Post War Era to the Present

1. Aleksandr I. Solzhenitsyn, *The Gulag Archipelago,* in three volumes (English translation: New York: Harper & Row, 1973, 1975, 1976).

2. Williams, Current and Freidel, *History of United States,* 795, from Wide World Photos.

3. For the full story, see John Barron, *Mig Pilot* (New York: Avon Books, 1980).

4. John Earl Haynes and Harvey Klehr, *Venona*: *Decoding Soviet Espionage in America* (New Haven: Yale University Press, 1999, a Yale Nota Bene book, 2000), 7 [hereafter Haynes and Klehr, *Venona*].

5. Ibid., 145-49.

6. Ibid., 155-56, 167-73, 201-206.

7. Ibid., 138-45, 207.

8. Ibid., 304-325.

9. Ibid., 207.

10. Ibid., 30, 48-49, 51.

11. Ibid., 191-96, 217-21.

12. Ibid., 207.

13. Ibid., 158-60, 207.

14. Ibid., 129-30, 207.

15. Ibid., 65, 207.

16. Ibid., 207, 228-29.

17. Ibid., 207.

18. Ibid., 207.

19. Ibid., 207.

20. Ibid., 207.

21. Ibid., 201.

22. Ibid., 206-207.

23. Ibid., 201.

24. Ibid., 196-201, 217-21.

25. Ibid., 207.

26. Ibid., 113-14, 186-88, 207.

27. Ibid., 90, 124-25. Charles Kramer, of the NLRB staff, also at other times worked as an aide to Congressman John Bernard, on the staff of four Senate committees, for the Agricultural Adjustment Administration, and the Office of Price Administration.

28. Ibid., 137-38. George Silverman, also at other times worked for the National Recovery Administration.

29. Ibid., 91. Regarding these last few notes, see also, Whittaker Chambers, *Witness* (Washington, D.C.: Regnery Publishing, Inc., 1952), 26-34 [hereafter Chambers, *Witness*].

30. Haynes and Klehr, *Venona*, 7, 21-22; and Chambers, *Witness*, 26-34, especially 30-33.

31. Haynes and Klehr, *Venona*: Treasury, 207, State, 201, OSS, 194.

32. Ibid., Appendix A, 339-370. The specific cables that refer to these individuals are listed in the Notes, 444-467. Specific cables are also frequently listed in the Notes relating to the rest of the text.

33. Ibid., Appendix B, 371-382. Sources are either listed in the Notes, 467-472, or referred to in some cases in the main body of the text.

34. All of these are identified in the Soviet cables deciphered by Venona. Ibid.: Hiss, 167-173; White, 138-45; Currie, 145-50; Duggan, 201-204; Lee, 104-108. Hiss, White, Currie and Duggan, were all identified by Whittaker Chambers. See *Witness*, 466-70, for instance. White was also identified by Elizabeth Bentley and Katherine Perlo, and Currie by Bentley: Haynes and Klehr, *Venona*, 129, 150.

35. Haynes and Klehr, *Venona*, 304-311.

36. Chambers, *Witness*, 559-573, especially 564-65, where the book records Chambers testimony about Hiss' sighting of a prothonotary warbler–confirmed by Hiss in his testimony, on 580–and his clandestine transfer of a Ford automobile. Chambers' testimony, 540-46, 559-573, 663-64, 691-93. Hiss' testimony, 550-56, 573-74, 577-599, 604-615, 637-662, 670-690.

37. Ibid.: Hiss denial of knowing Chambers, 550, 552, 556, 577, 593; changing his story, 577, 606; caught in lies about the automobile, 649-62, 664-69.

38. Ibid.: Hiss' and White's handwriting, 737-38, 748-50; Hiss' typewriter, 750, 781-84; copied State Department documents, 737-38, 742, 744-45, 748-750, 781-83.

39. Ibid., 463-70.

40. Haynes and Klehr, *Venona*, 90-91.

41. Chambers, *Witness*, 470, 739.

42. Ibid., 551-52.

43. Ibid., 574.

44. Ibid., 575, 618, 740.

45. Ibid., 741.

46. Haynes and Klehr, *Venona*: on White, 140-41; on Currie, 146-47.

47. Ibid., 141; Chambers, *Witness*, 676.

48. Haynes and Klehr, *Venona*, 140, 142-43; Chambers, *Witness*, 689.

49. Chambers, *Witness*, 691-92, including the footnote about Dr. Murray, head of the Psychiatry Department at Harvard, who sought to "diagnose" Chambers without ever having met him. Regarding James Reston, see 647-48, 710-11.

50. Ibid., 741-42.

51. The precise figures depend upon the measures and methods used. Using the Consumer Price Index - All Urban Consumers, with 1967 as the base year, based on the end of each quarter, yields annual inflation rates of 18.4% and 13.7% for the first two quarters of 1980. If instead, we compare quarters based on averaging the three months of the CPI, we arrive at 16.5% and 15.2% annual inflation rates for the same period. The CPI sequence by month for October 1979 through June of 1980 follows: 225.4 227.5 229.9 233.2 236.4 239.8 242.5 244.9 247.6. Source, the U.S. Department of Labor, Bureau of Labor Statistics.

52. Richard Harwood, *The Pursuit of the Presidency 1980* (New York: Berkley Books, 1980), 277, 6.

53. Ibid., 345.

54. Data sources: these figures are derived from Civilian Unemployment Rate, Seasonally Adjusted, and Civilian Employment Levels, reported by the U.S. Department of Labor, Bureau of Labor Statistics, and Gross Domestic Product, Seasonally Adjusted Annual Rate, reported by the U.S. Department of Commerce, Bureau of Economic Analysis.

55. Source, the Congressional Budget Office.

56. Source, the weekly data (ending Wednesdays) from the Board of Governors of the Federal Reserve System.

57. *Imprimis*, September 2006, Volume 35 Number 9. Reprinted by permission from Imprimis, the national speech digest of Hillsdale College, www.hillsdale.edu.

58. President George W. Bush, speech of October 7, 2002, in Cincinnati, Ohio.

59. Ibid.

60. Ibid.

61. Investors Business Daily, July 2003.

62. *Imprimis*, December 2006, Volume 35, Number 12. From a speech on November 9, 2006, at Hillsdale College. Reprinted by permission from Imprimis, the national speech digest of Hillsdale College, www.hillsdale.edu.

63. Ibid.

64. Ibid.

65. George W. Bush, speech of October 7, 2002, in Cincinnati, Ohio.

66. See the web site, http://www.usaid.gov/iraq/pdf/iraq_mass_graves.pdf. As of this writing, the site was last updated January 7, 2005. The site also relates the stories of three survivors who avoided detection, each by a different circumstance.

67. Ibid.

68. Chris W. Cox, *America's 1 Freedom,* May 2007, 40.

69. *The Federalist Papers,* No. 51, 324.

70. *Corpus Juris Secundum* (St. Paul, Minnesota: West Group, 2002), Vol. 15, 291.

Index

Liberty & Independence Press

To order by telephone, call 877-4 JULY 76 (877-458-5976)

E-mail: LibertyIndependence@gmail.com

Or order from our website: www.LibertyIndependence.com

By mail: Liberty & Independence Press
107 East 107th Avenue
Northglenn, CO 80233

Please send _____ copies of *America's History Revealed* at $15.95 plus $4.00 each for shipping and handling. *(Please add 2.9% sales tax for products shipped to Colorado.)*

NAME _____

ADDRESS _____

CITY _____ **STATE** _____ **ZIP** _____

TELEPHONE _____ **E-MAIL** _____

PAYMENT ☐ Credit Card   ☐ Check or Money Order
☐ Visa
☐ MasterCard
☐ Discover
☐ American Express

CARD NUMBER _____

EXPIRATION DATE _____ **CVV** _____

Please contact me regarding my interest in the following:

Future offerings from Liberty & Independence Press, such as *(check those that apply)*

☐ *Our Constitution and the Trial of Nicholas Throckmorton*
(A play based on an English trial in 1554, showing the need for the protection of our Constitution and Bill of Rights.)

☐ Other future works on Freedom, History, or our Constitution

☐ On Charter Schools

☐ On Character Education

☐ Other works by the same author

☐ Children's Books

☐ Having Phil Winkler speak to my group. See www.PhilWinklerSpeaker.com.